We Make Change

We Make Change

Community Organizers Talk About What They Do— and Why

Kristin Layng Szakos and Joe Szakos

With an introduction by Harry C. Boyte

Vanderbilt University Press

NASHVILLE

11 10 09 08 07   1 2 3 4 5

All photos in the book are courtesy of interviewees or the organizations for
which they work or worked, except for Sheila Kingsberry-Burt's portrait by
Billy E. Barnes, and Wanda Salaman's portrait by Rusia N. Mohiuddin.

This book is printed on acid-free paper made
from 50% post consumer recycled paper.
Manufactured in the United States of America
Designed by Wendy McAnally

Library of Congress Cataloging-in-Publication Data

Szakos, Kristin Layng.
We make change : community organizers talk about what
they do—and why / Kristin Layng Szakos and Joe Szakos.—1st ed.
    p. cm.
ISBN-13: 978-0-8265-1554-4 (cloth : alk. paper)
ISBN-13: 978-0-8265-1555-1 (pbk. : alk. paper)
1. Community organization. 2. Social action.
3. Community organization—Case studies.
4. Social action—Case studies. I. Szakos, Joe. II. Title.
HM766.S93 2007
361.2—dc22
    2006030887

To our parents, Judith Layng, Tony Layng, and Andy and Emma Szakos, who launched us on our way, and to our children, Anna and Maria Szakos, and foster daughters Tai, Toni, and Sherieka, who are the reason we do this work.

Contents

Acknowledgments

At the risk of making our thank-yous as long as the book itself, we want to acknowledge the wonderful help and support we have received from many sources. First, of course, we thank our families—the parents who brought us up to work for a better world and the children whom we hope we have taught to do the same.

Second, we thank the people who have helped guide us in our professional paths to this point: Paul B. Wice, Stuart J. Miller, Ellen Ruffolo, Earl Durham, Bruce Gottschall and Michael Schubert, Zsuzsa Foltanyi, John McCutcheon, and Hazel Clave. Others who offered advice and guidance for this project were Dave Beckwith, Dick Couto, Steve Fisher, Randy Stoecker, Rich Wood, Henry Allen, Deepak Bhargava, Seth Borgos, Mary Dailey, Gary Delgado, Pablo Eisenberg, Don Elmer, Gaye Evans, Kim Fellner, Andy Mott, Spence Limbocker, Pete Myers, Diane Ives, Charles Marsh, Mary Katherine O'Connor, Regina McGraw, Ben MacConnell, Gary Sandusky, Walter Davis, Zoë Lane, Greg LeRoy, Herb E. Smith, Jill Carson, David Rubinstein, Barbara Ehrenreich, William Greider, Sandra Mikush, Kathy Partridge, Lee Winkelman, Paul Loeb, Karen Waters, Wende Marshall, William Dietel, Idelisse Malave, Cathy Lerza, and Chuck Savitt.

We are grateful for the financial support this project received from the Mary Reynolds Babcock Foundation, French American Charitable Trust, Needmor Fund, Marguerite Casey Foundation, Charles Stewart Mott Foundation, Kendeda Fund, and Entelco Foundation. Gayle Williams and Tom David were willing to support the project when it was just an idea, and Diane Fenney, Dave Beckwith, Cris Doby, and Steve and Ann Stranahan joined along the way.

We couldn't have written this book without help from our trusty typist/transcriber, Claire Jolly.

We are grateful for the special talents of graphic designers Bev Sell, Kathy Reese, and Fred Schneider, and photographer Erin Garvey. Thanks to Larry Yates for providing lots of photos, to Laura Ramirez for photos and technical help, and to Joell Smith-Borne, Dariel Mayer, and Wendy McAnally for their extra efforts in putting this book together.

We'd like to thank the Virginia Organizing Project (VOP) interns, students, and others who reviewed chapters, helped with transcribing, made suggestions, and kept us humble—notably Allen Cooper, David Barish, Maya Stewart-Silver, Zora Tucker, Colleen Unroe, Mike Gifford, Kathryn McKinney, Helen Dempsey, and students in the University of Virginia Principles of Organizing class, Fall 2004, and their professor, Andrew Lawrence.

We appreciate the efforts of Connie Muscenti, Jennifer Niesslein, Gail Leondar-Wright, Betsy Leondar-Wright, and Sue Havlish in helping to spread the word about *We Make Change*.

Worthy of gratitude, too, are colleagues at the Virginia Organizing Project who allowed Joe to take a sabbatical for this project: Frank Blechman, Barry Butler, Brian Johns, Michele Mattioli, Jan May, Laura Ramirez, Ellen Ryan, Bev Sell, Ben Thacker-Gwaltney, Octavia Ware, Cathy Woodson, and Larry Yates. Thanks also to VOP leaders Jay Johnson, Andy Kegley, Denise Smith, Jason Guard, Sandra Cook, Del McWhorter, Jon Liss, Markell McPhearson, Mary Randolph-Preston, and Laura Lawson.

And we honor other friends, mentors and former colleagues: Nick Allen, Joey Childers, Joe Chrastil, Will Collette, Jerry Hardt, Billy Horton, Terry Keleher, Burt Lauderdale, Maureen O'Connell, John and Jean Rosenberg, Chuck Shuford, Patrick Sweeney, the staff of the Legal Aid Justice Center in Charlottesville, Virginia, and all the outstanding activists and leaders we have worked with over the years.

Special thanks to stalwart friends Dominique and Roger Micallef, Michele Whiting, Nathalie Guiral, Priscilla Wynn-Brown, Sylvie leManchet, Rebecca Hugot, Emily Dreyfus, Mary Newton, and Karen and Kelsey Waters for their love and support during the year of writing.

And, of course, to the organizers in these pages whose work gives us hope.

Preface

Kristin Layng Szakos

When I met Joe Szakos, it was inevitable that the question would come up: What do you do for a living? Mine was easy. I was a writer. Joe's answer was a new one to me. He was a community organizer. I had to admit I had no idea what that meant. He said his parents had had the same reaction. In our twenty-two years of marriage, I have grown very familiar with the world of community organizing, but I know that most Americans still have never heard of it.

Community organizers are the people who work, often behind the scenes, to help people come together to effect meaningful change in their communities by building effective community organizations. They are there with the neighborhood group working to bring bank loans to low-income homeowners. They are there with immigrant women organizing to get medical insurance for their families, with small-town environmentalists keeping a toxic waste plant out of their community, with parents trying to get schools to respond to the needs of children with dyslexia, with gay and lesbian students striving to create a safe space in their schools, with groups working to reduce the ravages of racism in their towns and institutions. Wherever there is a well-organized group agitating for progressive social change, chances are there is a community organizer nearby.

"Being a community organizer allows you to work with groups to make specific, tangible changes in a community while helping people learn important leadership skills," Joe says. "I love having the opportunity—daily—to help people raise their voices about the concerns they have in their communities, especially when it leads to major systematic changes."

Community organizers work at their jobs because they are passionate, because they believe that change is possible, and because they enjoy working with people. Although it's not an occupation that leads to great wealth, community organizers can make a living at it. Community organizers receive salaries, pensions, and health insurance. They raise families and send their children to college. They do well by doing good.

The National Organizers Alliance estimates that there are about 10,000 people working professionally as community organizers in the United States today. So who are these folks whose occupation remains a mystery to most of us?

This book is an attempt to explore the world of community organizing through the voices of real people working in the field—organizers in small towns and big city neighborhoods, women and men, some in their twenties, others in their sixties, of different races and economic backgrounds. It is our hope that through their stories the reader will come to an understanding of what they do—and why. We hope, too, that these stories may inspire a new generation to enter this exciting and meaningful field.

Preface

Joe Szakos

The anthropologist Margaret Mead is often quoted as saying: "Never doubt that a small group of thoughtful, committed citizens can change the world. Indeed, it's the only thing that ever has." U.S. history is full of stories about ordinary people banding together to improve their lives and their communities—and to change the world in the process. The abolitionist movement against slavery, the populist movement of small farmers in the 1870s, the struggle for women's suffrage, the Civil Rights Movement, the anti-war movement, the environmental movement, the movement that led to the passage of the Americans with Disabilities Act, the American Indian Movement, the gay rights movement, the anti-globalization movement: all of these have shifted the balance of power in some essential way.

Although it can seem so, movements like these don't just arise out of thin air. In every case, it is the work of people at the grassroots—people who bring people together to help them figure out what needs to be done and how to do it. Those people are community organizers.

So how come you never hear about them?

You can go to the library and get a book about how to be an astronaut, a teacher, or a firefighter. You can read biographies about baseball players, ballerinas, and politicians. But you'd be hard pressed to find a book in your local library about community organizers.

We hope to do something about that with the book you have in your hands right now.

This book is about many individuals who didn't just spend a couple of years working with a community organization before moving on to a "real" career. Instead, they are people—young and old—who have made community organizing their life's work, people who have helped develop thousands of leaders and have helped to build hundreds of effective community groups.

In the last few years, I interviewed eighty-one community organizers who work with large and small organizations all over the country, from Alaska to Florida. We have gathered their words to help explain what organizers do and why.

The original interview transcripts will be made available to writers and film-makers who want to use the information for research, articles, or documentaries on community organizing and social change.

I interviewed some people where they live, some at regional meetings and national conferences, and a few by phone. I made a real effort to find a mix of different kinds of people in the field: organizers with thirty years of experience and college-age organizing interns, organizers of different races, nationalities, genders, and sexual orientations, working in urban and rural areas in as many states as I could manage (28), on a wide variety of issues.

I also wanted to talk to organizers who worked with congregations, those who worked with membership-based organizations, and those who worked in coalitions, alliances, and federations. I sought out organizers who worked with a single constituency, such as low-wage workers or public housing residents, as well as organizers who worked with multiple constituencies. I was looking for some community organizers who focus on a single issue, some who tackle many issues at once, some who work at a neighborhood level, some who organize city-wide, some who work in multiple counties, and some who organize statewide or regionally.

In addition to these intentional variations, we discovered that there were others: some of the interviewees are organizing the communities they were born in, while others have traveled thousands of miles, across the continent or across the world, to work in new communities. Some are motivated by religious conviction; others are non-believers. Some come from families where activism is a valued heritage; others have shocked conservative families by their career choice. Some come from wealth, others from poverty; some from the inner city, some from the suburbs, others from farms.

Even though the community organizers in this book use different methods and models, have different philosophies and employ different approaches, what they seem to have in common is an essential optimism that with hard work and a plan, you can change things, step by step, for the better. And they all know that one person can't do it alone.

We have organized the book to try to give the reader a sense of what community organizers believe and do. In addition to providing fourteen individual profiles, we draw on all eighty-one interviewees in chapters like "What Is Community Organizing?" and "Advice to Aspiring Organizers." You can read the book from front to back or skip around to the parts that interest you the most.

Throughout the book, you'll hear the voices of organizers telling stories. Before you begin reading, though, let me share a story of my own.

As a young community organizer in the eastern Kentucky coalfields, my role was to prepare members of the newly formed Martin County Concerned Citizens for a hearing on a proposed Community Development Block Grant (CDBG). The county was trying to relocate the residents of the little town of Beauty out of the flood plain (and, we learned much later, out of the way of lucrative coal strip mine opportunities as well), but the residents—most of whom had lived there all their lives—did not want to move. One of my challenges was to help them to stand up to experts and bureaucrats even though more than half of the adults living in this Appalachian hamlet could not read or write. I recruited several new members of the group who could read to go door to door, reading the CDBG application to any residents who needed it.

The hearing was very technical, and consultants and experts were going on and on about acquisition and relocation benefits and definitions of terms like "dilapidated" and "deteriorated." With all the fancy talk, residents of Beauty were worried that their real-life concerns would be ignored.

Then Johnny Mullins stood up. Everyone in the community knew that Johnny Mullins couldn't read or write, so they were a bit curious how he was going to participate in this drama of "dueling experts."

"If you look on page 47 of the application, right there where the budget figures are," he said, confidently, "you will notice it's not the same as on page 14, where it gives the numbers about how many people would be moved."

The consultant for the county squirmed, obviously embarrassed by the inconsistency, but the biggest impact of Johnny Mullins' testimony was on the other residents sitting in the room. If Johnny Mullins could take on the experts and not be afraid, so could they! One by one, residents stood to speak. If the consultant didn't answer a question to their satisfaction, they would ask it again. If he used words they didn't understand, they asked him to explain.

After the hearing, Johnny had a big smile on his face. He went over to thank his friend, Hayes Maynard, a young laid-off coal miner. "Hayes, I want to thank you for reading all them fifty-seven pages of that application to me a couple times. And I'm sure glad I remembered it!"

The town of Beauty still stands where it always did.

Organizing is about giving ordinary people like Johnny Mullins and his neighbors the tools and the confidence they need to take on the powers that be.

Introduction
Seedbed of a New Movement
Harry C. Boyte

Co-Director, Center for Democracy and Citizenship

We Make Change is unique in a growing body of analytic and historical literature about community organizing that now includes several works by leading community organizers themselves. *We Make Change* profiles a diverse group of organizers, their perspectives, their experiences, their hopes, and their fears. What come through vividly are the gritty up and down experiences of organizing, as well as its relational and political qualities. These are people on the front lines of citizen action across the country, in a time when conventional wisdom holds that American citizens are simply apathetic and disengaged. *We Make Change* shows that organizing can be immensely rewarding, if also frustrating, difficult, exasperating—and hard work. It can also awaken new citizen energies and a broader sense of hopefulness about change.

We see interest in organizing among the several thousand students and young adults that we work with each year at the Center for Democracy and Citizenship in high schools and colleges around the country through our youth civic initiative called Public Achievement. More and more young people want to know about the sort of practical, progressive, and democratic organizing work that is illuminated here. For the most part, they also have to date learned little about such work, what it is, and how to connect with it through formal education. This collection holds potential for wide use in courses on organizing, urban affairs, and contemporary politics, as well as in the organizing field itself. It also may help to inspire a new generation of young people who take up organizing as career and as life work.

The diversity of approaches and philosophies present in *We Make Change* illustrates broad and growing networks of organizations and efforts, some in this collection and others not, but all part of a fledgling new citizen movement that I believe can be called "democratic" and "populist." The new populist movement gathers power for ordinary people to break up unjust concentrations of wealth and power; it advances community and egalitarian values; and it has a strong emphasis on civic learning and development of people's imaginations, skills, and public identities. Such networks range from left-leaning groups like the National

Organizers Alliance and ACORN, to the networks of what are called "broad-based citizen organizations" such as the Industrial Areas Foundation, PICO, DART, and the Gamaliel Foundation, which shun "ideology" but have a philosophically democratic politics, and are more reflective about democratic and religious values than the raw pragmatism of Saul Alinsky in the 1970s, the tradition that many of them claim. The larger movement also includes many new forms of organizing among young adults, new community-based approaches to organizing on the environment like those developed by the National Wildlife Federation, a new emerging community arts movement, and other strands. All these reflect values such as equality, community, democracy, concern for the poor, and diversity.

What unites organizers across networks and philosophies is what can be called the project of deepening democracy. All these organizers seek to develop the organized power of ordinary, uncredentialled citizens, especially in poor, working class, and minority communities. *We Make Change* does a splendid job of showing through stories and diverse voices how the development of citizens' power requires creating a counterbalance to the power of corporations and wealthy elites.

Readers should keep in mind two challenges that community organizers face as they do their work: technocracy and culture. In the first case citizens are disempowered in an information age not only by organized corporate or money power but also by organized "knowledge power." Decision making in most institutions is highly technocratic, or expert centered. Today, whether in the classroom or in the doctor's office, in the nightly news shows we watch or the public hearings we attend, many norms and practices marginalize and silence people without credentials, degrees, and specialized language. Knowledge power is more subtle and elusive than corporate power, but it is no less pervasive. People without credentials and recognized expertise are not often credited with having much to say. Progressive politics and large activist groups can sometimes reflect invisible, technocratic forms of power that are widespread in the larger society, especially if they are based too much on mobilization technologies like the "door-to-door canvass" and the Internet. In mobilizing approaches, in contrast to organizing, the issues are predetermined by experts, and ordinary citizens are slotted into predetermined roles. Dana Fisher's recent book, *Activism, Inc.*, shows how much the Democratic Party and many large progressive issue groups based on the door-to-door issue canvass have come to slight the interests and cultures of local communities as the result of technocratic trends.

Organizers, if they are serious about building democracy, have to deal with the postures and authority of technocratic elites as well as economic elites. Organizers help citizens to develop confidence, authority, and skill in the face of expert claims. In the best organizing work, organizers also sometimes help professionals to become "citizen professionals," "on tap, not on top," in the organizing phrase.

The second challenge community organizers in this collection face is culture; more specifically, the ways in which the dominant culture is sharply antagonistic to the values of community organizing. Though usually framed in terms of discrete issues, in fact organizing in a deeper sense is about building civic life, about democratic cultures rooted in real places. Organizing solves public problems, creates public goods, and creates public relationships. All of these dynamics go against the forces of "privatization" in the world today, not only of public goods but also of ideas—ideologies, religions, interests, life styles, a world of gated communities of ideas as well as neighborhoods. *We Make Change* is full of stories that rebuild a public world and public cultures—public goods, public relationships, public life with diverse views and interests. The distinction that many organizers make between organizing and mobilizing points toward this public-building process: Citizens in this collection are "at the table" with confidence and policy ideas of their own; they develop standing and power sufficient to be taken seriously. They renew public spaces and public interactions, shifting from the "superhero" view of elections and leadership widespread today in America, in which people look to others to fix the problems.

The privatization dynamic of the broader culture is inextricably tied to other trends, such as consumerism, the cult of efficiency, competitive success at any price, and radical individualism. Democratic organizing has to contend against all of these if it is to succeed. Many interviewees allude to such dynamics.

Yet there is also often a silence among organizers about the deeper cultural implications of their work. The silence can be traced in part back to the early 1970s, when progressive organizers and activists picked up the "bread and butter" issue language of Saul Alinsky, expressed especially in his 1972 book *Rules for Radicals*. What was missing from *Rules* and the issue organizing approaches that descend from Alinsky's book was the powerful cultural language of the populist movements of the 1930s and 1940s, Alinsky's own formative experiences. The loss of the cultural dimension can be seen in even a cursory comparison of Alinsky's two books, *Reveille for Radicals*, reflecting the rich cultural themes of the New Deal movements, and his 1972 book, which is wry, cynical about values, and almost entirely a-historical.

Other works on this formative period can usefully complement *We Make Change*. David Levering Lewis, *When Harlem Was in Vogue*; Lary May, *The Big Tomorrow*; Lisabeth Cohen, *Making the New Deal*; Michael Denning, *Cultural Front*; and my own works, *Building America*, with Nan Kari, and *Everyday Politics*, among other work, are resources. Organizing—whether in the community or in the motion picture industry, in the school or in the university—that is attentive to culture can also work large changes in culture. This is a lesson from the 1930s organizing in many cultural settings that complemented on the ground organizing in communities and workplaces. Today, there is a "taken for granted" stance about the dominant culture by many of today's progressive organizers.

Overwhelmingly, organizers in this collection, I believe, would agree that the values they fight for are sharply at odds with dominant cultural trends. But how many would imagine these cultural forces could be transformed? Such fatalism needs to be challenged. When community and citizen organizing explicitly begins to name and treat the larger cultural dynamics it is fighting, it will also come into its own in a new way, beginning to contribute to a wider movement for democratic change. It will become the seedbed for a new civic and populist movement in America.

This is a matter of some urgency. Today, many Americans see themselves outside of politics and public affairs, which they view with enormous distaste. Technical and administrative decision making, as well as strident, polarized political rhetoric, have gradually displaced civic wisdom that integrates different voices in problem solving efforts. Bureaucratic procedures and special interest processes have deprived citizens of the practical arts of deliberating and working together. Yet the public problems we face today are increasingly of the variety that can no longer be solved unless we revive the practical arts that are taught in community organizing. We cannot devise solutions to environmental hazards, for instance, unless citizens themselves take responsibility for reducing waste and recycling materials, unless farmers work to prevent soil erosion, unless community groups collaborate with industry to prioritize reducing toxicity in ways that do not destroy small businesses and jobs.

Government can facilitate some of these things, but it can never substitute for them. The problems of community development in inner cities, of school reform, of violence and public health problems, and many others present similar challenges. They are simply too complex and multifaceted to be solved unless we learn how to tap local community wisdom, community assets, and civic networks. Regulatory and therapeutic solutions that treat people as passive victims, needy clients, or righteous claimants do not work as policy. Nor will adequate solutions be found simply by applying market principles to public problems. Markets can help make many public services more responsive. In some forms they can enhance choice without compromising quality or equity. Yet neither markets nor government, alone or in combination, will foster long term civic health without the practical wisdom and public work of ordinary citizens.

For all that our society fills with constant chatter—24/7 news cycles, the explosion of the Internet, revelations of intimate secrets on television talk shows—there is also silence about the loss of public purposes, the erosion of a common public world, and simultaneously a sense of powerlessness to reverse these trends. The pollster Dan Yankelovich diagnosed the pattern a decade ago. Americans, he said, "feel a sickness in the very soul of society to which they cannot give a name." Since then, such discontents and patterns of retreat from the public world into silo cultures have accelerated, as Richard Harwood documents in his recent book, *Hope Unraveled*. We frequently encounter such sentiments— retreat from the common world, worry about erosion of common things, silences about the problem, and feelings of powerlessness—in our work at the Center for Democracy and Citizenship (CDC). From new immigrants to suburban parents, from inner city teachers to faculty and students in colleges and universities, people experience a "problem that has no name."

Broad social movements addressing problems of this scale cannot be brought into existence from scratch. They emerge from the coalescence, interconnections, and common sense of momentum coming from many diverse trends and directions. But conscious organizing that fosters deliberation, interconnections, public work together across lines of difference, and a common language can lead to increased confidence and hope that stems from seeing efforts in particular arenas as parts of a larger whole.

Scholars of civic trends, such as Carmen Sirianni and Lew Friedland, Peter Levine, and Cindy Gibson, argue that we are at the early stages of a new movement for civic life and democratic change in the United States. Gibson's white paper for the Case Foundation, *Citizens at the Center*, is a marker of this new movement and a distillation of some of its key lessons. Moreover, there are innovations and lessons in civic theory and practice to use in helping to realize this movement's potential.

Community organizing of the sort described in *We Make Change* holds great potential to "break the silence," and help advance the fledgling civic populist movement. Community organizing can build civic confidence and capacities so that people can take up the challenge of becoming architects of a democratic way of life, not simply democracy's spectators and consumers.

We Make Change

Ordinary citizens wield real power when they come together to demand change.

1

What Is Community Organizing?

Organizers across the country struggle to find a single definition that encompasses what they do. So far, no single phrase seems to fit the bill. There are almost as many kinds of organizer as there are organizations. But all share certain core qualities:

It's getting people to work together

> I'm changing the world. I'm making the world a just place. That's what organizing is about. There are many ways of doing that, but in the end that's what it's about. We're helping people change their reality. We're facilitating so that people can create a better world.
> —Guillermo Quinteros

> I help get together people who care about an issue. I help provide them with training and give them opportunities to speak out and make a difference on those issues that they care about.
> —DeAnna Woolston

> The organizer is the one who helps people to move from complaining to action to resolve the problem and get it fixed.
> —June Rostan

> A community organizer is someone who helps citizens organize effectively, work together effectively to make the changes that they want and to make their communities a better place. It's part teacher, part rabble-rouser, a whole lot of things. I guess one of the things I like about it is that there are a lot of different parts to it.
> —John Smillie

A lot of it is just talking to people. There's that Cesar Chavez[*] quote. Someone asked him, "How can you be a great organizer? How do you do it?" And he said, "Well, first you talk to one person. Then you talk to the next person." It's not quite that simple, but it takes that patience.
    —Abigail Singer

A community organizer is someone who works with members of the community to identify their concerns and problems and issues and hopes and dreams, and then brings those together in the form of an organization to act collectively.
    —LeeAnn Hall

An organizer is someone who brings people together to make change, to solve problems in their community or state or workplace by helping them develop the tools they need to work collectively.
    —Janet Groat

I actually like the NOA [National Organizers Alliance] definition, which is: "An organizer is someone who builds a democratic organization that develops the leadership of people to take public action." I think it's broad enough to encompass a bunch of people but also it should be clear that if you don't do one of those three things that's not organizing.
    —James Mumm

An organizer brings people together to sort out specific changes they want to see in the life of the community, develop strategies to get there, and then move into action to make the changes happen.
    —Ellen Ryan

In my journey to where I am now, I've had different and deeper understandings of what a community organizer does. In college I was exposed to the concept of community organizing at its very base level—what it is. That hasn't necessarily changed, but what I found out when I began to actually do the organizing work is that it wasn't just about turnout numbers, that it wasn't just about the campaigns, but rather the challenges around leadership development and development of political consciousness and crafting it together—what it means to craft an alternative world view.
    —Vivian Chang

I'm just thinking about how I got into organizing. I remember looking at this job description of the community organizer position for ORA [Oregon Rural Action] and all the things that are involved with it: Working on

---

[*]   Cesar Chavez helped to found and served as president of the United Farm Workers, a union of migrant laborers in the U.S.

local issues. Working at the grassroots level. Talking to people about what interests them. Traveling around the region and getting to know a particular region and the issues in that region really well. Doing all of that in an effort to make positive change and make a difference in how people can realize this idea of democracy. And to get paid for it, not a lot, but to have it be a real job. It was almost a no-brainer for me.

—Brett Kelver

Organizing is a way to help other people see that there are things other than going out and buying something new or having a few drinks, or all the other things we do. I think action is a great antidote to pain, and I want other people to know what I've experienced. And there's no other way to do that except jump in the middle and go for broke.

—Pennie Vance

It's about democracy

It's about citizenship—not the kind you get by being born in the USA or by swearing your allegiance to the flag, but what it means to be a member of a democratic society.

One of the things about democracy is that people have to participate. One way that an organizer works is to get people to participate and to help shape the decisions that affect their lives.

—Betty Garman Robinson

I'd like to think of a community organizer as an engine of the democratic process—the person who is facilitating citizenship. A lot of people talk about organizers empowering citizens. We don't. The fact is we show them that they already have that power, what power that you have as people. Even the word citizenship bothers me a little bit; I'd like to think that we're open to talking to people who aren't citizens. But in the more general sense of citizenship, we have rights living as human beings and we have responsibilities as well and that is informing people of both those rights and responsibilities and allowing them to decide.

—Matt Sura

In many ways I'm a teacher, not in a traditional classroom but in congregations and schools and neighborhood centers and union halls. We teach people about public life and how to claim an active citizenship, living out the democratic notions of citizen participation and the republican notion that there are civic virtues that have to be taught.

—Perry Perkins

My job as an organizer is to really be a facilitator—get information to folks so that they can participate in the legislative or governmental process in ways that'll help them.
—Presdalene Harris

An organizer wants the group of people she is working with to understand how the system works, as well as how to get what they want, and be able to bring enough pressure of various kinds to bear on decision-makers in order to win. A community organizer isn't as interested in a specific issue so much as interested in moving lots of people into active roles in public life.
—Ellen Ryan

Community organizing is about getting people to work together for a common good. What's so hard about that? Oftentimes people can't agree on what the common good is.
—Scott Douglas

It's about developing leaders

The role of the organizer is to use the language that exists in the community and tell them, "You already said it. You already know it." The idea is to reinforce it and to validate that voice that has been trembling to say something, to help articulate it."
—Diana Bustamante

A community organizer is someone who's catalytic. The best organizers don't have high ego needs. They're willing to submit themselves, in Biblical terms, to others. They're willing to subjugate their own ego needs in honor of the development of other people.
—Gary Sandusky

I think the definition of organizing is not even much of a big deal to me as much as it is how good you are at building relationships with people so that you can then go back to them over and over again and you can continue to work on things together.
—Donna Uma Aisha Brown

A community organizer is somebody who has vision for a more just and sustainable society and is working with members of whatever organization they work for to try and bring that vision into reality. The role of a community organizer is to develop leaders and to work with the leaders to be the spokespeople of the organization and control the strategy of the organization. I think that's probably the most important function that a community organizer serves: being a trainer, a motivator, somebody who

assists thinking through strategy, somebody who, more than anything else, asks the critical questions that help our members think about "Where do we go from here?" with whatever issue we're working on.
—Aaron Browning

I think a community organizer is someone who is there to motivate people, to encourage them, to help figure out strategy, access resources. To draw people into the work, to draw people into participation in the organization. To try to identify and cultivate leadership.
—Brett Kelver

An organizer, basically, is a person who sits in the back of the room and just watches people grow. He doesn't take a leadership position; he just asks the right questions so that people can, on their own, realize that we already have all the answers. In the end people can walk away from it with a sense of "I did it myself. Nobody came in and did it for me. I did it myself and as a result of having done it myself I know that anything that impacts my community, anything that impacts my fundamental quality of life, I can now handle."
—John McCown

A community organizer is somebody whose full-time job is to look for leaders and connect them with each other and with a strategy that the leaders and the organizers think makes sense around issues that they think are important, so that then they have power to do something on justice issues that are important to them. But the core of it is looking for leaders, finding leaders, developing leaders, and then connecting leaders to an organization and a strategy to build power.
—Allen Cooper

It's about power

We bring people together in the community to struggle for social change and political power.
—Jon Liss

An organizer is someone who works in a community to build a grassroots base of power to affect social and political change.
-Leah Ottersbach

I think that the community organizer is meant to mobilize people and help them build the power that they once believed that they didn't have to win on issues of justice in the community.
—Makiva Harper

It's about power. Organizers help community groups figure out how to build citizen power by working together.

A community organizer is someone who builds relationships with leaders and uncovers their self-interest, and gives them an opportunity to work in their own self-interest and address problems in the community that they could not address by themselves.
    —Jana Adams

Community organizing is about power and empowerment. I think a community organizer helps people who are not used to having power and not used to having a voice be able to come together and build people-power so they can make change happen.
    —Holly Hatcher

I really believe that long-term change is dependent upon community organizing. You can't sustain those victories without community organizing. I think you can bring about change, but the likelihood that that change is long-lasting significantly decreases, I think, if you don't have an organized group of people who are willing to defend those victories, and are willing to hold the people that they elect to the different branches of government

accountable for those victories. Or accountable, too, if they were to try to undermine them in any way. You have to be able to build the changes you make in society into the political culture and social culture of the state you're working in, or the country. I don't think you can do that without grassroots organizing.
—Aaron Browning

I think as a community organizer, my job is to shift people into reframing how they think about what's going on in their lives and get them thinking about what they can do. Community organizing gives people the voice and the courage to work together to make long-term changes in our society.
—Cathy Woodson

I don't like to think of it as empowerment, because I think it's not about giving them power but about activating the power that is in people. We all have it, it's just that sometimes we don't know we have it. Sometimes we've been suppressed or oppressed or depressed for so long until we've lost connection with our power. So I think it's about helping to power up individuals and communities.
—Sheila Kingsberry-Burt

It's kind of like . . .

I think of being an effective organizer as similar to being an effective coach. A coach needs to know how to play the game, but doesn't play the game for the team. A coach makes sure the team knows how to play the game, makes sure each player improves his or her skills, makes sure the team has a game plan suited to their level of ability and the opposing team they are confronting. Telling people, "Yeah, you really can do this!" or "No, you can't do that, you better practice first," is a key organizing skill. So you need to be able to be diplomatic, but also direct with folks. Sometimes being an effective organizer just involves showing people the ropes and calling a time out once in a while to rest and regroup. Other times it's teaching the fundamentals of the game.
—Ellen Ryan

Some organizers are architects, who become impatient without big monuments, and others are like teachers, and feel like their job is to make incremental contributions in a long stream of other people that will also make incremental contributions. I think the teaching-type tend to plug along and to stay in the work.
— Jeff Malachowsky

An effective organizer is part empowerer and part storyteller, telling the stories that persuade people that they can make a difference. Part cheerleader. Part leadership scout. You need to have the ability to recognize abilities in people that they may not have seen in themselves and talents that you can cultivate.

—Kimble Forrister

There are people who know the techniques well. There are techniques about how to run a campaign. Sure. We know how to identify people, get people out, and do phone banking. That's a piece of it, but it's not organizing. It's mobilizing, maybe. It's part of organizing, but it's not all of it. My take is that [an organizer is] really a facilitator who helps develop capacity in the community. The organizer is somebody who facilitates that whole process. In certain places there are organizers who are also leaders, because they come from that community. They are leader-facilitators. I don't see them as people who can completely disengage or be completely separated from what they are doing.

— Guillermo Quinteros

It's not . . .

Being an organizer is not the same as being an activist. For me, there's a distinction between working on issues that I care about myself, where I'm working as a volunteer with friends and neighbors to get something done. In that case I'm an activist, or hopefully a community leader, myself. When I'm functioning as a community organizer, I'm listening to other people, listening to enough people to identify patterns in what they are saying, and pulling those people together to develop a strategy and take action on something they want to accomplish together.

—Ellen Ryan

It's not for you to go in and solve people's problems for them, but to help people to come together to find a means to bring an end to their own problems.

—Steve Bradberry

I think the difference between service providers and organizers is that service providers just try to cover, or take care of the needs today but not tomorrow. As an organizer, you look at the long term. You help them to figure it out and become more conscious of how they can move from where they are now, from point A to point B. Because if you really want to make social changes, you have to base it in and engage with that which is in the community.

—Edgar Rivera

Organizing is not inherently progressive. There are a lot of right-wing organizers who do this, too. I'm only interested in what a progressive

organizer is, which is that you have to do the work in a way that creates justice, peace, equity, and dignity for people, in a way that protects the environment. It lets people love whom they want and worship how they want, without doing harm to others. That's the kind of organizer that interests me.
—Kim Fellner

A key feature is that the community organizer, for reasons of accountability, has to be grounded. They must be the exponent of some viable community

So—What do you do for a living?

Most folks don't know what a community organizer is. If you're sitting on a bus or a plane, how do you explain it to the person sitting next to you? What if it's your own family who don't understand?

Well, I still have to tell my parents every now and then. When I took this new job, they were like, "Now, what do you do?" My grandmother's starting to think that I am a spy of some sort. I give them the newsletter, try to talk them through it, but I'm not communicating very clearly.
—Kelley Weigel

When I told my mom I wanted to be an organizer she was so upset. She said, "You went to school for so long and that's what you came out with?" In her mind she saw White people with long hair and no shoes hugging trees or the northerner from New York or New Jersey coming down to the South telling the poor Black folks what they ought to do, and then leaving. So it's that mentality. I think that gives it a bad name.
—Octavia Ware

You could type in the search words "community organizer" and come up with some strange things. It seems like the outside world doesn't know what a community organizer is.
—Kelly (Corley) Pokharel

If I really want to engage people, I say, "It's a wonderful job. I get to work with people who are trying to make things better and help figure out how to do it. I help them figure out exactly what they want and who can give it to them, how to get those people to give it to them, and how to stay together while they do it."
—Dave Beckwith

organization. I think there are people who say they are community organizers who kind of float and do good. But if there's going to be a shift in power, unaccountable floating will not lead to that. Or it will not lead to a *sustainable* shift in power.
—Scott Douglas

Sometimes people understand . . .

With Latinos, it's much easier in some ways, because a lot of us come from a country where we had done this work, you come with experience. Or maybe they hadn't done it, but they had the knowledge of what an organizer is. For example, a lot of times when I go into the community, people say, "Oh, I know what you're trying to say. I know, you're trying to organize and make a revolution." They understand it that way. So even though people haven't done it, they have it in mind. They understand what organizing is and what it is we're trying to do. So, with Latinos it's much easier.
—Edgar Rivera

. . . and sometimes they don't.

I've had several reactions when I say I'm a community organizer. I had one person say to me, "Oh, you must have really clean closets."
—Vivian Chang

Two things happen when you say you're an organizer. They say, "Is that when you organize closets and offices?" I say, "No, I'm not that kind of organizer. I actually organize people. Think about the concept of organizing a closet and making sure things are where they belong. There's just a better view of your closet. My job is to look at the world as a closet and make sure people go where they need to go so that the world looks better."
—Lisbeth Melendez-Rivera

But often the question provides an opening
to talk about organizing to someone new.

An article I wrote about the labor movement starts out with me going on a plane trip. "What do you do?" the person beside me on the plane invariably asks. It's usually a businessman. On good days I tell them I'm an organizer, and I'll wait for their shock to appear on their face. On bad days I say, "I work for a non-profit." And on really bad days I think about opening a bakery and dumping the whole thing. After I tell them I'm an organizer, I ask, "Do you know what that is?" And sometimes people will say, "Oh, like for a union." Then you at least have a way of starting in. I say, "Well, union and community organizing are really related. It's looking around and seeing

The role of the organizer—A story

I help leaders sort through the data and information they're collecting in our research and help them think through what our plan of action should be. Often I'll come up with a draft of recommendations on how to go into a research or negotiation meeting. Then I help them to evaluate afterwards. It's my job to help the group come to a common interpretation of what just happened in that meeting.

This is a good story related to the housing that we've been working on. First, another organizer and I met with our spokesperson to be clear about our questions and our approach and to rehearse a little bit. Then we had a meeting for the seven people going into that negotiation meeting for housing for low-income families. Then we reviewed all of our roles and the demeanor that we wanted to take. We role-played every different kind of reaction that we could get from this guy. How do we want to react, as a group? We did all this practicing of how we're going to react to this official. Then we go to our meeting. We get in to see the official. He's smooth. He's a politician. He knows how to wine and dine.

So he is going on and on about how he agrees with us but why he just can't do it. "Here's why we have to keep it at 140 percent income" [housing assistance available only to those whose income is 140 percent of the median income]. It's basically B.S. And he's using big words that we don't really understand and concepts that we think we understand. He's kind of outfoxing us because he's been in this field for however many years. So in our evaluation afterwards, the leaders are a little bit intimidated and not sure what to think. They're saying, "Maybe he's right. Maybe it is impossible. Maybe he's doing all that he can do." Part of my job, as an organizer, is to agitate that a little bit and also help to facilitate a discussion so that no one person is dominating.

"Well, Reverend Gladd, do you think he's doing all he can do?" Then she said, "Well, it sounded good, but now that I'm out here I don't think so. Why can't we serve people making $15,000?" We start talking about it. If we left that meeting and just went our separate ways, I think half of our leaders or even all of them would have said, "Oh, he's a nice guy and I think he's doing all he can." But if we go through and interpret we can cut through that layer of B.S. We can interpret that together: "The stuff he said . . . there was no basis for that. He was just kind of giving us a speech there. He wasn't really giving us hard facts about why. And we do know that these other communities have been able to serve these people." So by the time we left we have agreement that this guy's argument did not hold up and that we're still going to fight this. What's our next step and how are we going to fight it? I think the organizer plays a big role in helping to facilitate all that.
—Haley Grossman

something that's not quite right, then working with other people to try and make that better. There are things like that in every community."
—Kim Fellner

That is one of the toughest things—explaining it to people. You ask a question, "What kind of problems do you see in your community? What are the things that you would like to fix or make better if you had a chance?" Then you pick one of them and you say, "Well, community organizing is taking this problem that you have and seeing if there are other people in the community who have the same problem and who would like to see it fixed. You try and find those other people and you get them to work with you to figure out who has the power to make a decision that would change this situation. Community organizing is about getting that group of people together and getting them to go and put pressure on whatever public official who has the power to change it and get it done."
—June Rostan

Profile: Brian Johns
A Day in the Life of a New Organizer

We asked Brian Johns, a new organizer, to describe a typical day, to give an idea of what life is like for an organizer still learning the ropes. At the time of the interview, in October, 2003, he was an organizer for the Virginia Organizing Project. He is now Political/Community Organizing Coordinator for the Service Employees International Union District 1199P in Philadelphia.

I have a great job. I have two main formats for a work day. One is the office day. I'll come in at 8:30 or 9:00. A lot of the work to set up meetings is done in between the meetings. The meetings are the really fun part, but you might have to call 150 folks to get ten out. A lot of those days are spent just calling people, or doing research. For example, I started working on a Virginia Housing Development Authority campaign. They had a $1.2 billion surplus that wasn't being put into use helping low-income folks get affordable housing. I would go in and look at VOP's database or contacts that I knew from different churches just from being in the Richmond area. So I create these lists. I call my office the "Land of Lists" sometimes, because you've got all these initial contact lists, and then you'll take a list of thirty, pare it down to the ten who've responded and who agreed to meet. Then once you meet with folks, you have another list of those who are really interested in acting on this. Some days in the office you're calling people all day—following up and setting up meetings.

Another office task might be research. We're starting a tax reform campaign; I didn't know a whole lot about Virginia's tax structure going in at all. So I spent some time recently reading a lot of the information on the tax system we have in the state and on some of the proposals that our statewide strategy team are working on to change that. I'm trying to make sure that I know enough to speak about it. So it's research, making calls, making lists, and following up from meetings. A huge part of it is follow-up.

We had a Dismantling Racism workshop in Petersburg on the ninth, and had about fifteen folks there. I'm calling all those folks and seeing what they thought about it, and really talking to them about some of the issues that were brought up. That's the same with any meeting. You want to come out of a meeting and sit down and really reflect on what happened. And then strategically think about what's next. "So we got this done, we got that done. What do we need to do to keep this thing going?" So that's the office days.

Then there are the individual meeting days, which are the traveling days. I'll try to set up three, four, or five meetings—however many I can on that day—and just go. For example, it can be going to ask for endorsements on the affordable housing campaign or campaigning to restore voting rights for former felons who had served their time in Virginia. You spend a lot of time meeting with folks to get endorsements, and with folks who work with voting rights or in civil rights organizations. Or churches, or different kinds of organizations that might be interested in signing on to work on the campaign.

And from those meetings you work out what people are willing to do. Some people say, "Hey, endorsements are a gimme. What else can I do?"

Then there are one-to-ones. One-to-ones are a huge part of chapter development. In Petersburg I started in December just talking to folks. I was mainly going into the community, figuring out what people were passionate about and what people wanted to see changed. These conversations can range from forty-five minutes to an hour and a half. It's just really finding out what people are interested in, and if they'd be interested in working with a group like VOP.

Also, we do a lot of planning meetings and trainings. The chapter in Williamsburg is going down to meet with the state senator and we've got a mix of a couple folks who have done this before and really been active in meeting with politicians, and a couple—"This is one of the first meetings I've been to in a while because I got involved with another group that didn't really pan out or something happened." And some have never been active before. And just really working with that group and saying, "Well, what do you want to say to the senator? What do you want to get across and how do you want to do it? Who's going to talk? Who's going to do this piece of the meeting, who's going to do that?"

So that's what some of my days are like. Really odd hours at times. Sometimes it's 5:30 or 6:00 getting home, and sometimes it's midnight. The first formal chapter meeting of a group includes a visit from a VOP State Governing Board member. The closest one that could go to Petersburg was in Lynchburg. So I left here [Charlottesville] at 3:00 in the afternoon for a 7:00 meeting. Lynchburg is west of here, and Petersburg is east of there. So hours are all over the place.

It's really a great thing, for example in Petersburg, to see a group go from these local, individual conversations to fifteen folks sitting in the room at a meeting saying, "We've got a real problem with drugs in the city," or "with kids on the street during school hours," or "with landlords raising our rents but not providing the services. What can we do about this?" and really look strategically at these kinds of things.

That's my typical day. It's either in the office or on the road for meetings or trainings. Today was an office day; we got back from a retreat this weekend so I had lots of follow-up to do.

I'm still struggling a lot with the whole aspect of not overworking. I'm getting into this mindset of, "We could all work on this forever, and what change are we going to see?" It's truly easy to get into the thing of, "Well, if I just make these twenty-five more calls today that's one step closer to the goal."

My life, I would say, is pretty consumed by organizing. But I am learning how to set some of those boundaries. You need a day off or an afternoon off every now and then, and understand that that's acceptable. I think the organization does a good job of making you see that as well. But at the same time it's what I love, and this is how I want to live. I tell people I'm always surprised every time I see the paycheck—it's like, "Whoa." This is something I really love doing.

Profile: Don Elmer

35 Years
and Going Strong

Don Elmer is Organizing and Organizational Development Specialist for the Center for Community Change in Washington, D.C. He lives in Issaquah, Washington. He was interviewed in May 2003.

I grew up in North Dakota. My father was an evangelical preacher with the Evangelical United Brethren Church. He was assigned to German-Russian territory in the south central part of North Dakota because he had grown up in a home where they spoke German.

This church eventually joined with the Methodist church and became the United Methodist Church in 1968, but I would consider parts of the North Dakota conference at that time to be in the fundamentalist tradition. It was fairly insular. It did a great job of building community internally, but if you weren't part of that church you were an outcast. It was considered dangerous to associate with people who were not "saved." That was probably one of the most troubling things for me while I was growing up.

A lot of my friends, growing up, were not part of our church. It was always troubling, to me, to think that these kids that I really loved were all going to hell. There was just this thing in my head that didn't make sense, even though I totally bought the religious tradition of that time.

When I was nine years old I went through what they called a "conversion experience." I was "saved" when I was nine. My father was the evangelist at that time—we used to have evangelists come through all the time, and at that point it was him. The thing that I remember most is at that moment feeling that I was okay just the way I was without changing a thing, which was one of the more profound moments of my life.

There were 400 people in the town, and each summer, for two weeks, there would be this revival meeting. Two thousand people would show up. At the beginning, I didn't understand what that was about. I found out, years later, that it really was an ethnic gathering of German-Russians throughout that whole region of North Dakota and South Dakota. I didn't know that anything existed like an ethnic community. I thought it was the community I grew up in.

One of the things that happened there that had an impact on my life was that they would have not just missionaries from overseas, but people from Africa, Asia, and South America. Because I was a preacher's kid, a lot of times those folks would come and eat with us at our house. It was just mind-blowing, because everyone else looked the same in our community and many of them looked down on others that were different.

During that time, sitting around the table, it was like dying and going to heaven and finding all these interesting people from all over the world. It just took me a long time to realize that that experience had a lot to do with my being drawn into organizing.

I ended up in Chicago, in a multi-ethnic setting. That made a whole lot more sense to me. It was like a moth to a flame. I was going to find a church that was more inclusive and that didn't condemn people for who they were. That was the piece that drove me. I ended up going to seminary in Chicago. While I was in Chicago, at seminary, I used to run into Saul Alinsky. Alinsky used to come to my seminary—at that time it was called Evangelical Theological Seminary—and there was a college right next door to it. So he would speak at the college and then he would come over to the seminary and would be looking for organizers. He was abrasive and entertaining. We just all loved the guy. He scared the hell out of our professors. It was a big deal.

One experience after another led me to people who had worked with Alinsky in one form or another. The first experience was with Shel Trapp, who at that point was a pastor with the Evangelical United Brethren Church on the near north side in Chicago. I was assigned to his church for my field work. So the two of us would work together. We were both conservative as hell: no drinking, smoking, dancing, whatever. But he used to hold a dance in his church and we used to change all the prayers, so those were the most radical things we did in church.

Then I ended up going to do an intern year with Rev. James Reed at another church in Chicago who had worked with Alinsky on the south side. It was the defining moment of his life. He ended up getting thrown out of that particular church, but it really shifted the way he looked at life. I was this country boy from North Dakota. The first day I got on the job, the whole church and the pastors were out in front of an all-Black public housing complex. The marshals were evicting everybody, so they would take the furniture down, and we would take the furniture back in. At the end of the day, the two pastors were jailed. I just freaked out. I loved it and was scared shitless.

I was married at that time, and we ended up going to the Peace Corps for two years in Korea. It became an experience that allowed me to digest what had happened to me in my intern year. Again, it was in a different culture. I would get up in the morning and look at my face in horror. I looked so ugly. I wasn't Korean. My nose was way too big, and people would throw stones at my face and call me "big-nosed American." There was a lot of hostility there because of the presence of the American military.

I remember walking down the streets and I got kicked in the groin outside a bar. I could barely walk. I hated all Koreans for two weeks. Through that experience, though, I began to see how rage and anger are part of life. I came to terms with being in Korea and understood the reasons I was kicked. I also began to understand that I needed to have some boundaries about me; it was okay to protect my own interests. It was a good setup for my organizing experience.

I came back and then headed for seminary to finish up. By that time I had integrated a kind of theology that fit my circumstance better. The seminary and the students I dealt with well, but a lot of the professors turned on me and decided that I was too radical to be there. A lot of these folks were friends of my father and they thought that they were protecting me from a bad environment. They tried to tell me that I needed to go home to North Dakota to be a pastor, which I had intended to do.

But interestingly enough, after that experience, I decided that I would work for Alinsky for one year. He was mostly traveling at that time, so I would work with somebody who had worked with him. I would work for a year and then go back home to be a pastor. Obviously, I never got back home, which I've always been grateful for. I found something that really fit me. This was the Northwest Community Organization, and it was the home of the organization in Chicago where the anti-redlining movement had started.

After two weeks on the job it was like dying and going to heaven. It was like I had found my niche. It was so exciting. I could hang out with ordinary people, people from every ethnic group imaginable—Poles, Blacks, Puerto Ricans, Ukrainians, etc. We had them all in the same meetings. I took them by car to the meetings. When they were alone in the car, the Poles would call the Blacks "niggers," and the Blacks would call the Whites "honkies." Everyone found a racial slur. But when they would get to the meeting, if the target or enemy up front tried to polarize the crowd by attacking one group or another, they would all get up, no matter what they had said in the car

• • • Jesus' way was to turn the other cheek and to be totally vulnerable and in some ways invite attack. What I had to learn is that Jesus was not a namby-pamby. He threw tables over in the temple. He called the religious leaders of his time "vipers" and worse. So I had to integrate the strength and power with the vulnerability and gentleness that I learned as a kid. Jesus lived out both. • • •

and say, "Don't ever talk to my brother like that again." There was this sense of unity.

I found out, years later, that I had organized, along with a woman organizer who was under my supervision, the first campaign against a bank to get them to invest in the neighborhood where they had made all their money. That started to scatter all over our area, then the city, then the country. It eventuated in CRA [Community Reinvestment Act] legislation, first in Illinois and then nationally.

This path that I'm describing is from September of 1970 on. In a way, community organizing became my way of expressing the faith. I ended up being ordained as a United Methodist minister because by 1970 there had been the merger between the UBE and the Methodist Church. My particular appointment was what they called "specialized or extension ministries." So my ministry was considered to be community organizing.

Keep in mind the time period that was going on. In the midst of all that, Martin Luther King was coming through town and there were riots in White communities trying to keep Blacks out. By the end of seminary I was going to all the anti-war marches. All of the women's movement stuff was happening in that period, too.

I wanted to do an expression of faith where I didn't have to talk about it. The talking about it was contaminated by my upbringing, which seemed very coercive and pushy. Organizing gave me an opportunity to live the faith. It was joyous! It was fabulous!

Jesus' way was to turn the other cheek and to be totally vulnerable and in some ways invite attack. What I had to learn is that Jesus was not a namby-pamby. He threw tables over in the temple. He called the religious leaders of his time "vipers" and worse. So I had to integrate the strength and power with the vulnerability and gentleness that I learned as a kid. Jesus lived out both.

In 1973, I became the director of the Northwest Community Organization [NCO]. I learned a phenomenal amount from Shel Trapp. Again, it wasn't an accident that I got drawn toward him. I have to tell you this story.

When I became director of NCO, Trapp left me a poster to put over my desk. It said, "Yea, though I walk through the valley of the shadow of death, I fear no evil, for I am the meanest son of a bitch in the valley." Trapp was a former Methodist pastor and left the church to become an organizer. He came out of a faith commitment as well. We were like brothers in that sense. He was tough and I was gentle. He hoped I'd learn to be a little tougher, which was reflected in the poster he gave me. I always hoped he'd get more gentle. Over time, I found my own strength and I began to see the gentleness in him.

I thought for a long time that the reason that I was a successful organizer was that I was learning from Trapp how to be tough. People would laugh at me, years later, when I would describe this. They would just say, "That had nothing to do with it. We always knew you weren't like Trapp. People used to come to your meetings because you knew how to build relationships." I could fill a room faster than anybody, but I often didn't know why they were there. I had to learn strategy. I had to learn how to think methodically. Trapp was brilliant as a tactician and strategist; I learned that from him.

There were a couple of things we were doing at the same time. The organization had to be renewed. It had been built in the old style of Alinsky organizing as a combination of church, community, and labor (if there was labor there), and so on. At the beginning of NCO it was made up of churches, civic groups, and settlement houses, with churches being the most powerful. Twenty-two congregations were pulled together by Monsignor Egan, and they were told to each give a certain amount in dues. They came up with the money! It was astounding. All the money was raised at the beginning and then was put in the bank. Then there were the settlement houses [social service agencies]. What would happen there is they would supply an organizer to organize their constituency around the settlement house. Then there were civic associations in the community that established a democratic structure for each part of the community. This was a large area, 160,000 people on the near northwest side of Chicago. Tom Gaudette was named the first director of NCO after Alinsky and Monsignor Egan launched it.

All Gaudette would have to do would be to walk in, meet with the pastor, and ask the pastor to bring his key leadership—anywhere from ten to fifteen people—together the next week. Gaudette would then meet with the pastor and the leadership to find out what the issue was that they were most concerned about. Then they would set a meeting a week later with the alderman. Let's say it was garbage, because in that neighborhood their garbage often did not get picked up. They'd get the alderman to show up and 500 people from the congregation would show up. I was astounded when I would listen to Gaudette talk about it, but it was understandable. It was during a day when the pastor was the key leader of the parish and community. He was also usually the key leader of the entire ethnic community. So you could get thousands of people out by having these twenty-two pastors pull people into the organization.

By the time 1970 came along, the role of pastor in the community had eroded. Institutions in general were not trusted. So that the same pastor who had announced a meeting at Mass and got 500 people to show up was now lucky to get five!

So when Shel Trapp became director in 1970, he had to figure out how to renew an organization that had gone stale. He had to take an experience that he learned on the west side of Chicago, in a neighborhood that had been all-White ethnic and had turned Black overnight. The neighborhood just emptied out. There were no churches to organize there, no settlement houses to organize there, no civic groups to organize there. So they transformed block clubs that had been formed by Blacks in the community to create a sense of community into action arms of the organization. That transformation became so successful that, for a period of history in Chicago, people forgot how Alinsky had originally done the organizing and thought that the only way to organize was through block clubs!

So the system of organizing in Northwest Community Organization of relying on the churches and settlement houses fell apart. Trapp used block clubs to renew the organization. This system of using block clubs helped renew the civic associations, but it also prodded the churches and settlement houses to continue to play a role in the organization.

I came to NCO the same day that Trapp became the director. I didn't know that I had put together some of the first block clubs in the organization. I was just doing what Trapp told me. I didn't know the history. That's one of my lessons too—I think that we forget about our own history and the history of the organization at our own peril. When crises come along, then you no longer have the tools to look at them from another position and come up with ways to deal with it. So we renewed the organization, but unfortunately we lost the history.

We won incredible things. The neighborhood was what they called an "urban renewal designated area." It was supposed to be torn down and all the poor people thrown out. It was supposed to be middle income and rich. We were able to stop that and it became one of the first areas of Chicago that stabilized as a multi-ethnic neighborhood. Hyde Park was high-income and had a mixture, but this was low-income. Then we started all these campaigns around CRA legislation, FHA kind of problems where people thought that they were buying a house that was up to code. Most of these people who were buying were Blacks and Puerto Ricans, people of color. They thought it was guaranteed by the government, but it turned out that they were falling apart.

What we did is we organized all of these homeowners and went after FHA. It was a long campaign. What came out of it was reimbursement legislation through the federal government. These people were reimbursed for the repairs that they had to make on their homes that weren't up to code. So that kind of stuff was going on.

We launched all of our campaigns from that meeting. We had Westside Coalition at that time, which were organizations from NCO all the way to OBA, where Gaudette was, in Organization for Better Austin.

I want to go back for just a second. During my first week at NCO (Trapp was the director), I ran into an issue in my assigned neighborhood. Chicago had a lot of "panic peddling" at that time, which is where a real estate operator would come to a White ethnic family and scare the hell out of them with "the Blacks are moving in," and all that nice language, and "You better sell now, or you're not going to get anything for your house." So they would literally pick up in 1970 a house for, like, $2,500, for example, and sell it to a Black family for $19,500. So both sides would get screwed.

One of the issues we had was against Mayor Richard Daley. We had gone all the way through his system from the alderman on up, because we had a huge number of open and abandoned buildings in the neighborhood, and we needed them torn down. They were so bad that they were being used as shooting galleries for drugs. People would start fires in them, and the fires would spread to other buildings. It was just a mess. They were so far gone they couldn't be repaired. So we went after the mayor. I think we must have had 500 buildings, something like that. They needed to be torn down. The alderman and everyone else in the bureaucracy kept saying that there was no money for demolition. This went on for weeks with no results. It was getting very dangerous.

We finally got all the way to Mayor Daley. We sat in his office until he finally came to talk to us. By the time he came to talk to us we had gone through his system so thoroughly that he couldn't say, "You did it wrong." So he finally said, "Well, tell me what's going on." So people would tell their stories about what happened. Kids would get raped and buildings were burned down. He had tears in his eyes. He said, "It's true. We don't have any demolition money to tear down the buildings. But I will guarantee you that we will tear them all down starting tomorrow. I am designating the fire department to tear them all down." So he had the fire department of the city of Chicago tearing down 500 buildings. The firemen hated us, but the community just loved it. So that kind of stuff was going on.

I became the director in 1973. I was interim director first. At that time we would have an annual meeting. It was what we called a congress. The organization was in very bad shape when Trapp and I came in at the beginning. The organization didn't really represent adequately the Puerto Rican part of the neighborhood.

The first congress that happened when I was alone was incredible. I knew that we needed more Puerto Ricans on the ballot and that we needed more Puerto Rican representation. But a group of Puerto Ricans were really mad by then, and they came in and tried to take over the meeting. Some of them went after one of my organizers and almost beat him up during the congress!

We had to delay the congress for two weeks because it just got totally out of hand. But by the time it was over, part of the Puerto Rican group left and the representation of Puerto Ricans, Blacks, and Whites on the final slate represented almost exactly the numbers who lived in the area. Everybody had their fair share of representation.

One of the things that you should know is that things got really rough in organizing all over the city. At NCO things would get really nasty at meetings. People would fight and get up and shout racial epithets. That kind of stuff was awful. But we just thought it was Chicago and that was

What makes a good community organizer?

Some of this stuff may sound kind of canned. The piece that's always been the most important for me has been the listening. These days I would call it "deep listening," without interruption. In the old days I would listen just long enough to get what the issue is and then launch into what needed to be done.

Now I have a little more patience for just listening, period. To get to know someone on a deep level so that you can figure out what their own self-interest is and who they are as people and help them to move toward in terms of what their dreams are about. Yes, there are battle tactics and all that kind of stuff along the way, but the really important thing is to help people connect with their dreams.

Another way of putting it is to help them connect their external lives with their internal lives as well, so that their lives are not split and dualistic and moving in a direction that isn't very satisfying. Part of it is to try to help individuals with this, but then try to help individuals connect to the community so they are not isolated. The people in the United States often atomize each other into individuals. You need to build a sense of community and build a sense that this group of people has the capacity to do and be history, not just hear about history. They can fully engage in the moment of creating something new.

I think that one of the characteristics of effective community organizers is that they really have to know themselves as well as the person or group that they're working with. If there isn't that capacity for self-understanding, the organizer is a very limited, mechanistic kind of guy or woman. That kind of stuff came to me much later in life. It's crucial, because otherwise you're just stirring things up without understanding what the hell life is about. You get other people into trouble and then you shrink back into the shadows. That's really a chickenshit way of dealing with life.

A good organizer should really understand the political milieu that people are part of and understand the history and what's going on. I think that's really important.
—Don Elmer

the way things were. People were crazy. What we found out later was that our organization had been infiltrated by not only the FBI but by the City of Chicago Police Red Squad and by the state of Illinois. It was during a time that Mayor Daley was freaked out with all the dissent and civil rights stuff. So he was interested in getting rid of all the organizations that he thought were communist or subversive organizations. Even if they weren't, they would trump up the charges and try to destroy the organizations.

I left as director in 1975 and became the director of a group we had put together, the local equivalent of NPA called MAHA [Metropolitan Area Housing Alliance]. It was during the time that we passed the national legislation on FHA and CRA in 1977. I had a staff of thirty-five people who came from all over the city and represented the twenty-five Alinsky groups. We'd have a meeting every week and then we would do actions all over town. Some stuff was rough. There were internal battles that were really tough. It took a lot to hold it together.

One of the lessons I learned the hard way was that you don't try to mix a national organization and a local organization or a local coalition all in the same room. We had the national and the MAHA organization in the same office, one big, open room. We would make a decision in the staff meeting and by the following morning it would be undermined by the national staff because it didn't quite fit in with what they wanted nationally. It just got incredibly hard to deal with. My staff was just so mad all the time, because we would make a decision and it would get undermined. We finally actually built a wall down the middle of this huge room. We said, "This side is MAHA and this side is NPA."

There were a number of buildings in our neighborhood. The landlords would run them down. They would get people to pay the rent but they would never fix them. Then, at some point, they would get someone to burn down the buildings so that they could get the insurance money. The mob was involved in this and Alderman Keane as well. He ended up going to prison.

We asked the state of Illinois to come in and investigate it. We found out later that instead of investigating these landlords and real estate operators and insurance companies, they investigated us! We sued FHA for not securing their abandoned buildings and the case ended up in federal courts. The federal courts had to share with us the information they were using against us in the court case. After I had left NCO, the new director, Eunice Sweedenburg, and I went downtown to the federal building. They showed us this room. It was filled with all the files from NCO. They were in better shape than all our own files were. They knew everything that went on. Our attorney couldn't tell us what the FBI had said about us, but locally they said that I was running a subversive organization out of the back of my car. They were trying to drum up stuff about my background in North Dakota. They were getting into meetings and disrupting meetings and breaking up meetings and trying to destroy us.

We asked what the FBI had done. Our lawyer said he was sworn to secrecy, but he said, "Don, just rest assured that every time you took a dump it was in the report." So we knew that people were inside. It was phenomenal that we lived through that. In fact, the organization thrived and worked well despite the infiltration. It was so chaotic internally that you had to be steady as a rock.

Judy, my wife, was accepted into law school in Washington, D.C. So

I decided that I would go there with her and try to put an organization together there if I could. I had a group of forty Black congregations as a sponsoring committee. It was phenomenal. It was just wild. At that time, I didn't know church-based organizing. It was a neighborhood that was made up of all rental units and it was turning over from all Black to all White overnight. Developers would come and throw people out of buildings as large as 450 units. They would revamp them and resell them as condominiums and make enormous amounts of money. So that was the threat.

We put together a tenant organization to stop the condominium conversion. We actually won, but with a lot of help from the economy at the end of this process. I built the organization from '77 to '78. We launched it in '78. In '81 we pretty much stopped the condominium conversion but we also turned a lot of these buildings into co-ops where the tenants could buy into their building as a co-op and they could stay.

The organization was called Washington Inner City Self Help. The only thing bad about that name was that the acronym was WISH. For a community organization, that didn't seem quite tough enough.

I learned another piece there, in terms of race. What I decided when I came to town was that because we'd never had enough people of color on our staff prior to this, that this was going to be a Black organization. I promised the organization when I built it that my job would be to train Black organizers. One of them would follow me when I left. I didn't know the power of actually saying that up front, at the beginning. That was really what made it work. At the end of the process we had plenty of people to choose from to be the director.

Then I went to Denver. I wanted to do church-based organizing because I'd heard a lot about it out there. The [Denver] sponsoring committee was put together by IAF [Industrial Areas Foundation], but it had taken six years and IAF still hadn't sent in an organizer. The group got mad and hired me instead and threw IAF out.

So I came in to try to be the first director of a congregation-based organization in Denver, without ever being trained to do it. That was very difficult. It turned out that things worked out, but it wasn't easy. I had to take all the organizers in the neighborhood organizations (eleven) and work with them. I included them on my staff. The Catholic community organizers (four) were also on my staff.

I had to try to come up with a unified process so that the organizers around town wouldn't attack each other or undercut our new organization. Then I ended up being able to slowly but surely pick the ones who would be best in congregations. They had to know the congregation structure and at the same time work with the community organizations in town so that there was a blend of neighborhoods and organizations.

We ended up being able to build to a convention of a thousand people. We had some great stuff on the issues. We ended up winning a state utilities commission through the state legislature. The campaign started with our going after the state utility company for outrageous rate increases. They refused to negotiate, so we passed state legislation to hold them accountable on a regular basis. We also started a campaign to clean up the Rocky Mountain Arsenal, which we won several years later [cleanup of nuclear and chemical pollution].

It was at this point in my life, at the end of MOP—that was the congregation-based organization in Denver—that my life fell apart. I was exhausted. I wasn't taking care of myself. My marriage was falling apart. I didn't have a personal life. I ended up with a divorce and that was what got my attention.

I decided that I had to live my life a different way. One of the things I had to change was this drive where organizing was the only thing in my life and there were no boundaries. So I ended up with a Buddhist meditation practice and some counseling. I discovered that there was someone alive and well inside of me and that I needed to find some balance between my internal and external life. I had to pay attention if I was going to first of all survive, and then thrive again.

I'm sixty-one years old. I started organizing when I was twenty-nine. I went straight through with no breaks, no vacations or anything, until 1985. During that period when everything fell apart I actually started to consult with groups around the country and got interested in building new organizations from that experience. During my time with the Center for Community Change, I've been able to help build twenty new community organizations (mostly congregation-based).

During that interim period of '85 to '87, I ended up doing part-time consulting and I worked as a chaplain at the University of Colorado, Denver. Then in '87 I was hired by the Center [for Community Change]. That came at a perfect time in my life. Andy Mott came through town and kept asking me what I was doing. Eventually he said, "Why don't you think about coming to the Center?" I said, "What about all the groups that I'm working with?" He said, "Bring them in. We'll give you a paycheck every month. You don't have to charge."

I ended up doing just that! It was a very creative time for me. The Center at that time gave me the space to do what I wanted to do. It felt like what I was called to do, just being a support system to community organizers and organizations in the area and also to help build new organizations.

I think turning into a consultant suited me after that period of time because my experience was actually very grounded in good organizations. I was lucky. I got trained by one of the best at the time in Chicago in the '70s. That gave me a foundation that I really have been grateful for. I learned organizing from the ground up and I learned it from the issues and through building structures and through building coalitions all the way to the national organizations. I felt grounded in that. I had this two-year hiatus where I was much more introspective and was taking care of myself.

One of the things I discovered with true meditation and being more reflective was that I could sit back a bit and not be quite so wedded to outcome. I could spend two weeks with some folks and not be wedded to a particular outcome. I think that's necessary for a consultant. You really can't meddle in the same way and don't have a right to. It's more healthy to be able to see that the process flows.

You have to build a relationship over time, that's the other thing. The people that I started consulting with on my own, in 1985—I literally spent fifteen years with them. Some of them would come in and out, but a lot of them stayed many years.

What else did I learn? That was one, the thing about letting go a bit. Being able to trust the process that they would have their own solutions. I can bring in ideas from the outside if it's appropriate, but I don't lead with that. One of the dangers with the Center was that they didn't charge. I think one of my learnings is that when I was working alone I needed to come to terms with my own value and that I needed to pay attention to my own needs in terms of money. I could have been much more clear about what I needed and then gone after it, and not felt guilty because these organizations didn't have much money. All organizations have enough so that it doesn't have to be for free.

The Center actually became a really good hybrid for me. We have people who come up with expenses when they're able to, but with a brand new organization we'll do something for free because we've raised money based on it. So that's a bit ambivalent even yet, but I think the important thing is to have integrity with whatever you're working with. If money isn't involved, you have to be clear about what the group wants and be able to think about how you're going to deliver it if you can. If it isn't working out, you need to be able to turn around and say, "I can't stay here. I have to terminate this agreement."

Where Organizers Come From
Childhood Memories

Many of the organizers we interviewed recalled their childhood experiences as being formative in how they came to see the world, leading them to become organizers when they grew up. For many, their parents played a strong role in forming their ideas and beliefs. But their childhood experiences are incredibly varied; there doesn't seem to be any pattern to how future community organizers grow up, except that—somewhere along the line—they learned that the world needed to change, and that they could help make it happen.

Where they come from

Many were from small towns and rural areas.

> I grew up in Billings, Montana. My grandfather homesteaded about twelve miles from where we're sitting, at a place called Rattlesnake Butte. This is my dad's father, so I was born and raised in Yellowstone County and that's where I started organizing. I grew up here, went to high school here. When I graduated from high school I went to the University of Montana in Missoula. My family still lives here. My parents are still alive and they live about five blocks from here.
> —Patrick Sweeney

> I'm from Virginia originally. I grew up in a small southern town down in southeastern Virginia. Smithfield was what it was called. It had a population of 3,000 or so. I spent my whole childhood there. My family name was Gwaltney. In Smithfield that meant that I was upper class in terms of socio-economic status. There's Gwaltney meat products and the packing plant thing and everything. That's my family.
> —Ben Thacker-Gwaltney

I grew up in River Rouge, Michigan. This is a very small down-river community that borders the city of Detroit. You can actually stand in three cities at one time if you bend over a little bit. They are very small communities. Up until I was a teenager, the areas were very, very segregated. I don't think that people started moving across borders until probably the '80s.

My people originally come from Mississippi. My grandmother and my grandfather on my father's side came out of Mississippi and settled in Little Rock, Arkansas. Then their children moved. The boys moved as young men to Detroit. The girls moved to Seattle, Washington. I'm the first generation born in the North.

—Rhonda Anderson

I grew up in northern Wyoming. All of my grandparents were born in Poland and immigrated to Wyoming. My grandfather took over a small homestead, so my father grew up on a ranch, which is also the ranch I grew up on. It's quite small. Coal mining's what brought them to that part of the world, so my father also worked in the coal mines. Of course, the working conditions were deplorable. My grandparents worked in very tough conditions. I didn't realize that I was poor because everyone else was poor, too, so there wasn't a great deal of money in the community. Only as a teenager did I begin to be aware of some things. I was always aware that I

Children can be an important part of community action. Members of the Idaho Community Action Network greet the Immigrant Freedom Riders at a migrant camp outside Boise.

was Polish, and I was always aware that that was a bad thing. There were all those denigrating Polish jokes. So I became aware of prejudice very early in life.

—Pennie Vance

I was born in Casper, Wyoming, and my dad worked in the energy industry, so we lived all over Wyoming. I went to school at the University of Wyoming and got a degree in elementary education and graduated about the time all baby-boomers graduated.

—Vickie Goodwin

I was born in Albemarle County, in the Charlottesville area. I am the oldest of four girls, which I think has a little bit to do with where I am now. I grew up on a family farm: nothing fancy, playing outside a lot. I went to the University of Virginia, which is also in Charlottesville. I've done most of my work life in Charlottesville. I'm a pretty one-area girl in a lot of ways. My experience is local work.

—Julie Jones

I grew up on a farm in central Illinois. I went to a small rural school. It was a consolidated school of eight different towns because none of the towns were big enough to support a high school. My mother is a Democrat, and my father is a very conservative Republican, so we always had lively, spirited political debates around my house. In high school I started going to political conferences and doing political volunteer work. It's a very, very conservative Republican area, and I would seek out the losing Democratic candidate and volunteer some time after school.

—Emily Gruszka

I grew up in upstate New York, in a small farming community called Steuben of about 200 people, mostly small dairy farms. It's an area of upstate New York that was settled largely by the Welsh in the 1800s, so a lot of Welsh people live in the area—Roberts, Owens, Williams, Hughes, Jones. Pick your name.

My dad was very active in politics pretty much all his life. He served as a county supervisor and a justice of the peace, and was pretty active in Democratic Party politics, so I'm sure some of my interest in organizing came from that experience. My mom has always been the conservationist of the family, so she cares a lot about the environment. She was actually a hunter most of her life, whereas my dad could care less about spending any time outdoors, and an outdoor adventure for him was mowing the lawn. I spent a lot of time with my mom, doing that kind of stuff. I probably got some of my appreciation for environmental justice, environmental issues, from her.

And then, certainly, my dad ran a farm co-op, and actually just retired.

Our next door neighbors owned a small dairy farm and I started working there as a teenager. So I worked on farms, and I think that cultivated my love for family farmers and agriculture.

—Kevin Williams

I grew up in a rural part of Connecticut. My father is a self-employed homebuilder. My mother didn't work outside the home; she did a lot of work at my dad's business. I just came from a real blue collar, middle class background.

—Sara Kendall

I grew up in a little town in western North Carolina called Valdese, this small textile, bread, and furniture town. I was the middle child of three from a working class family. My father worked in the bakery, in the wrapping room. Then he delivered bread. He had a bread route from the time I was in eighth grade. Then later he went to work in the town's water filtration plant, and then finally to a small factory that made vats. My mother was an office worker for over thirty-five years at the office at the bakery. It was a big bakery, an industrial bakery.

There were 111 students in my graduating high school class. Most of the kids came from working class families.

I grew up in the Presbyterian Church and was very active in the church youth group. I was active in Girl Scouts and a lot of things in school: high school drama, public speaking, and debate. We debated whether there should be health care for the elderly. This was in the '60s. I debated the pro side on that, and the people who debated against us said that having health care for the elderly was socialism. I'm glad that we have it and so are a lot of elderly people. So that's where I come from.

—June Rostan

I grew up in a little town in rural Ohio called Dover. It's kind of strange mix between an agricultural community and a community that has a lot of steel mills around it. I was always interested in ocean issues and natural history, and I grew up spending a lot of time in the woods and my mother taught me a lot about just being by myself, so that's what I grew up doing.

—Pamela Miller

Others lived in big cities or in the suburbs surrounding them.

I'm from New York. The place that feels most like home is Queens. We lived there for much of my childhood, though not all of it. We also lived in Manhattan and Long Island. My family was very public-service oriented. There was a tradition of civic engagement and political engagement. That was virtually all of my family. That manifested itself in activities that I would not be part of. They were generally Republicans and had a more conservative view of the role of government and fiscal spending than I do. But I actually think I gained a lot from that background, in terms of the importance of being involved and the idea that people can make a difference.

—Janet Groat

I was born in 1958 in New York and grew up in New York. Eventually my folks moved to Long Island. My dad was a builder who went bankrupt and became an architect. They moved down to D.C. because there were more jobs down here in the '60s.

—Jon Liss

I grew up in New York City, which is a special thing all on its own. I went to public school in New York.

—Kim Fellner

I was born in Nashville, Tennessee, on December 4, 1946. My nickname as a child was "Baby Douglas" because my father and mother could not agree on a name for me before we left the hospital. So I was signed out of the hospital as "Baby Douglas" and that stuck.

My mother was a lifetime maid who worked at other peoples' houses. I was often always put down at school because my father was a deliveryman. He was the sole employee of what we then called a "feed store"—a hardware store with rabbit food, chicken feed, bales of hay, kindling—in the middle of urban Nashville.

—Scott Douglas

I was born in Cambridge and grew up in Massachusetts and New York State, primarily. My father was a professor and we moved around based on where he was teaching, but it was primarily in Schenectady, New York, in a working class neighborhood and then in Amherst, Massachusetts, which is a groovy college town. My grandmother was an immigrant from Italy and worked in the sweatshops in New York City and Philadelphia as a seamstress and my grandfather was a taxicab driver. His extended family lived in the Bronx and had a small family tailoring business.

—LeeAnn Hall

I am a second-generation child of Taiwanese parents, the middle child, and I was born and raised in the San Francisco Bay area, which is where I spent most of my life growing up. I am the daughter of a really strong line of women figures in my family, really just strong. My grandmother survived by sewing clothes, and was widowed at a very young age. She totally made it on her own sheer power, and I draw a lot of my strength from her and from my great-grandmother and from my mother—all very, very strong women in their perspective on life and instinct to survive.

—Vivian Chang

I grew up in Louisville, Kentucky, which is where my mom's family is from. I never knew my biological father. He sort of left the picture when I was about two and my mother was pregnant with my younger brother. I grew up in Louisville, first in the house next door to my grandmother and then in some low-income housing. Then my mother remarried when I was maybe six, seven, eight. My dad adopted us, so he's my dad. He brought three children from a previous marriage and then they had a child together, so there's six of us.
    —Leah Ottersbach

I grew up in Boise, Idaho. I spent the better part of eighteen and a half, nineteen years there. Third generation Idahoan. My mom is a fourth and fifth grade teacher, and my dad sells real estate.
    —Aaron Browning

I grew up in Maryland, in the suburbs, in I think what might actually be the oldest subdivision in Anne Arundel County, Maryland. Not a good neighborhood, because it was old and very sort of working- to middle-class, but on the beach so it's a little more valuable now. Sort of classic suburban schools. Where I grew up I remember woods but now it's shopping malls and housing developments.
    —Bob Becker

I grew up in a suburb just north of Chicago, in Winnetka. I lived there until I left for college. If you know Winnetka, you know that it's a fairly White, conservative, uneventful place. I didn't really know what activism was, growing up, until I went away to school.
    —Abigail Singer

I was born in Huntsville, Alabama, and lived there until I was about ten. Both my parents worked for IBM when the company was doing a lot of work with the space program in Huntsville. Then they closed that facility down and transferred people to a lot of other places. We ended up moving to Lexington, Kentucky. So I consider most of my growing up to have happened in Lexington and central Kentucky.
    —Brett Kelver

For several of the organizers, their childhood involved living in a foreign country, either as a native or as an immigrant. For others, their parents' immigrant experiences helped shape their lives.

As far as growing up, I don't remember and it doesn't have any impact until I was about six when we moved to Vietnam. My dad was training English teachers. For the next seven years or so we lived in Southeast Asia while he was doing that work. That had a very substantial influence on my life. Issues of race, power, and colonialism . . . those things were very real. My dad was progressive and he was a social scientist. So he had a pretty enlightened attitude about those kinds of things.

Then we came back to the States and it was '64. Fairly rapidly we were dealing with the Vietnam War and Civil Rights.

—Larry Yates

I was born in Barcelona, España. Spanish was my first language, my mother tongue. My second language was French. My legal father was British. My biological father was a Catalan businessman and deep-sea diver with whom my mother carried on a twelve-year affair. I grew up in a mostly English-speaking family, but I did not speak any English myself until I was sent off to boarding school at the age of eight and was forced, for sheer purposes of survival, to learn it. I fled English boarding school when I was sixteen and entered the American College in Paris. In Paris, I spent most of my time in cafes discussing Marxism after navigating my way through the madness of the Place de la Concorde on my Solex [motorbike]. Winter holidays, I returned home to Franco's Guardia Civil with their machine guns positioned on each street corner, and summers to the ecstatic freedom of the Mediterranean beach scene, dancing all night and watching the fishermen pull in their nets at dawn.

—Brian Shields

I was born in El Salvador, and I grew up there. Basically, the things I did there were going to school, helping a little bit working with my grandparents. I immigrated to the United States during 1979.

I left my country because all these massacres started in El Salvador . . . there was the army, and I didn't want to be recruited. I decided to leave, and also I was looking for that American Dream.

—Edgar Rivera

I was born in the Dominican Republic, in the capital, Santo Domingo. My father is Black Dominican, from a very poor urban family. They were rural at one point, but during the dictatorship they ended up moving to the capital. My mother is White American; you can actually say old school WASP from the U.S., old settler families in the U.S. So she moved down there and I was born down there with my two brothers.

My father was involved in movements of resistance against U.S. imperialism. So my political development—the development of my analysis—really started from the get-go. I was born during the 1975 civil war. Marxist values were the foundation of our family.

In 1981 we went into political exile outside of the country. My father had an opening at the United Nations and went there. My mother, who was American, was very happy to come to the United States because it had been a very difficult seven years. My father started work with the U.N. We ended up only being in the U.S. for a couple of years before we went to east Africa. I spent some very formative years in Nairobi, in Kenya.

I would have to say that those are the primary formative parts of my personal experience that have influenced the development of my politics. It's being in a multi-racial family with Marxist analysis. It's being a person who's traveled and lived in other places from a very early age.

—Ana Lara

I was born in Carolina, Puerto Rico. My parents separated in 1973 or something like that. In 1975 my mother decided that she wanted to move to New York City, so she moved to the Bronx with my sister and myself. At that time, I was like eight years old. I didn't know any English. At that time the slumlords—the building owners—were setting some of the buildings on fire so they could get insurance money. I didn't know that at the time. The only thing I knew was that my mother kept moving from one building to another building to another building.

—Wanda Salaman

I was born in San Juan, Puerto Rico. I am the child of mixed class background parents but grew up middle class within the standards of Puerto Rico, which is probably working class here. It's a different scale. I grew up with parents who were incredibly civically conscious. My father was a Rotarian who believed that civic duty was part of the work that one must do when one is given certain advantages in life. I was blessed with a godfather who was incredibly politically active. He was a member of the Independentista movement in Puerto Rico. He got harassed a lot about that. So I had a lot of political talk and I had a lot of this idea that privileges in life come with a duty. It wasn't just about sitting on your ass and enjoying what you had. You needed to give something back.

—Lisbeth Meléndez-Rivera

I was born in Los Angeles. Both my parents were Mexican immigrants: my mother from the state of Coahuila, my father from the state of Sinaloa. They met in Los Angeles and got married there. I was born there. I was the third child. Then we moved to San Luis, Arizona, which is right on the border with San Luis, R.C. Sonora, on the Mexican side, so it's a border town. My father had a grocery store but then he closed it down. That coincided with my father and my mother separating for other reasons (not the closing of the store). My brother was about six months old and I was three when he left the home. We grew up with my mom as a single parent.

I started working in agricultural labor when I was about eleven or twelve. Then we made the trek to California—my mother, my two sisters, and my younger brother—in the summers to go to work in the various crops. In Arizona we worked picking cantaloupes. We also picked lemons and oranges and worked in packing sheds. In California we did everything:

lettuce, tomatoes, green peas, green beans, prunes, cauliflower. We did the whole spectrum of agricultural work.

Because my mother couldn't make ends meet, my sisters and I worked three days a week, either Friday, Saturday, and Sunday, or Saturday, Sunday, and Monday. We had to miss school to work. We worked in the fields. I remember going to the labor trucks and being there before the school bus picked up the rest of our classmates. When we were delivered in the agricultural buses, we would stay inside so that the kids from the school buses wouldn't see us. We worked over twenty hours a week. That was before high school. Then in high school I worked in a grocery store and later at a department store as a bookkeeper.
—Diana Bustamante

My parents are immigrants, one from Germany and one from Austria. My grandmother lived with us when we were growing up. What was interesting about the household was that my mother's parents were concentration camp victims. I never knew them. They were killed before I came along. My mother was a war orphan and left home when she was twelve. She never saw her parents again. My father was a college student when he left Vienna. He ran away and his mother survived. She's the grandmother who lived with us. So we had a bilingual household, German and English.

I think a lot of that framed the people that I and my brother and sister became. My parents took away from their experience the really important values. Living through terrible things does different things to different people. It makes you brave in different ways and scared in different ways. I think my parents, to our good fortune, took away the lesson that you are always accountable for your own behavior and responsible for the well being of your community.
—Kim Fellner

Other influences

*For some of the organizers, race was a central factor
in determining the later course of their careers.*

I always feel as though I got into social justice work through my family. I feel like, in some ways, being born with more melanin in my skin in this part of the world under the historical context of America, the date of my birth was probably the date of my activism. My grandparents and my parents lived in Alcoa, Tennessee. My mother wanted me to be born in a hospital, so she was driving to Knoxville, Tennessee, which is about eighteen miles, to get her checkups and doctor visits with an African-American doctor. She had to be rushed to Knoxville General Hospital when I was born because that was where the African-American doctors could work. Consequently I'm

from Alcoa but I was born in Knoxville because of racism. I feel like that's where my activism starts, on May 5, 1951.
—Donna Uma Aisha Brown

I'm from Sparta, Georgia. It's the third largest county in the state as far as area, but it has a population of about 8,900. Much was accomplished by my father, who was hired in the early '60s by Hosea Williams as a field organizer of the SCLC [Southern Christian Leadership Conference]. He worked with them for two or three years and I guess he became disillusioned. He felt that it was one thing to be able to sit at the counter with White people and have lunch, but he thought that his efforts could be better used if he would organize to make sure that Blacks had the money to buy a hamburger once they were able to gain access to the restaurant. I remember us marching for thirty days straight to desegregate the schools. In our household everybody had to march. Mama and all the children: everybody in that house who had legs had to march. And the other families in the community felt the same way, so we crowded the streets every day for thirty days. It was like a big party. The young people who became elected officials at that time were my heroes. I really looked up to them.
—John McCown

I was born and raised in Chicago, in the South Shore neighborhood. I started in Montessori School until third grade. Then I went to a small Lutheran school. There might have been about thirteen people in my graduating class. One of the interesting things I began to realize about that experience is that the majority of the teachers were older Black women, so I might have been one of the last generations in the Black community to get that whole thing about, "You have to work twice as hard and jump twice as high in order to compete in the world." I think as I got older that played into why I do the work I do.
—Steve Bradberry

I was born and raised in Montgomery, Alabama. I grew up in an area of town called New Town, just outside of downtown Montgomery. We were really blessed. The neighborhood I grew up in is considered low-income. Most of the people there are pretty poor. Some were actually middle class, but New Town had the reputation of having more lower-income families than middle-income families. In fact, it's not far from one of the projects in Montgomery. Going to an integrated school meant there was tension. But at our end of the street, our house tended to be the house that a lot of the kids would come to.

My parents were strict in terms of having very definite ideas about how they were going to raise their kids. They worked really hard. I appreciate it now, as an adult, more than I did then. They were instilling in us a set of

values, a value system. As my father would say, it had nothing to do with anyone else around us. People might say, "Well, you're from a certain neighborhood, and kids from there have certain experiences." That had nothing to do with us. Education was key in our house. I often tease my nieces and nephews now, because they might get a stomachache and not go to school. My mama was a nurse. If we got sick she'd doctor on us that morning and send us right out the door to school. We got perfect attendance because education was such a big deal in our family.

—Presdelane Harris

Presdelane Harris, age 12

I grew up in Richmond, Virginia, born, raised. I went to public schools, elementary and middle school with all African-American students. I never attended integrated schools until high school. I was in the first group of students that integrated Highland Springs High School in Highland Springs, Virginia. It was a new experience for the majority of us. I had to learn how to deal with things I had never dealt with before. My family members never talked about racism. They were more focused on protecting me from racism than actually sitting down and teaching me about racism, so racism was a new experience. In my experience, teachers had always been working hand in hand with students and very supportive, and all of a sudden you've got a teacher calling you a niggra and having to sit in the classroom with only one other Black kid in the classroom, there's just two of us. The teacher is describing historical events and talking about the niggras, and the White students are laughing and giggling about it and the Black kids are having to sit there, not responding and not able to tell the principal. Parents reported this to the principal but nothing ever happened. That was life at Highland Springs High School for me, but we learned to survive. We learned how to work together, the fifty-four Black students in my class. We were never selected to participate in school activities so we just made our own and made sure we all got home from after-school activities by car-pooled rides. We attended sporting events, plays, and school concerts as a group.

—Cathy Woodson

I grew up in San Diego. My dad was in the Navy. When I was about three we moved into military housing in San Diego, in a community called Linda Vista. I remember moving there. It was called Kay Park at that time. One of the interesting things about being a Navy family is that everybody is sort of categorized and segregated according to rank of the head of the household.

So we started out in Cabrillo Heights, which was sort of the tenement-type apartments, when my dad was an E2 or something like that. Then we moved to a house in Linda Vista, in Kay Park, just before he became a chief. That's an entirely different type of environment, sort of suburban.

My father was always sort of militant and strong. He was very aware of his African-American heritage and always made sure that we were educated in that regard. He did work for the military in terms of diversity training, back in the '60s and '70s. That was pretty unusual. What I remember is that we always had all the Ebony history books and saw every public broadcast on anything related to civil rights. He would also teach classes to the sailors and the officers on Black history and race. He would try them out on us in the garage. He'd bring home a projector and films that he'd check out from the Navy library. He'd sit us down with all the kids in the neighborhood. He had a chalkboard and everything. He'd show us the film and then lead us through a discussion. We always thought it was fun. You got to see a movie.

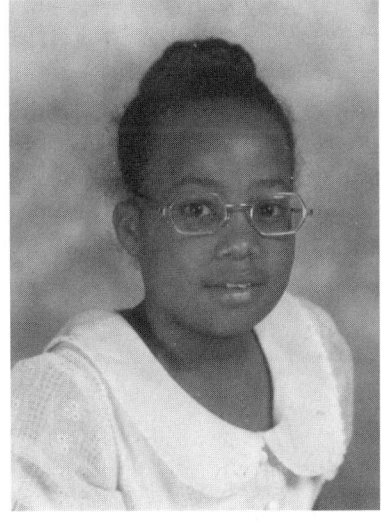

Karen Waters, age 8

My parents divorced when I was twelve and we moved into almost an all-White suburb. We lived in a subsidized low-income housing project. There were four of us kids. That was a culture shock to us, to move into an all-White environment that way. I remember going to school and there were just a handful of Black kids. Our first week of school some White kids threw water balloons at us and yelled "Niggers!" My sisters transferred out of school. They were old enough to say, "We're not going back." My mom allowed them to ride the transit bus for about an hour every morning back to our old neighborhood to go to school. But I was too young, and would've had to go to a different school, so I didn't have any choice. I just had to make it work.

—Karen Waters

For others, it was the experience of being an outsider, looking in at the culture around them.

I grew up in rural Colorado in Leyden, a former coal mining town of only twenty-seven houses. Leyden is west of Denver, between Golden and Boulder. It sits over part of the northern coalfields, which were established at the same time as the southern coalfields. The southern coalfields have a history and aura about them, because the National Guard actually opened fire on miners on strike there at the turn of the twentieth century. It was called the Ludlow massacre and the incident is part of United Mine

Workers of America union history. The northern coalfields operated at the same time and at the same point in history.

The Leyden mines provided most of the coal for the Denver tramway system, but the tramway system shut down in the late '40s. That prompted Leyden mines to shut down after they lost their key customer. My parents moved to Leyden just after World War II, along with a bunch of other vets who used their benefits to acquire homes. By then, there was only one former mining family left.

Leyden was built as a company town. The Leyden brothers built the houses at the turn of the twentieth century to provide housing for their miners. The houses were company—all tiny and all looked alike. The houses consisted of 640 square feet of floor space, tarpaper-covered wooden buildings with pyramid-shaped corrugated tin roofs.

Leyden was a defined community. Everyone knew everyone else. We had really limited water resources. One spring served the water needs of the whole town. Most people worked at Coors, which was not too far away, or at the railroad. It was a very blue-collar town.

We were located within the sphere of the Denver metropolitan area, but essentially rural. I was born in 1951. In the '50s and '60s, the suburbs of Denver started to grow. This prompted major changes in Leyden. During my lifetime, the two-room school got consolidated into the larger district; the one-gas-pump store went out of business; the water system got absorbed. Leyden went from being a fairly independent community to being an extension of the Denver metro area. We were the remnant of rural poverty. People from the suburbs would drive out on Sundays and point at us, the kids with coal dust streaks on our faces, and the grim little houses where we lived.

I got bused to suburban schools, which gave me this deep sense of being on the outside looking in. We all knew that we were from Leyden. Everyone could figure out who we were. That experience was extremely formative. We could be real clear about the fact that they had "it," and we didn't.
—Gary Sandusky

I grew up in southeast D.C. My strip was middle class, but all around was the inner city and low-income housing projects. My grandmother raised me and it was just her and me. I'm Grandma's baby. I was a Huxtable kid. I went to church and did ballet and swimming and traveling. Life was good. She had her knees operated on so we moved to Crewe, Virginia. She wanted to go back to her home where life was slower and that kind of thing. So I moved to Crewe from D.C. at the age of fourteen or fifteen. I think I cried for a week. I graduated from Nottoway High School. I remember the first time I was walking into the high school. A male classmate and I were walking through the door together. He stepped in front of me and opened the door. I just kind of stood there. I didn't know that men opened doors for you, so it was kind of like a whole new culture for me. That was life growing up.
—Octavia Ware

I was born in Louisville, Kentucky. My father was a Presbyterian pastor and from a farming community near Louisville. We moved from Louisville while I was a baby, so I have very few memories of Louisville as a child. We moved to Whitesburg, Kentucky, up in the mountains of southeastern Kentucky. He served a church there. Then we moved out to the western part of the state, to Madisonville, when I was in about the second grade. My father was called to a church there. We were there for about three or four years and then we moved to Charlotte, North Carolina, where we lived for about six years, serving the church there. In the middle of my eleventh grade in high school, we moved to Dallas, Texas. I finished high school and began community college there. So I really don't have any roots. We moved a lot. We never got settled and made long-lasting networks of friends. I've always been adapting and learning.
—Robert Owens

An amazing number of the organizers we interviewed are preachers' kids.

Maybe, as Dave Beckwith says, these parents gave their children a sense that one's career should reflect one's faith, and that working for and with others for a better world is something to be strived for.

My dad's a pastor. He was active in civil rights and peace work, even in the '50s and '60s. He's an American Baptist minister. In some ways, the model of what it is to be a man was created in my mind, very early. A man believes in something. His work is about that. His life revolves around his work. His family and his relationships are all one piece. A key piece of that is what you believe in. So that was the model.
—Dave Beckwith

I grew up in Colonial Heights, Virginia. It's not the most open-minded place in the world. I moved there when I was seven. My parents are both Presbyterian ministers, so I grew up in the Protestant/Presbyterian tradition. We moved there because my dad got a job in Petersburg, which borders Colonial Heights.

Probably the first or second year, we came out of our driveway—we lived really near the high school—and on the side of the school in huge letters is graffiti mentioning "Colonial Whites." And when I think of Colonial Heights that always pops to the top. It's about ninety percent White. Very conservative, very Republican. It's an interesting place to grow up. Right across the river is Petersburg, where my father's church was. It's about eighty percent African-American.

I knew from the beginning that I was different from most folks in the town, coming from a more progressive background. I grew up in the church, in this culture of service. At least in Presbyterian churches, there are a lot of opportunities to do service work. For example, we went to the

soup kitchen every year and helped serve. Didn't really think much about it. We'd go to Petersburg to do that. Or go on mission trips: "Let's go work on somebody's house. Hundreds of miles from here. It'll be a good time, we'll get to swing a hammer, see a different place." So I was brought up in those traditions of doing mission work and service work.
—Brian Johns

I was born in 1951. I grew up in Mississippi in the '50s and '60s. I was very fortunate. Both my parents were native southerners but were very clear to me that the system of segregation was morally wrong. That was at the center of our families, of our lives, and of my understanding of faith. It was definitional to my growing up. Our dinner table was always a conversation about current events, which in Mississippi meant that it was a conversation about civil rights. It was a really formative thing for me. On top of that my dad was a pastor and I grew up in a church environment where faith was very important. I think, looking back, there was always this tension in my family life where the notion of faith was permeating all of who you were. I was told that segregation was going away, but at the same time I was told that we couldn't do anything about it. In fact, we had to be careful who we told that we felt this way. I was never comfortable with that, so there was always this tension in me. I was always looking for ways to act on that.
—Perry Perkins

I grew up in Nashville, Tennessee, for the most part. I'm fifty years old now. My dad was a Church of Christ preacher and a sociology professor at David Lipscomb College. He had grown up picking cotton in Mississippi, and went away, got liberal on the race issue, and decided he wanted to come back to the South and change things with regard to race issues in particular. He believed that his best venue for doing that was as a teacher and preacher. He was a big influence on me, as was my mom, of course. She has always stayed involved in my work and helped me think through ideas.

All through junior high and high school my dad and I would talk about what Lyndon Johnson was doing in the War on Poverty, and what Martin Luther King's work meant and all that. That was a big issue of discussion for us. I went away after college to the northeast to work in poverty ministry in New York and New Jersey, but ultimately wound up coming back down south to Alabama in 1991.
—Kimble Forrister

Profile: Teresa Erickson
Organizing in the West

Teresa Erickson is the Staff Director for the Northern Plains Resource Council in Montana. She was interviewed at the Western Organization of Resource Councils (WORC) Board and Staff Meeting in December 2002.

I grew up in Western Colorado, the daughter of an underground gold miner. My mother is part Mexican, part Indian, and those two people had much influence on me in terms of how I think about this work. Partly because of being the daughter of a miner, and being sort of ethnic, we saw a great deal of injustice: labor injustice in terms of my dad and then ethnic injustice in terms of my mother.

I grew up in Telluride, which is a ski resort now. That experience made me dislike ski resorts because that town is nothing like it was when we grew up and none of the long-time natives could manage to stay there. It's now very rich. I mean ultra, ultra rich. An incredibly beautiful mountain town that is littered with enormous second homes and other development which is quite unappealing to me.

We moved down the valley because my father's health was so bad that he couldn't live at the altitude anymore, even though he was born and raised there, because he had silicosis. When we moved away from Telluride, my dad had to move to a mining camp, and I was raised by my mother and her two unmarried sisters in a down valley town called Montrose. So it was my sister, myself, my mother, her two sisters—we have a very strong female orientation. My poor dad, who came home every ten days, had to deal with this gynarchy or whatever.

It influenced me. They, my two aunts, more than anybody drilled into my sister's and my head that you never rely on a man for money. They gave us this sense of independence and neither of us had that drive to get married to be able to quit work and be supported by a husband. They taught us how to take care of ourselves, including managing bills, repairing things, and doing garden and yard work.

I went to school at the University of Northern Colorado at Greeley and really my pursuit then was to have fun and see more of the world. I had no academic ambitions; I mainly just wanted to get out of Montrose. Greeley is way out in the eastern part of the state. It's flat land and I had never been to such a place before. When I would come home on weekends and bring my friends with me, people could not believe that we grew up in paradise. It wasn't until I was nineteen or twenty years old that I realized that we grew up in the most beautiful place on earth, envied by everyone who didn't grow up there. I became very attached to my homeplace at that age, interestingly.

I had no academic goals so I took home economics classes and shop classes and stuff like that because that was more interesting to me. I was a geography major. I took a class called "Diet for a Small Planet" and read the book by Frances Moore Lappé. It politicized me incredibly—and it was a home economics class. It was a cooking class mainly, but the book, the politics around food, the politics around organic, whole food versus processed food just shaped my thoughts so much. It pushed me towards getting involved in the Greeley food co-op. I didn't even know what a food co-op was or the structure of co-op. So through that class, I got involved in the food co-op, and through the food co-op, I met people who worked for CoPIRG [Colorado Public Interest Research Group]. I went to work for CoPIRG for about a year after I graduated, and that's how I heard of the term "community organizing." Through CoPIRG I was exposed to a lot more thought about social justice, strategy, and taking on the bad guys. It wasn't really organizing—I mean they called it organizing, but it was justice and getting into that tense, conflict-oriented work. My first job was being a mediator of landlord-tenant problems. I had just been a student, and so I totally took the side of the tenant until I saw what students did to properties. And then I realized, "Oh my god, there are two sides to this story."

CoPIRG gave me experience on other issues like wilderness, energy, pollution, things like that. After about a year at CoPIRG, for a lot of reasons I decided to keep seeking life adventures. I had $300, a dog, an old Datsun 510 station wagon with all my worldly possessions in it, and I decided to move to Ecotopia, to Oregon. No particular reason except that I had heard that Oregon was progressive, but I decided to go stop in Montrose on my way. So I stopped, saw my folks, and met some people who were going to Mexico. They needed someone to go with them to babysit their kids. So I went, spent all my money, had a great time in Mexico but came home broke. So, at least for a while, I was stuck in Montrose. I got a job waiting tables there.

Then I worked for the District Attorney as a Child Support Enforcement Officer and then was recruited by the Department of Social Services to be a caseworker. At social services, I worked in nursing homes, which was just the most depressing job on earth. Compared to my previous jobs, it expected so little of me that I organized a local community group while

What makes a good organizer?

Optimism. Love of people. I don't mean to sound arrogant because I'm not a perfect score on all these things, but you have to have a lot of love for things: for people, for the world, for trees, for dogs, animals. I mean it just seems like that helps you overcome enormous odds.

Being lighthearted, although I don't know, I could contradict myself on that too. Sometimes I really enjoy working with people who are very serious about this work because they are so into it, but I think what helps you survive the dark times like we're experiencing with the Bush Administration now is being lighthearted about it.

Being irreverent; being able to be irreverent in almost any circumstance has helped me many, many times.

Being disciplined. And appreciating discipline, honoring discipline that people really work to keep details and to keep on task. I mean organizers who have discipline are amazing, amazingly effective.

I think you have to be outgoing. I have yet to see a shy person succeed at organizing. Sometimes people can overcome being shy, but it eats them up and makes them unhappy because you're exposed to so many people all the time.

People who think strategically like Baldemar Valesquez. The minute you meet Baldemar Valesquez he starts to size you up and size up your issue and wants to talk to you about how to leverage power. I don't know if that's something you learn or if that's something that's just inside of you, but it's a characteristic. Maybe it's what you work towards becoming, but people who have a strategic mind, who are critical thinkers that question things, make effective organizers.

Then I think there's some sort of indefinable thing that some people have in them, like they enjoy the fight. It's so stimulating to them. I like Oprah Winfrey a lot and have read some of her stuff. One of the things that she says that I find really interesting is that she has a term, she calls people who like to work hard "staminists." She said that she spent a lot of her life being criticized for being a "staminist" and was told she ought to get a life and all this sort of stuff. But it's what she liked to do, and she has a lot of energy. I think staminists do well in this work.

—Teresa Erickson

I was working. I was so used to having a high work ethic working for CoPIRG and then working for the District Attorney, that when I went to social services, I could do the job with one arm tied behind my back. And I hate being idle. So I surreptitiously did a lot of the basic work to organize a group, using pragmatic intuition—I didn't really know what I was doing. There were a lot of us who lived in Montrose who were alarmed at some of the things that were happening environmentally, as well as the rising electric rates. Fighting electric rates was one of the first issues I got involved in.

My sisters and I formed a group called Uncompahgre Resource Council and became extremely controversial right away. We had such an unusual profile for "environmentalists"—we were local from the community, daughters of an underground miner, sort of hispanic-y looking. People wanted us to be spokespeople for our organization. So we were leaders in an organization that we formed. Within a very short period of time, we realized that if we were going to get serious, we had to raise money and make the organization much bigger. We then created a larger regional group and knew we had to have somebody working on this full-time. So we did that, and I applied for the first job opening. I was on the board of directors and applied for the job and got hired as the staff director for the Western Colorado Congress.

WCC had its first annual convention and we brought out a speaker that somebody in our group had heard about, this cowboy from Montana named Wally McRae. He came out and he spoke about community organizing even though he wasn't an organizer. He was a leader. He was so charismatic and so articulate that he just swept the crowd. And then he went back home and talked to the staff director there, Pat Sweeney, now my husband, and Pat called us up and said, "We're always looking for organizations that are similar to us and Wally told me about you guys. Can I come down and meet with you?" And it was Pat that really began to paint the picture about community organizing for me.

What have been some of your proudest achievements as an organizer?

God, I wish I had some that just leaped to my mind. Well, forming the Western Colorado Congress, especially not knowing a thing about what I was doing. I was very much the driver of that, just out of pure instinct. And even though it has its flaws, structural flaws, because I didn't know what I was doing, I am proud of the fact that it's still alive. It just celebrated its twentieth anniversary [in 2002]. It's kicked some ass.

Then we've been fighting this awful railroad that hasn't been built yet, and it's proposed by a speculator who wants to shorten the route of the coal mines from Wyoming and cut through Montana, a short-cut railroad up to the Midwest. It's a horrible idea because it would run through one of the last fairly undeveloped river valleys called the Tongue River, which is a prairie/desert river [valley] that is very sparsely populated.

The Northern Cheyenne tribe lives right there. One of my proudest moments in this organization is knowing that, if not for me, I'm not sure the organization would have dealt with the Northern Cheyennes like we have. We have cultivated them, the tribe itself formally as well as many tribal members, into very strong allies—and not without hurt and pain because reservation work is very hard. You have to be willing to be subjected to racism by Native Americans against you because you're not a Native American.

I think that working with tribal folks raises this very complex set of oppressive characteristics that you must juggle in order to be successful, and you have to be really willing to be vulnerable, to be criticized. But the power of the reservation is huge, and we're fools if we don't see how powerful the reservation is. For just sheer straight-out strategic reasons we should get involved with tribal people.

Then for greater reasons of unity and overcoming racial problems, we should seek Native Americans as allies when we have a mutual self-interest. I'm proud of the fact that I pushed us to be deliberate in seeking the Northern Cheyenne as an ally.

And that railroad is still not built. It hasn't gone away in terms of a proposal, but we have clearly won on that over and over and over again. We also built a coalition with unions, so here you have cowboys who don't get along with Indians or unions, and the Chambers of Commerce in these small towns all working as one really well functioning informal coalition. And it was fun. Every single piece of it was fun, except some of the dark nights when I thought we might lose. But it's probably one of the things I will forever look back at in my life and think, "That was some fun."

• • • I'm a true believer. I believe organizing is the only way to really change things. I definitely believe deep in my heart that community organizing is the only hope we have for a better world. That's why I stay in it, and I enjoy it. There are times when I get up, and I can't wait to go tackle this or go some place. I'm thrilled a lot of the time. • • •

One experience that defined my career to a certain extent was a ballot measure, I 122, a statewide ballot measure that we initiated and coordinated with seven other organizations in Montana. This ballot measure would have outlawed a practice in this state that allows hardrock mining companies to pollute directly into rivers, giving them a "mixing zone" that is as big as it takes until it's diluted to the point where the water meets state standards. Some of these mines have mixing zones that are miles long, and they have polluted over 3,300 miles of rivers.

So we ran this ballot measure, and we were up against huge out-of-state and even Canadian mining companies who outspent us ten to one, and we lost.

But we built this incredible grassroots structure across the state, and Northern Plains did all the mechanics for it. We figured out how to have area captains in each county and defined the job of an area captain. We got eight groups for the first time ever to merge all of our membership lists. Then we sorted them by geography, and we recruited people out of our mutual lists to be area captains and volunteers. We had a network of 900 volunteers who did a lot of things. We held town meetings and public debates, and we did literature drops. We could not fight them dollar-for-dollar in advertising, but we fought like hell and we lost. And we lost forty-three to fifty-seven, so it was a decisive loss.

It taught me the power of television to the average voter. Before the bad guys' advertising came on TV, we were polling sixty-nine percent. We were winning big. And then when TV ads hit we just death spiraled. We couldn't come back up. Now I'm proud of it, but it shook my faith. I had a crisis of faith for about three months. I was demoralized by thoughts like, "People are sheep; they're so stupid they fell for phony ads. . . ." You know, I was really hurt. I was hurt that agriculture, our base, went with the mining companies because the mining companies zeroed in on rural areas and said, "You're next. If you pass this ballot measure they're going to come after your cows that poop in the creek," and all this sort of stuff. But after much reflection, I later believed that, shit, we hung on to forty-three percent. Forty-three percent saw through three-and-a-half-million dollars worth of advertising. I finally recognized the greatness of this accomplishment.

At the same time that happened, there was another ballot measure to outlaw corporate spending in ballot measures, and it passed big time because people are weird voters. They were disgusted at all the confusing and outrageous ads on TV, so they voted against our ballot measure, but they voted for something they did understand, which was to take corporate spending out of ballot measures.

The anti-corporate spending measure was eventually struck down as unconstitutional, but that took two years. So there was a two-year window of time in which no corporation could spend money on a ballot measure, so we ran a ballot measure to outlaw open-pit cyanide heap-leach mining in the state. It passed and it passed decisively, like 58–42. Ten days before the election, the ballot measure that outlawed corporate spending was found unconstitutional, but the corporations only had ten days to do anything and by then it was too late.

I define a lot of things as pre-I 122 and post-I 122. I learned so much from that campaign, and it was a great experience, but it hurt me deeply that we lost. I'm convinced that you can't run any ballot measures with an ultimate "yes" vote if you have such a well-financed opposition.

I think most voters are only influenced by what they see on TV; they don't encounter contradictory information. They don't go to meetings to learn more about these things. It just told me that as a society we're in deep doo-doo because so few people have developed roots in their beliefs about issues. And only grassroots organizing will give them those roots; it is the only answer, and it's the hardest hill to go up.

One of the reasons we hung onto forty-three percent is because we had town meetings, we had discussions, and we forced people to choose, to think about, "Where do I stand on this?" Our voters were deep—they chose to believe us and to this day, that forty-three percent number shows itself time and again in voting for or against progressive issues.

I'm a true believer. I believe organizing is the only way to really change things. I definitely believe deep in my heart that community organizing is the only hope we have for a better world. That's why I stay in it, and I enjoy it. There are times when I get up, and I can't wait to go tackle this or go some place. I'm thrilled a lot of the time. I mean internal hassles, like staff fighting or board fighting and stuff like that, are the worst. You know if anything could drive me out of this work, it would be that. But I stay in it because I enjoy it and because I really feel good about the fact that we are making a difference.

3
How I Started Organizing

We asked the organizers how they got into organizing in the first place. What was the trigger that made them choose this line of work? For some, it was just how they grew up; organizing ran in the family. For others, it was the time they grew up in. In the 1960s and '70s, change was in the air, and many young people were caught up in creating it. For many, the job as an organizer grew out of their own activism. It was the issues that brought them to the field. Some came to organizing young, some in college, and some only after years of doing something else.

The answers are as varied as the people who gave them

For some it was how they grew up; organizing ran in the family.

I was born in the D.C. area. I lived for a year in the Catholic Worker House there. My parents are very political. My parents actually met when my dad, who is a lawyer, offered to defend my mother for free one time when she got arrested at the Pentagon back in the '70s for an anti-war protest. So I grew up with politics and activism, very much focused on the anti-war movement with a very big emphasis on nonviolence as a practical tactic and philosophical underpinning of what I was working on.
   —Nicholas Graber-Grace

I started to work on these issues in the community because in my family we have our history. My brother was in the university and he was a leader. We were in a very bad government [in Bolivia]. It wasn't democratic; it was a military government. My brother was doing a meeting about the community—what can I help in the community, what can I do for a better life, what can I do for the poor? The government took my brother and put him in jail. My mother was very sad, and we were looking everyplace for my brother. We thought maybe we could not find my brother any more because of the political issues, and we thought maybe he was dead.

When I went to the police they said, "We don't know what it is, we don't know what it is." My mother was very sad; we were trying every day. After that we found my brother but he was very, very sick. It had been a very traumatic experience for him. When he came outside my mother said, "You don't have to do any more political activities. You have to stop." My brother said, "No, Mom. We have to do it again, and more, because I have my experience. And we have to change this life because we need a better life for the poor."

So we started to work on political issues.

—Alicia Ruiz

I actually found out about organizing back in 1960. It might have been a little earlier. It might have been 1959, when the Freedom Riders came through Warren County [North Carolina]. My grandmother let me go with them to introduce them to folks. I was five or six, but I was that kind of kid who knew people. People knew me and liked me and expected me to do things. Even though I didn't know that's what you called it, I think that was my first encounter with organizing.

—Sheila Kingsberry-Burt

I'm in my later fifties now, so I was growing up during the Civil Rights Era. I went to college in '64. I think between that as a backdrop and the riots in the cities in the mid-'60s, I felt particularly drawn to organizing as a way to understand a lot of what I saw going on around us. There was a lot of injustice and a lot of sense of communities up in arms. There was a need to help people really have a chance to become all they could be.

—Ken Galdston

For others, it was the times they grew up in;
in the 1960s and '70s, change was in the air.

In the 1960s I got very intensely engaged in the anti-war movement and SDS [Students for a Democratic Society] and really went about as far out as it could go. I was in the streets and got fairly crazy. I belonged to a collective. The war really was my focus because emotionally it was such an intense thing. But I was thinking about the other issues and I had been involved in some peripheral Civil Rights stuff. I went through the split of SDS. I was there when it happened in Chicago. That was very dramatic and kind of pissed me off at the time, because I didn't think we should be doing it. But I went along with the people I was associated with, who were some of the people who started Weathermen. So I was with that. That was the first time I lived in the inner city. I was in a collective in Baltimore, which was a very half-assed collective . . . we weren't very effective. . . . We went into a high school once and held the teacher aside while we taught the class, those kinds of things.

Then I went to Cuba, for the first Venceremos Brigade at the end of '69. Oddly enough, that really kind of calmed me down. I saw, in Cuba, that the process of political change and political transformation was ongoing. It hadn't ended when they captured Havana. It had *started* when they captured Havana. I came back with more of an attitude of "This is a long struggle. We're not going to have a revolution next week."
—Larry Yates

When I was in high school, I toured Colorado as part of a gospel duet, playing guitar and singing gospel songs in the mountain towns. I walked the straight and narrow and made good grades. Then I got to college in 1969, and discovered drugs, sex, and rock n' roll—and the movement—which were all inextricably linked. If my experience had been limited to opposing the Vietnam War (which was of personal interest because I didn't want to go) that wouldn't have been enough to keep me involved in organizing. Meeting real people and developing relationships with those who had literally put their bodies on the line while organizing the Denver-based Hispanic Civil Rights Movement was like a conversion experience for me.
—Gary Sandusky

I went to Maryville College in the fall of '65, and got introduced to a few professors who were questioning the wisdom of our being in Vietnam. I got involved in the anti-war movement, such as it was on a small campus like that. There were about 900 students at Maryville College when I went. My father had been in the Marines in the Second World War, and was very much involved in the American Legion. It was not easy for me, in terms of my family, to be against the Vietnam War. There was a combination of working against the war in Vietnam, and working some on issues around race. Maryville was a predominantly White campus. There were nine Black students. The Civil Rights movement was going strong in the mid-'60s, so that was a part of our thinking.
—June Rostan

I went off to school at the University of Michigan, in Ann Arbor, 1974. I rapidly became attracted to the anti-war activities and organizing on the campus, and by late 1974, I was pretty much devoting myself full-time to organizing anti-war activity around the state.
—Jeff Malachowsky

I got into this partly because of politics and interest in elections, electoral politics, even in college. I grew up through the Vietnam War and the war protests. I was in college during the years when Students for a Democratic

Some start as canvassers in voter registration drives. Approaching strangers to talk about change is good training for future community organizers.

Society, SDS, was active on campus, and where people were challenged to act on their beliefs if they were anti-war. At that time, certainly many college students, including myself, were. That sort of sparked me to think more about how policies get made, who had the power to decide things like whether we should be in Vietnam or not, whether money should be spent building up the military versus helping people pay their health insurance, all these kinds of questions.

 —Patrick Sweeney

For many, the job as an organizer grew out of their own activism.
It was the issues that brought them to the field.

I had left West Virginia to go to college, and when I came back, my main goal was to figure out how to nail the coal companies. I didn't really know how to do that. I started doing some research into coal and particularly property taxes, because the state was supposedly reforming the way they taxed coal. That was the summer right after I came back, and in the northern part of the state there was a meeting of some environmental organizations, and they had invited this guy, Joe Szakos, who was working for Kentuckians For The Commonwealth at the time, and they were so

generous that they gave him ten minutes to do a presentation as a part of their day-long program. And he talked about the five goals of organizing—Kentuckians For The Commonwealth's Five Goals of Organizing—and that presentation really got me excited about organizing, because it was just about finding people that want to change something in their own community. It doesn't matter what it is, but it's finding people who want to do something and then get them together, and then together to figure out how to build power to change that. That made so much sense to me, because up to that point, most of the activism in college was advocacy—research and advocacy—with a lot of hand-wringing about doing *for* other people. Organizing cut through all that garbage, because you don't do anything for people other than find out what they want to do something about, and then agitate them and teach them how to act on it. That made a ton of sense to me, just given my experience growing up in West Virginia, because I remember going to meetings where these people would be having these high minded conversations about the working class, and what would be best for the working class. And I would be thinking about Ed Mullins, my neighbor, who taught me how to fish and was a coal miner, and at that point had been locked out of his job for over a year and had spent a year and a half on the picket line, and I thought, "What would Ed think about this conversation?" Ed would think it was a whole bunch of crap. But as I thought about organizing, I thought, yeah, I could go and sit down with Ed and say, "Ed, what do you think needs to be different here, and who else do you know that wants to see that different? Can we get them together, and can we start figuring something out?"
—Allen Cooper

Organizing was just something I started doing. There wasn't any one event or huge change in my political analysis. It was just a natural progression of seeing what was going on in my community and reacting.
—Abigail Singer

It was luck. I felt like I was being led to it. I'd been interested in environmental issues from high school, but had really no idea how to plug into them. I'd always felt drawn to social justice issues for most of my life, and environment in particular. In college I was active with getting the recycling set up better on campus and with the Student Environmental Action Coalition. But it always seemed like there was a lack of hands-on work being done. It was always just writing letters or making phone calls or picking up bags of aluminum cans.

Right after I graduated from college this group SEDG [Shenandoah Ecosystems Defense Group] was getting started in town. The first meeting I went to they were talking about going to camp out at this timber sale, and actually walk the area that was going to be cut. It was about getting to know the land in order to try and protect it. That really drew me to it. And from there I just learned as I went and got steadily more involved as the years went by.

—Christina Wulf

When I graduated from college, I traveled overseas for a year with a working holiday visa. I was able to travel and work. I went to Australia and New Zealand for a year and met a lot of activist folks there doing women's rights and environmental issues, just a broad spectrum. It really meant so much to me to meet people on the other side of the world that had very similar values. That really did a lot for me.

Then when I came back I didn't know what I wanted to do. I don't think I'd ever really met an organizer. I didn't know what that was. I just knew what an activist was. I was looking for a non-profit job, but there's no social justice section in the classified ads. There's no non-profit section in the classified ads either. So I started talking with some of my friends that I'd done work with in the past. One of them was the Louisville organizer for KFTC [Kentuckians For The Commonwealth]. They were hiring a legislative coordinator. Of course having my degree in social studies—I also had a minor in Women's Studies—just seemed like a perfect fit. I remember I wanted it so bad. I was like, "This is the coolest job ever."

I was so nervous at the interview, but everybody was so down to earth and laid back. So I started as a legislative coordinator and met all these organizers. I was like, "This is my calling. This is what I want to do."

—Leah Ottersbach

Some came to organizing young...

In high school, in ninth grade, I organized the students and the parents to basically get a teacher removed from the school because she was incredibly racist and had set up a classroom dynamic that was incredibly destructive. I just knew it wasn't right. I didn't have the guidance at that point to be very constructive about it, so I got into fights with her. I was constantly being sent to the guidance counselor. The vice principal of the school, Brenda Smith, took me aside and said, "You know what? You have leadership potential, but you're using it in destructive ways." She said, "What you're doing is powerful and good, but you need to learn some constructive leadership skills." So at fourteen she started me on this path. I imagine she talked to my teachers, because people responded to me in that way. I organized and had the teacher removed. The students and the parents got together and she was removed from the classroom.

—Ana Lara

One summer I was with my friends and we didn't have anything to do. This kid said, "Why don't you start a girls' baseball team?" So I started a girls' baseball team with my friends in the neighborhood. At the place where we

Young people bring energy and
passion to community groups
working for social change.

were playing there was this old guy whose name was Ashley Hakogo. He
was a community leader. I joined a youth group in an apartment building.
The building was like sixty or seventy apartments and maybe like twenty
families left in that building. All the kids that were part of the youth group
lived in that building—the reason that they had a youth group was so that
they could patrol the hallways to make sure that crackheads or drug dealers
were not in the building stealing the windows and stuff like that. We used
to go to monthly community meetings for Cratona Community Coalition,
where the old guy, Hakogo, was the president of the neighborhood
association. So locally I was doing stuff with the youth group, like cleaning
baseball fields and community gardening and doing volunteer services at
the hospital with the older folks. It was making sure that we were active and
keeping us out of trouble.
   —Wanda Salaman

I think there were a lot of different things that planted seeds for me to get
here. There's this guy who I went to high school with (in the '50s). His name
was Husaini Oakley. He got suspended for handing out a pamphlet around
the school blasting the ROTC [Reserve Officer Training Corps], saying that
it shouldn't be a class. People in the ROTC shouldn't get credit for science
when they're just playing army. That was probably the most radical thing I
had ever seen in my entire life: someone actually typing up a letter with his
own name attached to it and passing it out to the school blasting the ROTC.
It maybe wasn't the best way to go about things. It probably hurt some
people's feelings and whatnot. It started dialogue. If you start a dialogue on

a subject, then you will think. And I thought, "That's what organizing is all about. You start to think." You automatically start to do things, because with certain knowledge you automatically have to take actions.

I went to a National Student Congress in Ohio the summer of 1958. That was probably the beginning of my consciousness. Here were students debating segregation, debating apartheid, and talking about the Algerian Revolution. I was like, "Oh my gosh, there's this whole world of people talking about these incredible issues."
—Betty Garman Robinson

The first time I got a sense of [organizing] was in high school, when I lived in Livingston [Montana]. The Northern Plains Resource Council was active there. One of the big issues was whether they were going to put a dam above Livingston on the Yellowstone River. The Allenspur Dam was to provide water for all these coal plants in eastern Montana. Everyone in Livingston was pretty worried about that. So I started following Northern Plains at that time. They had tables and fundraisers in Missoula and I got to know them there.
—Dennis Olson

I've always tried to figure out exactly how I got here. Looking at my parents, you wouldn't guess that they would have a daughter who would decide to be an organizer when she grew up. I grew up in a pretty apolitical family. The politics, when they were discussed, were pretty conservative.

As a girl, I started going to a camp called Nature Camp. It was a great experience because all of the counselors were college students, so it wasn't taught by the little old ladies or even adults. Most of the counselors were seventeen to twenty-five, with twenty-five being pretty old. Most of them were closer to twenty. They were the perfect folks to inspire someone like me. You're outside with them for two weeks and they're teaching you about nature, about how streams work and how forests work.

At the same time they're telling you a little bit about college life and what's cool. A lot of them were just getting involved in environmental politics on campus. A few of them were willing to bring their politics to camp. You'd go take a hike to a clear cut and then you'd get a little bit on the politics of clear-cutting. I wasn't thinking about it then, but now I think that was the roots of understanding a little bit about how policy affects what I care about, which would be the forests that I'm walking in or the stream where I live.
—Julie Jones

. . . some in college . . .

When I was in college, my advisor, who had just moved to Vermont from Montana, was a member of Northern Plains [Resource Council]. . . . I had no clue what I was going to do with my degree after I had graduated, and he set up two internships with environmental organizations in Montana. One was Northern Plains and one was with the Montana Environmental Information Center. I got the internship with Northern Plains and moved to Montana for a summer. I don't think I knew much of anything about it beforehand. I had not had any contact with labor organizing or any other sort of organizing that I can really remember, so it was that direct work experience.

—Sara Kendall

I found out about community organizing when I was in college. There was an ad in the student paper and it just said, "Care about neighborhoods? Come to a meeting!" It was an information session on an internship program the college was offering in community organizing. I started as a student intern doing neighborhood organizing in Providence, Rhode Island, in 1976.

—Ellen Ryan

I went to Chicago in 1954 as a senior in college. A recruiter, Andrew Billingsley, talked to our sociology chair about work with the American Friends Service Committee as interns in community service. So off to Chicago three of us went, and one girl went to California. I was assigned to the Urban League and did community organizing. I think there were two full-time people in that department.

We organized block clubs. There were telephone calls coming into the office all the time saying things like, "We don't have any police protection on this street, on 32nd and something." My job was to go out and talk with them: "What do you want to do about it?" And then help them make the slingers. I learned to operate a mimeograph machine. Then we'd go out and distribute them.

"Would you have this meeting at your house? Would you tell your neighbor?" That was what I did for six months. I worked full-time as an undergraduate student. We lived in the Quaker house, on 56th and Woodlawn. So that was my first real experience with community organizing when I knew that's what it was called.

—Marie Coles Baker

I found out about organizing during my senior year in college. I was trying to figure out what I wanted to do after I graduated college, if I wanted to go to grad school or if I wanted to go straight into the work force. I really didn't know what to quite do with my sociology major. . . . So I sat down with my career services center and they did a profile of some of my interests. About a week later, they sent me this e-mail about the DART Organizer's Institute. I'm reading it and I'm like, "Oh my. This is it. This is it!"

—Makiva Harper

When I was at the University of North Carolina at Chapel Hill, the state was trying to locate a nuclear waste facility as well as a hazardous waste facility. Essentially they had joined two compacts with the surrounding eight states where they agreed somebody would site those two facilities and they drew straws and North Carolina lost. During the four years that I was in school I watched the state siting process as they just bounced around from one poor Black community to another. I listened to the reasons why they were thinking of putting it here as opposed to there. And also I was very involved with getting students to support the communities that were organizing against these facilities. It just introduced me to a new way of trying to think . . . I had never heard of community organizing before that. But suddenly, these communities that had no power and no right to be able to hold up this huge process were really quite effective. I also watched as they struggled to get beyond just the "No, we don't want it here" to "What does it mean when you were successful and the state just moved to the next town over?" All of those questions were really rich and helped kind of set me on a path.
—Lisa Abbott

I just happened to be in the right place at the right time. When I was in college I thought for a while that I was going to be a Sino-Soviet Affairs kind of person. I took a lot of Russian classes and a lot of political science classes. Then in my last year of college, in 1968, I went to canvass for Eugene McCarthy for president, for a weekend in Indianapolis. At the end of the weekend I called my parents and said, "I don't want to go back to school for this term. I want to continue with this campaign." My parents, bless their hearts, packed me some clothes and shipped them to Nebraska or wherever the next stop on the campaign was.

I had a chance to canvass for Eugene McCarthy in Indiana, Nebraska, California, and New York. I got to see a little bit of what the country looked like to other people in other places. So that was interesting. Indianapolis was really different from New York. It really had a wrong side of the tracks where all the Black people lived, unlike New York City where I grew up, in the middle of Manhattan. It never occurred to me that there were places like Indianapolis . . . . The whole journey made me see politics differently. It was a different feeling.

Eventually I went back to graduate school in Pittsburgh. There was a community organizing effort going on around the university. The neighbors around the university tried to fight the university's expansion into the neighborhood. [The university] wanted to eminent-domain a whole piece of the neighborhood and build more buildings. Part of that included Forbes Field, which was the old baseball stadium in Pittsburgh. So this group of neighbors had formed and were leafleting the university. I took a leaflet and I went to a meeting. Eventually I became very active in that group and eventually I became the organizer. Through that I got involved with Model

Cities and other agencies that were involved in the neighborhood at the time. It was a wonderful experience.

—Kim Fellner

I got politicized during college. It was mostly about issues of race. Being at an institution like Cornell, it was a rude awakening. I had grown up in mostly homogenous areas, in terms of ethnicity. I grew up in almost all Mexican-American communities, all Chicano communities. Clearly we experienced racism, but it was institutional, not on an individual basis. So it can be more subtle. Cornell did away with the subtlety, and I started to get much more involved in the activism that was going on there on campus. A friend of mine, who was a graduate student there, had heard about this thing called environmental justice and had heard about the Southwest Organizing Project. So he gave me a brochure or a pamphlet or something and said, "You might want to check these people out."

—Robby Rodriguez

I wouldn't have gone down this path at all if I hadn't had a friend open the door into leftist politics for me at UVA [University of Virginia]. I didn't really fit in at this school. All I wanted to do when I first got here was be a successful Black man, which is radical in itself. It was all about getting a nice job. Don't go to jail. Pay my taxes. Be a good person. I became a radical Black person because there are more people in my age group in jail than in college.

I always identified with bettering society, but I thought this was my way of doing it. When I got here I realized that it wasn't for me. I looked at the social scene around me, and the social scene was basically assimilation. All I knew is that I didn't want to be them, "them" being the stereotypical UVA student, but that they were a success, as our culture defines it.

Someone opened this door for me. I started writing for *Critical Mass* my second year. Through that I got involved with the Green Party. As soon as I got involved with *Critical Mass* I started to open up. I got involved with other things and became known as "that leftist guy on grounds." I got invited to join other organizations. I remember one day when Bokar Ture, son of Kwame Ture, of the Black Panthers, asked me to join the executive board of the Griot Society. I don't think I've ever been that flattered in my entire life. The son of a radical comes up to me and asks me to join his group. I always thought I wasn't Black enough to join the Griot society in that full-out way. I guess I was.

I'm going out to Oakland this summer. There's this group in Oakland called the Center for Third World Organizing [CTWO]. They focus on organizing in minority communities. They have this program, the Movement Activist Apprenticeship Program. So I'm doing that. They place you in Oakland for a week. You do their tutorial sessions for a week. Then they place you in a group somewhere in the nation. It could be in Oakland

with them or it could be in San Francisco, Chicago, New York, L.A., or D.C.—it depends. Then you're there for a couple of weeks and you come back to CTWO to wrap things up and tell everybody what you learned. Then you have a graduation ceremony. At the ceremony there's people there who are scouts for groups who are looking to hire community organizers. Basically it's six weeks of getting hardcore, in-the-field experience. It's nitty-gritty stuff, like fundraising, door-knocking, flyering, having press conferences. Then you come back and say what you learned. Then you get a job, hopefully.
    —Lamar Glover

I found out about it when I was about to complete my master's degree at the University of Idaho. I didn't take the usual master's degree in forestry. Most course work focuses on topics such as "The Impact of Spruce Budworm on Douglas Fir in Northern Idaho," or some project like that, but my emphasis was on public involvement. I looked at public involvement in national forest planning processes. I also took classes at the business college, and at that time, Robert Redford was experimenting with an institute for resource management. His institute was with Washington State and the University of Idaho, and there were some very interesting courses they were offering, like legal courses. I took some courses through there, and got exposed to different ideas and different people. And I had a really good course that I took in journalism. Michael Frome was the teacher at that time—he's written a number of books—and he's the one who exposed me to other groups in Idaho, mainly environmental groups, that were working on a variety of issues.
    —Kevin Williams

. . . some only after years of doing something else.

For nineteen years I was a Lutheran pastor. I picked up a doctorate in Historical Theology along the way from the Iliff School of Theology in Denver. I came into organizing late in life, after I'd left the ministry and spent some time sort of bouncing around figuring out what my second career was going to be. I finally decided that what I was, what my background made me, was an executive director of a small, locally-based non-profit organization. And so that's the kind of job I was looking for, and it just so happened that the job I was able to get and was most interested in that came along, that fit that description, was to be the staff director of Dakota Resource Council, which does community organizing in North Dakota. So I accepted that job and started in mid-December of 1993.
    —Mark Trechock

I substitute-taught. I had been active in the Democratic Party, doing fundraising and that sort of thing, and then I sold Tupperware for fifteen years. My best friend was the chair of the Powder River Basin Resource Council and she kept trying to get me to join this organization. They had a very good organizer in Douglas at the time, Jane Abbot, and Jane came to see me. I told her, "Come to see me after payday, because I can't afford to join right now," and she actually did call me the day of payday, so she caught me before I spent all the money. So I joined Powder River.

I realized that the things that they were doing were the sort of things that I supported and cared about. And I've always felt that people working together can accomplish things. It seemed to bring together all the things that I'd been working on in my life. It was fundraising, it was teaching people about the political process, helping people get involved. In many ways, community organizing seems to bring together all the experiences I had before, in teaching. Working with people in order to show them how to accomplish the things they want to accomplish.

Then my friend [. . .] commented to the director at that time, Chesie Lee, and said, "Vickie would be a good organizer." And I'm like, "So what's an organizer do?" and they tried to explain it to me. It was one of those times when I was thinking that it would be nice to do something different. So I thought, well, I haven't done a resume in a long time; I'll do a resume and apply. It can't hurt. So I applied for the job. I got hired. I went home and talked to my family about the travel and the things I understood about the job and they were very supportive. So I just sort of fell into it. I've been doing it now for thirteen years.
—Vickie Goodwin

I worked for the Appalachia Service Project, Inc. Let me preface this by saying ASP does great work and it played a major role in moving me from just seeing injustice to working for change. Basically, it's set up so that four people our age [18–23] run a center for a summer, from providing food for the volunteers to picking which houses get worked on to figuring out what the schedule is for each day and what work gets done. That summer we worked on twenty-five peoples' houses, but we didn't do a thing to make sure their kids wouldn't be in the same position. That didn't sit right with me.

I think the breaking point for me was a man named George Mullins. George Mullins was in a wheelchair. He was about seventy-two. He had lived in a hollow in eastern Kentucky his whole life, lived in that house four-fifths of his life—he'd gone away for a little bit for military service. He had lived alone for at least twenty years, and this man was an amazing carpenter. But week after week he had to hear us tell him, "No, I'm not sure we can do it this way." He'd say, "Well, maybe you could nail this piece over there," and the groups would say, "Nah, I think we're going to do it this way." He was really having trouble with folks coming in to work on his house, which was something he could do himself. He just didn't have the resources to do it. We were sitting on his porch and talking about a number of things, and he told me this story of a mental institution and the tests they had to see if people were sane. What they would do is turn on a faucet and have a bucket underneath. They'd fill up the bucket with water and hand the patient a spoon and tell them, "Empty the bucket." If the patient used the spoon and tried to dish the water out they would not be released. But if the person were to reach out and cut off the faucet, then they knew that it was time to start thinking about how to transition that person back into everyday society. So George told me this great story, but at the same time it wrecked me. Because I began to ask, "Whoa, what am I doing here? How am I taking part? Am I even looking at the faucet or am I sitting here with twenty spoons and handing them out?"

—Brian Johns

I was working with Appalachia Service Project [ASP] in 1980–81, in the summers and after that, and at that time, there were a handful of folks in eastern Kentucky who were getting started with a new organization called the Kentucky Fair Tax Coalition [KFTC]. I actually had a couple of them come speak with our youth groups at ASP about different issues in central Appalachia. It made a huge impression on me, partly because of the work in and of itself, but also in comparison to—kind of in contrast to—what ASP was doing, which is work I valued then and still value now, and have a lot of respect for, but it is clearly a sort of band-aid approach. What these community organizers [from KFTC] were doing was trying to figure out how to attack the root causes that were underlying the situations I was seeing on a daily basis, that were pretty horrendous in many cases, in terms of housing conditions, etc. It wasn't the first time I had ever heard of organizing, but it was sort of interesting to be able to see it begin to unfold.

—Burt Lauderdale

I began as an intern, actually as an undergraduate, working in battered women's shelters in Tennessee. That was a personal calling because of my personal experience. I wanted to help other women. That's when I began to learn that the personal is political. What had happened to those women and what had happened to me was not an individual problem. It was not just one family's problem. It was a societal problem. It was a systemic problem. My political consciousness began to be raised through that work.

—Jane Crowe

I graduated from seminary in '93. I spent some time doing volunteer mission work in Nicaragua with the United Methodist Church. Then I came back and worked in the office that had sent me for about a year. I worked in some non-profits around Atlanta in refugee resettlement. I was food coordinator at a homeless shelter. I worked at a camping store and bookstore, some of the retail world, for very low pay. I think it was sub-six dollars an hour. It was when I was at the bookstore that I made a connection with a group in Atlanta called Urban Training that did community organizing. They mainly worked with community groups in low-income communities. They focused a lot on public housing. I did an eight-month internship with a veteran organizer there, a fellow named Dewey Merritt. He taught me a whole lot about poverty and community work. I was really excited when I realized that there was something called community organizing, bringing people together to make change in their communities.

—Ben Thacker-Gwaltney

Just after seminary (I had entered seminary with a focus on urban ministry, because I had been doing these different projects with the Church of Christ in the northeast for seven years at that time), I was looking for a new direction because I felt that a White guy from the South was not really the right person to be working in the communities I had been working in. People of color probably needed to be taking the leadership there.

I thought that one of the things I had been effective at was persuading church folks back in the South that poverty was an appropriate concern for the church. This is from an evangelical church that usually looked at the soul, not the body, and didn't care about mundane concerns like poverty and food. I had suggested to my brother, who had a summer off before law school started, that he check with Kim Bobo at Bread for the World whether they might have some work he could do for the summer. And he worked in the organizing department for a few months there.

Dirk (my brother) told me that this organizing job was perfect for me because it was the perfect blend of poverty concerns, faith concerns, and politics. And those are my big three topics. Those are the things I talked about in the dorm until late at night, many a time. But when he was describing it to me, when he was coaching me about going through the interview at Bread for the World for one of their open positions, I was asking, "Well, what's organizing? What skills do I have?" And he said, "Well, you know how to lead a small group, right?" I said, "Yeah, I know how to lead a small group." He went on, "You've got people skills; you can do public speaking."

—Kimble Forrister

I worked for the chaplain's office at Brown the year after I graduated. At the end of my time at the chaplain's office, the students with whom I was working and I organized a conference on American labor issues and history. The keynote speaker was Reverend Jim Drake, who had worked for sixteen years with Cesar Chavez and the farm workers in California. He had been persuaded by the Board for Homeland Ministries of the United Church of Christ to see if he could take what he had learned organizing farm workers in California and apply it to woodcutters in the rural South. Eventually about twelve of us from Providence, Rhode Island, went down and worked with Jim in the Southern Woodcutters Assistance Project, which eventually spun off into the United Woodcutters Association.

I found my calling at that point. It was through community organizing that I realized that you brought the faith and the public arena together. I loved that work. In the two years that I was in Mississippi I had a chance to go to a ten-day training that the Industrial Areas Foundation [IAF] put together. I loved the fact that there was a system of thinking about this. I was certainly very attracted to the fact the IAF—and then, as I learned, others as well—were organizing using religious congregations as a foundation for that organizing. That certainly met my interest in the church and in faith. I went to Mississippi thinking I would just stay for a summer and I stayed for two years.

—Paul Cromwell

I was in my mid-40s when I came to organizing. I think the majority of non-profits focus on direct service. In my work (with a non-profit transitional housing program), I thought I was doing something to help. But in the back of my head I kept thinking, "Wouldn't it be wonderful if we would work ourselves out of a job? We shouldn't be doing the same thing year after year." People used to look at me like I'm crazy, "Work ourselves out of a job? What are you talking about?" But it just seemed like there was something very wrong with our system that some people have so much and even I feel like I have more than a lot of people I know, and why is that?

—Cathy Woodson

Profile:
Nicholas Graber-Grace
Organizing with ACORN in Florida

We asked Nicholas Graber-Grace, a new organizer, to describe a typical day, to give an idea of what life in an urban, membership-based organization is like for an organizer still learning the ropes. At the time of the interview, he was the Lead Organizer with Orlando ACORN (Association of Community Organizations for Reform Now). He has since become Head Organizer with Broward County ACORN in Ft. Lauderdale, Florida.

Right now I am working here in Orlando as the Lead Organizer for Orlando ACORN. I am out in the field every day working to build an organization of low- and moderate-income families and people. I talk to folks every day who have a sense of disempowerment and who don't feel connected to what's going on. I'm working with them and getting them involved. As ACORN members they begin to meet other folks. They begin to take positive action in their lives.

We have a small staff. There's a Head Organizer in the office and then I'm the Lead Organizer. We have one person on staff right now that has a week under her belt and is just getting up and running. We had a couple other people that we trained in Orlando that have not taken to organizing. We're in a process of building a staff now. We want to get up to five organizers. We've got somebody who's supposed to start next week. If we can get somebody every week, then hopefully we should have a stable office then. We also have political staff running canvass operations to gather signatures for the minimum wage petition. We've got about thirty to thirty-five canvassers working out of the Orlando office on a daily basis.

We work from 11 to 9 Monday through Friday and then from 10 to 2 on Saturday. I wind up working a little more than that just because I have other stuff I need to get done. We come in in the morning and focus on training and role-playing. We have to get ourselves mentally prepared to be out in the field for that day. Each Monday we have a staff meeting where we set some goals for the week. We evaluate the week before and figure out where we are as an office and what we ought to be doing. In the mornings we make some phone calls related to a certain campaign we're working on and do some Internet research. We do whatever it is that we need to do that is office work in the morning.

Then by about 2:00 or 2:30 we're headed out to the field to go door knocking. We try to door knock at least four hours a day. That's a process where we recruit the membership of the organization. We're out in the field doing new doors, where we're just doing cold calls to people. We're finding out what the issues in the neighborhood are and what are the things that people right here are concerned about. Recently I've been doing some tenant organizing so there have been a lot of issues in terms of landlord accountability and maintenance.

The main issue is, what does this person care enough about to actually fight for? What is this person passionate about? When you're knocking on somebody's door they might say, "Oh, I'm concerned about the street lighting," which is true. But then when you sit down and talk to them a little more there might be something a little bigger and a little deeper that they're more concerned about. You work through that conversation and really dig through that bigger issue that they care about enough to actually get involved. So you do that and we come back with one, two, three members a day.

You do follow-ups and meetings. You'll be following up with people who hadn't joined the first time you spoke with them. You'll do second visits with people who are new members so that you can get them up to speed on exactly what we're doing right now and how they can make their priorities a part of the organization's priorities. We do a lot prepping with our leaders in terms of just meeting with our leadership. "Okay, so we're doing X, Y, and Z. How can we actually get the rest of the membership involved in that?" One of the good things about ACORN's model—and, I would presume, a lot of organizing models—is that there's way too much work for the organizer to do it. If the organizer were to do all the work, then first of all it would never get done, second of all the organizer would burn out, and third of all they wouldn't build a mass movement. So it's really important, in our model, to focus on leadership development and training our members so that they're the ones doing the work in the field.

Then by 7:00 p.m. or so we come back to the office and we're on the phones from 7 to 9. We also do nightly check-ins and talk with staff about how the day went, what could have been better, what they're struggling with right now, and what we need to work on. What are the issues and can we make a plan to deal with those? So we check in and make phone calls in the evening. Those phone calls are important for turnout because we have a lot of events that we need to get our members out to so that we can actually win the campaigns that we're working on. At 9:00 we're done and people are free to go home. Oftentimes we'll go out after that to a local bar or out for a bite to eat. We did that a lot more when I first started because we had a very young staff and there were a lot of people starting at the same time. We still do it at least once or twice a week, I would say.

The recent membership drive, which we finished a few months ago, has gone really well. I was organizing in a couple of mobile home parks. There were a lot of problems in terms of disrespect and managerial misconduct towards residents. There was discrimination towards Latinos. The rents were being increased every year. It was a situation in which everybody owns their own mobile home but pays a rent for the lot that they're sitting on. It was a very exploitative situation. One of the best parts about it now is that the chapter there is challenging the rent increase, and I'm only marginally involved in that. As an organizer, it's to the point where the members just give me a heads up on what they're doing. I help talk them through some of the possible scenarios and strategize a little bit, but they're pretty on the ball for everything that they're doing. That's awesome, because it gives me the time I need for training new staff and all that.

Profile:
Kelly (Corley) Pokharel
Just Starting Out

Kelly (Corley) Pokharel is the Executive Director of CASA of McHenry County (Illinois). At the time of this interview in December 2002, she was an organizer for the Northern Plains Resource Council in Montana, where she had been working for six months.

I was born and raised in a suburb of Chicago called Crystal Lake, a northwest suburb. I spent my whole life there. I'm twenty-five years old.

My parents tell this story about when I was little, I was the "fair" kid. I had an older brother and a younger sister, and I was in the middle. I wanted everything to be fair. If I was getting punished for something, my brother had to be punished, too. And the punishments had to be the same. I wanted everything to be equal. Even if I had to be punished for it, I wanted things to be equal. I just grew up with that attitude. There's no reason that people should have to suffer for the benefit of others. One should not be given an advantage at the expense of the other. I knew I wanted to make a difference in that sense.

I attended college at Augustana College in Illinois, and then I went to graduate school to get my degree in social work at Washington University in St. Louis. About a year after I graduated from there I ended up here in Montana.

I really didn't know anything about community organizing until I went to graduate school and took a couple of clinical social work classes and was terrible at it. I thought, "Well, I still really want to do social work. There's got to be something else out there." One aspect of the social and economic development concentration was community organizing. So I took some community organizing classes and community building. I just loved it. It seemed like a perfect fit. I felt like I had a knowledge about it. The things I didn't know really interested me; I wanted to learn more. That was the first time I ever knew that there was something called "community organizing" as a profession.

I did three field placements. I did one in north St. Louis with an almost entirely African-American population. Those who weren't African-American were elderly White widowed women who had lived in the neighborhood all their lives. It wasn't necessarily a safe neighborhood, but they did a lot of work on housing issues. They wanted to fix up homes and help people get loans to do that. They wanted to make the streets safer. There used to be a lot of prostitution and drug dealing a couple years before I got there. So my first internship was with them. It was pretty basic. I didn't get to do a whole lot of community organizing, but I got to watch other people do it. I really liked it.

Then I did a second one with Missouri Coalition for the Environment. I was interested in the environment and I liked people; I knew there was a connection there. I found it at Missouri Coalition for the Environment. That got me into more organizing and less watching people. I did research. I held my first educational session for community members. I was the one to call people out and get them excited. It was pretty exciting for me.

Then my third field placement was in Nepal, at a place called Nepal Water for Health. It was a local NGO that worked with communities helping them install safe pumps and wells. We also helped those communities manage the systems once they were involved.

With all of my field placements, I was allowed to choose where I wanted to work. This allowed me to connect my experience to my interests. I think the most important thing that I gained out of those experiences is that I had the chance to go out and see what a community organizer is. My classes were helpful, but classroom work is never one hundred percent of what you need to know.

At that point I really didn't know what I wanted. I knew I wanted to be around people. I knew I didn't want it to be a job where I had to sit behind a desk and do research all the time. I knew I didn't want to do policy. I wanted to be on the ground making change. As far as my interests fell, I wanted to work with women. I wanted to work with the environment. I wanted to work with human rights issues. It was just a matter of finding the right place for me to fit in.

We had a career counselor, and she would send out e-mails of jobs she had found out about. Most of the jobs that came out were for clinical social workers. You could type in the search words "community organizer" and it came up with strange things. It seems like the outside world doesn't know what a community organizer is.

I researched every job I applied for. Usually it wasn't extensively, because there were so many different ones. My second interview with Northern Plains was with a board member, which was good. I wasn't just interviewing with a staff person. She gave me a different perspective on what this organization was and what she thought about the position I was about to go into. By the third interview, I called and I set up an appointment to talk with one of their organizers. I wanted to say, "Okay, tell me. What exactly is your day like? What do you do? What do you enjoy about this and what don't you enjoy?" That was the most helpful, to have someone say, "Okay, here's a typical day for me."

The first three months I was there I was shadowing the organizer whose position I was taking over. She was still staying with the organization, but they were switching her to a different chapter. I got to shadow her for the first few months. That was helpful, because I got to see how this organization runs a meeting and how you write an agenda. I learned through her the expectations the organization should have of me. She introduced me to the leaders and other members. I thought that was very helpful, to have someone there that I could go to. And not just her; everyone in the office was the same way. I thought it was really difficult to learn some of the issues. Some of them are incredibly technical and some of them I still don't feel that I have a grasp on. I'm not sure, at this point, what could be done differently. I was given a lot of material to read. I had separate, one- or two-hour interviews with people who were very familiar with those issues, to update me about them.

Our training process has since changed. Now new organizers are placed with a mentor for their first six months to a year, to help guide them through all of the ins and outs.

In no way do I think that my training is done. It's not done, and I think everyone in the office knows that. For me, personally, after three months of shadowing someone, I was bored. I was ready to do something, and I wanted it to be on my own. I'm the type of person who has to do something to learn it. Watching someone is helpful, but until I actually do it myself it doesn't stick. Ideally I wouldn't want to shadow someone. There are certain situations and times when it would be nice to have someone there to guide me through it. Overall I like the independence, the challenge of taking off on my own. But that's different for different people. With that said, I don't think a "sink or swim" policy is a fair one. People learn in different ways at different speeds.

The biggest thing that has helped for me has been to sit down with people and look at them face-to-face and talk to them one-to-one. There were a couple people when I started who I felt had absolutely no confidence or trust in me. People would look at me and say, "Oh, you're twenty-one. You've just graduated from college."

I know that's not the case and the people who hired me know that's not the case, but the people I'm working for don't know that. I felt like I had to prove myself to them.

I used to think that everyone thought that social justice was important and that fairness was important. And if you took a survey people would say, "Oh yeah. I'm for social justice. Everything should be fair." But when it gets down to the nitty-gritty, all the minute language, I don't think people necessarily believe that. I think people look out for what's in their best interests. And I can't blame them. Sometimes you need to look at the big picture and look at your best interests in the long term or in relation to others' best interests. But the people I work with, I feel, do believe social justice is important. That is what they are seeking: justice.

I'm about to go home for Christmas and my family's going to ask, "What do you do?" It's good to prepare. I would say, "As a community organizer, I work with farmers and ranchers to protect their water quality, family farms and ranches, and unique quality of life. We usually work on issues to protect their land, their property rights, their water, and the air that they breath. So we work with people to bring them together, to have power in numbers. We work with them to give information to them and get them to talk to their legislators. We help them get power to make change in their community."

It seems like we have a big lack of community in this country. No one knows their neighbors. No one talks to the people they pass on the street. Everyone teaches their kids to be afraid of strangers. How are you ever going to learn anything about anyone? How are we going to bring people together if they're too afraid to talk to each other and too afraid to share ideas with each other? We need to start young and tell people, "It's okay to play in the front yard and say hi to someone who walks by. You should go volunteer and meet new people. You should get out there and not be afraid of people. Find out what makes people tick, what they are interested in, what concerns they have."

Why Organize?

We asked the organizers why they do this kind of work. What is it that keeps them at it day after day, year after year, when others lose heart or follow other paths?

Wow! They pay you for this?

It's like Lou Gehrig said: "I'm the luckiest man in the world. I get paid for doing what I love to do." I sort of stumbled into it, actually. I saw the need to transform the world. My ability as an organizer helped bring people together to help make that happen. After the lean years of being a courier and a cab driver, it was like, "Wow, you can get paid for doing this!"
  —Jon Liss

I feel that through the happy circumstances of my upbringing and my persona I've been passionate about justice issues since my teen years. When I had the opportunity to do work to fight for what mattered, I went and did it. I have never, for a moment, looked back or regretted it. I feel like my life has been blessed that way. I've never been unemployed a day in my life since the day I walked into my first union. It's like, "I have done exactly what matters to me and what I love every day since." Who can say that? I am so lucky.
  —Kim Fellner

I think it's a wonderful way to make your living. It's very good work to do. I think for people who feel like they want to do more than just a nine to five job and effect change with their lives, it's probably the best thing that you can do.
  —Sara Kendall

It's such a great field. You get to be with people and in the drama. You get to move things. It's magic. It's wonderful. I have been involved in campaigns that have delivered real resources to people who really needed them. They decided they wanted it, went after it, and got it. When that happens it's magic.
—Dave Beckwith

It feels good to do good . . .

It makes my heart beat fast. It's been a challenge every day and I like that. I've never, ever had a moment of being bored or disengaged. I like the people. I like the members. It gets messy and there are times that are hard and there are times that people are just yelling at you, but it's about being part of a team of people that don't have a lot. Working with them has usually been an honor. It's the sharing, the commitment, and the sacrifice by people who have had so much less than I've ever had. They're willing to make that sacrifice to improve things. The courage that people have and the dedication . . . that's who I want to hang out with. That's my community.
—LeeAnn Hall

There's no other feeling like seeing people actually create change. It's amazing when people realize that they already have what they need to get what they want done. They realize how to make someone else change their mind. That's really cool. There's lots of autonomy. There's lots of opportunities for creativity. You have to be creative. It's fun, it really is. At the end of the day, it's a fun job.
—Karen Waters

It's actually a lot of fun. . . . You get energy from people and you learn from people. It broadens your worldview. You get to meet all kinds of people. It gives you this real rush. A lot of us feel disenfranchised in society, whether we're White and middle-class or not. We feel that we don't have any control and the world is crazy. When you're organizing you get to have a voice and you get to have some power. . . . You get to feel that power and that solidarity with other people.
—Jane Crowe

The people you get to work with—and the opportunity to change lives.

You know, it's about seeing that spark that happens in people's eyes when you realize that something is possible, when you see someone just move from a place of, "That's just the way it is, what can we do about it?" to "OK. Let's do something." Not only that, but "It's wrong, and we need to do something about it." It's about seeing those small moments of

Members of Tenants and Workers United demand child care reform from local officials in Alexandria, Virginia.

transformation and that's what drives me, I think. It's becoming clear as I talk about it. It's that moment that makes everything worth it and it's just never a question for me why.

—Vivian Chang

I feel so blessed to be in this work, but I think the other great reward—and it's not limited to any one organization—is that look in people's eyes when they win an issue that they thought was pretty impossible, or the one that's like, "You know what? You *can* fight City Hall. You can make a difference." There's also the look in people's eyes when you bring diversity together. You see folks who commonly would not be rubbing shoulders together, either along racial, gender, religious, or neighborhood lines, working together and loving the work they're doing together.

—Paul Cromwell

I stay because I like the work. I'm committed to the people, to the community. Sometimes I think of myself as having the spirit of Harriet Tubman. "You're going to be free, or else. You're not turning back now." This just has to be done. I also don't know how much longer I'll do this work. I'm

fifty-three years old. Like I said, it's labor-intense and stressful and hard. But I enjoy myself too.
   —Rhonda Anderson

I'm really drawn to the work of going out there and helping people to change their situation and empowering people. I think it is just an amazing concept to be out there and to think about doing it because it's ordinary people becoming such powerful institutions. I love that. Every person has such an interesting story or opinion and it is just a matter of finding out where that person can fit in, how you can help that person in your neighborhood. That's why I'm drawn to it.
   —Emily Gruszka

I was involved with the Black Power posse, so I know a lot of activists, people whose names and faces are in the news and who are well known. But here were these people, these older men and women, who were doing tremendous things for people who they didn't know. People who they would never meet or would meet just this one time. They were giving willingly of their time, not looking for any press or anything like that. They were just trying to do something about it. They'd come out and volunteer, and then they'd just go home to their kids and grandkids. It wasn't a big deal, it was just something that needed to be done and they did it. The opportunity to work with people like that is a tremendous thing. And it also just fits in with my own personal philosophy.
   —Steve Bradberry

It's certainly not the money—

I took a $20,000-a-year pay cut and sold my house so I could do this.
   —Pennie Vance

I couldn't have needed a job too badly because the pay wasn't that good. The starting salary at that time [1984] was $800 a month. And I was coming out of college with a master's degree. One professor on my graduate committee at the business college argued strongly for me not to take the position. He said, "You do not want to take this position, because all you will do is organize potlucks." That was his definition of a community organizer, I guess. And actually, I've organized a lot of potlucks over the years, and they're great. I haven't regretted it for a minute.
   —Kevin Williams

I think that it's a hard profession. It's not really well paid. It's very demanding. It's hard to maintain a private life and a family. So I think there are a lot of things that work against people staying in organizing. I think those who stay in it stay in it because there's something in them that won't

let them let it go. I think once you've done this work, it's very hard to see other avenues by which you can have the same kind of impact or can see where a true, participatory democracy is really working. There're other things, certainly, that one can do to better society and for justice, but there's something pretty unique in organizing in the sense of its participatory democracy aspect. I think the people who get hooked on that really get hooked on it; therefore, the pay and the drawbacks don't drive them out of the profession.
 —Paul Cromwell

Our culture creates the expectation that you should be terribly financially successful. You should have the best car and the newest TV and the most expensive computer game. If you want to be an organizer, I think you have to choose something else. [Financial success is] just not as important as engaging in relationships and creating change and fostering a sense of community and culture and cultural values. It's not the same. If you don't have the framework to work from then I think it's really hard to stick with organizing. That's where the reward is. It's not in getting paid. It's not career advancement. It's not stability.
 —Gary Sandusky

We have organizers who left corporate America, making a lot of money, and much prefer the work at ACORN [Association of Community Organizations for Reform Now] because the reward is there. I have friends who make a lot of money in corporate America, but they hate getting up and going to work.
 —Steve Bradberry

There's so much that's hard to put a price on. What are the rewards? What are the satisfactions? There's no price tag for that kind of stuff. I'd rather be doing this than making three or four times as much money doing something that doesn't touch my soul or my spirit at all. And I'm able to do that because it pays me enough for the basic things that I need.
 —Brett Kelver

And it's not easy work.

I struggle a lot with family. I'm married and I have a family. I've noticed many organizers don't, and I know why: the hours are rigorous, and it is a tough job. I struggle with balancing work and family and travel. It seems that I travel quite a bit, and I hate to be gone too many days at a time, but it happens sometimes. I do. I mean there are days I could walk out of my office, lock the door, and never go back because sometimes you feel like all you do is set up meetings. You set up meetings and then you set up more meetings and then you set up lobby days and then you set up rallies and

then you set up more meetings. Sometimes it feels like you're a hamster on a wheel—and then something really great will happen.
—Robin Bagley

I think I'm stubborn and that's why I'm in it. I feel like I haven't learned enough yet. By the end of this year, I may come to point where I understand enough about organizing to feel like I've had some success. In essence, that's a fifteen-year training period. I think that's about right.
—James Mumm

I remember when I first came to KFTC [Kentuckians For The Commonwealth] and I was in Frankfort, I would literally skip up the halls toward one of my friends and I would be like, "I love my job! I love my job!" I had this tremendous energy and enthusiasm. I was just very hopeful and optimistic. That first session we got smashed. That squashed me. When I came back that next year I still had energy and enthusiasm, but I wasn't exactly traipsing down the halls singing, "I love my job." I think we live in such hard times. We get beat down.
—Leah Ottersbach

But it's worth it.

It can be the most rewarding and most challenging job in the world. I really like the challenge, and at the same time it's really great to see people start believing in it and to start believing in it myself. To say, "Hey, this process works." That's what keeps me going.
—Brian Johns

The thing that attracted me early on is that you can do this work your whole life and do something different every day, if you want. You get to do work that has meaning. I'm grateful. I look at my dad, who died at forty-three of a heart attack. I never heard him say he liked work. He didn't even have to say anything. You could just see how awful it was. He wanted us to be something more.
—Ray Higgins, Jr.

This is what I like to do. I see it as a contribution. It's very exciting, in terms of where we are. It's part of what I believe. It's also because I've been challenged. I'm doing something different. At the same time I'm creating opportunities, I have the financial support for what else I'm doing in my life. I could get a job with better money, but this is providing me with what I need and I'm doing exactly what I want. It's that kind of balance. I'm doing things and I'm learning a lot. I'm trying new things.
—Guillermo Quinteros

[You've got to have] some sense of working toward that long-term goal, moving bit by bit and putting something together in small pieces. It's something that is going to be worth fighting for in the long run. An organization is going to have some power and actually be able to affect society in the long run. I don't know of anywhere else that you can be a part of something like that. Maybe in the church, but most churches have swung far afield from any social change efforts like that.
—Ben Thacker-Gwaltney

I stay because I am in a set of collegial relationships that deeply enrich my life. I haven't found that anywhere else. I stay because I'm pretty damn angry and this is a place where that is appreciated. It's lifted up and tempered and controlled. I stay because it's a place of intellectual development inside a context where you're doing something with significant meaning. The intellectual exchange moves from the abstract to the concrete. I've thought about leaving and haven't because it's pretty invigorating. When it quits being invigorating, I'll leave.
—Perry Perkins

Some do it because they believe that organizing is the best way to effect change and they want to change the world . . .

I honestly do not believe that we can bring about lasting change without grassroots organizing. I don't. That's one of the reasons why I continue to— why I want to be an organizer. And one of the things that I think will keep me in this type of career for as long as I possibly can.
—Aaron Browning

I think there are a lot of different ways to make change happen. For me, there's a certain purity or goodness about working directly with people. Especially in the context of the idea that we're supposed to be living in a democracy where all of us have a voice. So working to get people involved in decision making and proposing change seems good and basic. Once it's done, it's really hard to change back for the worse, because you've gotten people charged up and involved. So it has a longer lasting feel.
—Brett Kelver

The dream of America is an engaged populace where people have rights and responsibilities. At a goofy, romantic level, I believe that. I believe that the people who live with the decisions should make the decisions. That's what democracy is about and it's a fundamental value in our society. People have basic rights. We have a Bill of Rights, but if we don't fight for the rights to make them real they won't exist. They're not real if they're not real in the lives of everyday people. If they're not real in the lives of people who have the least amount of power in our society then they're not really rights.

Members of the Pioneer Valley Project in Massachusetts meet to set goals, review victories, and present awards at their 2004 annual dinner.

There has to be a vigilance about that. And I do this because it's fun. It's fun to win. The actions are fun. The people are fun.
—LeeAnn Hall

I think organizing is important. Just the basis of organizing, where it comes out of community discussions and community effort to solve shared problems. It made a whole lot of sense when I was introduced to it. You want things to happen, and you have to influence the power structure to make it happen. You don't have dollars, but you definitely have people. To have people you have to organize. I wanted to see some real change happen that would affect the things that I think are important. Other people think those things are important too, and we can come together to make it happen.
—Julie Jones

I think it's really hard to explain why you get involved with social justice, period. Clearly my family, particularly my father, had a lot to do with it. Growing up in the '60s had something to do with it. As far as why community organizing rather than some other kind of advocacy or some other things that I have done and a lot of people I know do—I think it works better. I'd say it's a question of efficiency. The way to make social change is to get as many people involved in it as possible.
—Larry Yates

I became a community organizer because I wanted to do something that would be important for all people—and for personal reasons, I would like to see life a little bit different for my grandchildren, great grandchildren, whomever is to follow after me, even my son. I do not think we have to live through the same issues that I grew up with. I think people do make a difference. People working together can make a difference, and if I can be a part of that here in Virginia, that's very important to me. We have a long history in Virginia of people not being active. Activists, as some of them refer to themselves, say they're tired; it's too hard here. And it **is** hard, but that's why I became a community organizer—to do something, to make changes in Virginia. I want to see some things change in the state of Virginia, which then ripples out into bigger parts.
    —Cathy Woodson

I'm a true believer. I believe it's the only way to really change things. I definitely believe deep in my heart that community organizing is the only hope we have for a better world. That's why I stay in it, and I enjoy it. There are times when I get up, and I can't wait to go tackle this or go some place. I'm thrilled a lot of the time.
    —Teresa Erickson

I am convinced that for long-term change in this country, community organizing is the key. I guess I have become something of a true believer, in terms of theory of change, that this approach, this piece of social change work is the key. We are pretty far from doing it well enough to realize the potential or the change that we want to see. So I stay and I keep struggling with how we do it better.
    —Burt Lauderdale

I feel like I'm actually doing something to change the systems in our country that are unjust and unfair. I think we have it pretty good; I don't want to be cynical. I think we're pretty blessed to live in this country. But one of my interns says, "Good is the enemy to excellence," and there's no reason why we can't try to improve things. I think that I became an organizer because I want to make this country live up to all it set out to be.
    —Holly Hatcher

. . . others because they feel called to this work.

I think it's about passion. For me, it was definitely a calling. If you're really passionate or feel like you're called to something, I think you're more likely to stick with it even when it's tough. You know that if you were to quit you wouldn't get the same fulfillment from other work. The passion can be different things for different folks. For me it's definitely a connection to my faith and what I understand, from my faith, about how we're supposed to be as a society. I thought, "God, you are so amazing to me." I was struggling so hard trying to go through other doors. I always tell people, "I can't say anything except God put me into the work, because I did not come here looking for this." But here I ended up.

I tell people, "This work gets frustrating, no doubt. It gets difficult. It just gets hard at times. But I count myself so blessed because I can honestly say, for the most part, 'I like my job.'" I know so many people who can't say that.

—Presdelane Harris

Sometimes I say that the reason I do it is to piss rich White men off. But it's not really that. . . . To me, this is my calling. I'm not here to make a whole bunch of money. As long as I'm living all right and can pay my rent and have my cell phone . . . those things are basic things of life. They're not necessities, but they are things I choose to have. I do it because this is what I want to do. This is what makes me happy, that I can help change people.

—Wanda Salaman

I believe the work is my calling. It's not working for the Justice Center that I think is my calling. The call is to liberate the captives. Give sight to the blind. Set at liberty the poor. Really do something to help people. Value the life that is in all of us, the life that is in them. . . . What better service can you give than to help create better quality life for people? There's a scripture that says, "The well don't need a physician." I don't need to work for people who don't need help. They don't need anybody to do things. It's the people who are poor, the people who are oppressed, the people who are disenfranchised—they're the ones who need help finding their voice. I am that voice. Nobody's been more economically challenged than I have been in my lifetime. I've experienced some of the very same problems of the people that I serve now. So I genuinely believe that it is my duty, my responsibility, and my calling to do so. That's why I do it. I do it because it's the right thing to do.

—Sheila Kingsberry-Burt

I just got drawn to it like a moth to flame. It set my life free. It was like being let out of prison, where my natural curiosity and capacities could grow. If I look at why I stayed, I think part of it was that I came out of a religious tradition. It wasn't just to be an organizer; it was to live out the faith in some way. So it had a grounding in something that was more long-lasting and more meaningful to me at a deeper level.

—Don Elmer

My mother was like "I don't understand why you can't just do this after work. Why can't you go back to school and get your law degree?"

What I said to her was, "Do you question why Padre Julio is a priest?"
"No. That's his calling. God calls him to do that."
I said, "So have I been called to do what I do."
—Lisbeth Meléndez-Rivera

For all it is a way to integrate their values into their work life—
to walk the walk, to sleep better at night, to never have to wonder,
"What if I had followed my heart?"

I have no ambition to separate my work from my life, and supporting
organizing gives you the best opportunity to have your work and your life
be as one.
—Scott Douglas

I'd always wanted to figure out how I could have a job that would help
make the world a better place, and well, here was a way to do that. It was
consistent with my values in life, the things I believed in.
—John Smillie

I think it was mainly my heart that told me it was the right thing to do. . . .
Organizing is a vocation. It makes me happy as a person. It's part of who I
am. I think we all need to strive for that.
—Kevin Williams

And my choice at that time was, I was offered a permanent position to
go work—this is like one of those life decisions where you're like, "Oh my
god, what if I had chosen . . ."—I had a job offer from US West, the phone
company, to go be a manager, . . . but for whatever reason, I just knew
that wasn't what I wanted to do, that I wanted to do something more
meaningful. I literally was at the point of "What am I going to do?" when I
got this phone call from Steve Johnson, and he was like, "I think you should
go apply for this job" and I was like, "Okay." I am not a spiritual person by
institutional standards, but I do think that there is an element of community
organizing that involves an aspect of spirituality that involves faith in
humanity, or faith in the advancement of the common good . . . that we do
this work because we believe it's right. . . . I just wouldn't feel comfortable
doing something else.
—Kelley Weigel

I have a Baptist-Pentecostal background. I'm settled on what my faith
principles are and what I believe. You have to treat people right. You have
to be fair. You have to be just. You don't have to like me to do that. You just
have to do it. You have to work toward that. This society may never reach
that perfection because this world has issues, but you ought to be doing

everything in your power—at least where you live, work, and breathe—to help it to become a more just society.

—Presdalene Harris

I'm able to stand on the outside and call for people to do the responsible thing. One of the fun things for me in Alabama has been—I guess I've just been invited to do this for the third time—to serve on a panel of the "shadow government" for Leadership Alabama on the day that they have on politics in Alabama. It's me and the head of the business council and the head of the teachers' union and the head of the farmers' federation, which in Alabama is the source of much evil: They're the ones that resist all positive change, mainly under the guise of keeping taxes low. The panel talks about how decisions are really made and that sort of thing. I think they mainly put me on that panel for the moral juxtaposition. There was this former judge, now dean of a law school in Alabama, who stood up and asked the question: "I want to ask this question of the three other panelists besides Kimble: How do you sleep at night?" And they got a big laugh and I don't know if those guys turned red or not, I didn't really look at them. I think I was turning red. But it does feel good to be confident that you're fighting for something good, not for pure self-interest. You're really fighting for the good of the whole society.

—Kimble Forrister

Soon after graduating from high school I enlisted in the military. Soon after that I found myself in Vietnam. Vietnam was the place that totally changed my life. Before going to Vietnam I was basically just a person that didn't really think. But while I was in Vietnam someone asked me, "Why are you here?" And I couldn't answer that question. Ever since that point, I determined that no matter what I was doing or where I was, if anybody ever asked me what am I doing this for, I will have a reason for it.

—Jerome Scott

I think people who stay with organizing have a sense that this is going to be a long road and the only way that the road is going to get any shorter is if we stick to it. It's easy to walk away, but I don't think I ever could. If I were to ever walk away I would lose the reason I get up in the morning. This is my life's work. It's not a job. I think the people who stick with organizing tend to share that. This isn't just something that we do. It's not something to pay the bills. It's not something that we think is nice and fun and interesting or good work experience or a resume builder. It's something that we know has to be done and we're going to be here to do it.

—Nicholas Graber-Grace

Profile: Rhonda Anderson

Organizing for Environmental Justice

Rhonda Anderson is an Environmental Justice Organizer for the Sierra Club. She has been organizing off and on for twenty-five years, first as a labor organizer with the Service Employees International Union, and since 2000 as a community organizer for the Sierra Club. She lives in Detroit. She was interviewed in August 2003 at a Dismantling Racism workshop in Albany, New York.

I'm a single mother of four. My oldest son is thirty-six, the second is thirty-four, the third is a girl and she's twenty, and the baby girl is twelve. The oldest actually passed in 1985, but I always include him as if he still is. That's my way of handling it. I think it would just be too difficult for me to just say, "I only have three children," when I know I have four. He was killed. He was attending Wilberforce University, and I was just so proud that we were able to get him to that point. Actually, he was killed by a drunk hit-and-run driver.

I'm going to be very honest with you. My thirty-four-year-old is in prison. He's in there for the second time. He should be home hopefully in November of this year.

My twenty-year-old daughter is expecting. She's not married. She's not working. The father of the baby is not working. This poses all kinds of stresses, dilemmas, and all kinds of things because I was expecting my children to be quite different. And it's not so much that I'm so disappointed. I am somewhat disappointed. But I think it speaks volumes to the fact that my family is actually a normal family in the city of Detroit, where over half of the families are headed by a single woman, without a man in the home. The children are growing up without that father figure where they can learn so many things. I now believe that that father figure is crucial to the way that children will develop.

So that's who I am. I'm a Black mother, a single mother, the head of the household. I'm the primary income earner and the only income. It's also the reason that I do the work that I do, because in my attempt to save my children I've learned that I have to save the other children too. I can't

• • • I'm a Black mother, a single mother, the head of the household. I'm the primary income earner and the only income. It's also the reason that I do the work that I do, because in my attempt to save my children I've learned that I have to save the other children too. I can't separate my children from the other children. So I work very hard to change the conditions that our children have and that we have. Being an organizer, I think, is an excellent way to try and change things. • • •

separate my children from the other children. So I work very hard to change the conditions that our children have and that we have. Being an organizer, I think, is an excellent way to try and change things.

I grew up in River Rouge, Michigan. This is a very small down river community that borders the city of Detroit. You can actually stand in three cities at one time if you bend over a little bit. They are very small communities. Up until I was a teenager, the areas were very, very segregated. I don't think that people started moving across borders until probably the 1980s.

I've lived in Michigan all my life. My people originally come from Mississippi. My grandmother and my grandfather on my father's side came out of Mississippi and settled in Little Rock, Arkansas. Then their children moved. The boys moved as young men to Detroit. The girls moved to Seattle, Washington. I think that my generation was the most privileged generation. We lived a good life, basically, even though we were very poor. We had so many excellent opportunities. I don't think the fifth or sixth generation has had as many opportunities as our generation has.

I graduated from high school when I was eighteen. I had two children. I had my first child when I was sixteen. I had my second one when I was eighteen. I graduated from high school with my class, walked across the floor, and got my diploma. I had to rush home because I had to get back to my children. My grandmother was at home babysitting for me while I went to my graduation ceremony.

The first job I had was at a small Black hospital. It was started some time in the '40s, and it was at a time when Blacks could not go to the White hospitals. I sat on the negotiation committee because there was no one else to sit on it. The representative from the union recognized me, saw me and listened to the things I was saying. I think he was impressed with my abilities to comprehend some of the things that were going on. I think he was also impressed with the fact that I was kind of aggressive in attempting to get the things that the membership really needed. So he asked me if I would like to work for the union, and I said yes. This was after working for the hospital for ten years. I was an in-patient and out-patient billing clerk.

I also worked every other clerical position in the hospital—collections, switchboard, cashier, all of those positions. So that's how I got into it.

I worked as a business representative for Service Employees International Union for about nine years, negotiating contracts, representing the members, and things of that nature. At the same time I had opportunities to organize within labor. So that was my first introduction into organizing. The type of organizing I did then was where we would go into a facility that was not unionized, blitz the place, stand out front handing out papers and things of that nature. We would go to homes and make house calls. We actually had to organize from scratch, giving people information on what a union was and what the benefits of a union were. So that was my introduction to organizing.

Actually, I didn't like organizing. I hated it. I would do everything I could to avoid it, because it meant doing some very one-to-one things. I was so shy. I especially hated making house calls, and that was a crucial part of organizing. You have to go to people's homes. First you've already made your introduction, probably talked to them, told them, "Look. We're here and we're trying to organize a union. Are you interested?" If they said they were interested then we would give them a card and ask them to sign the card. We were trying to compile an estimate of how many people were interested and how many people were not. If they signed the card, then the next step would be to visit them at their homes and talk to them one-to-one about forming a union or maybe being a part of this very secretive committee. We had to keep it very secret, for a while anyway. Later on down the line things came out and everyone knew who the leaders were. That became the very difficult part for the people that were working on this committee.

I'm the type of person that, when I start something, I'll stick with it almost until you kick me out. I stayed at the union position for about nine years, starting in April of 1980. In 1983 there was tension going on between the president and the vice president of the union. Something happened and every person on staff—every board member, every clerical person—received a copy of the union's own payroll records. It was very easy to look at it, just one glance, and see that all the Whites were being paid more than all the Blacks, and all the men were being paid more than all the women. Now if you know anything about labor, you know that that contradicts everything that labor is about. My job was to make sure that people were not discriminated against, that they received fair wages, and that seniority was the rule.

After we made this discovery I was faced with one of the most difficult decisions of my life, and that was what to do. We knew that we were being discriminated against. It came down to the Black women, and there were only a few of us. When I started this position in 1980, it was actually the result of the affirmative action law that was just passed in 1979. So one of the things that this particular labor union was trying to do was get Blacks in. So since I was Black and a woman that was another one of the reasons that I was picked. There were three women on staff, two Black and one White. We were the ones that stuck it out. We filed EOC charges against our local union and the international union. This was the Service Employees International Union. All hell broke loose. When they discovered what we had done they came after us with everything in their arsenal. Service Employees International Union was, at that time, I believe the fifth largest union in the United States and one of the only growing unions.

I remember the president of the union, Dick Cortz, flew in from Washington, D.C. He let us know that he was going to kick our ass. We were doing something that we shouldn't have done. We knew we needed some protection, so we tried to form our own union. The first people that we talked to were representatives of the UAW [United Auto Workers]. We asked them if we could join their union. The lady came, had a meeting with us, and asked us to sign cards. We signed cards, saying "Yes, we want to be part of your union." The same lady came back and told her boss. Her boss told my boss, "Look, your staff is trying to organize."

All hell came down on us. We were given organizing assignments that no one in their right mind believed could be successfully completed. And we completed them. We did it. We would go into areas where we had no assistance from anyone and we would organize. It became very stressful and very difficult. Ultimately, we did form an association. We couldn't go with the UAW because they said, "No, we won't do that to a fellow union."

During that period my father and my oldest son passed in the same year. Between the stress of trying to fight that union and the personal things that were going on, it just became too much. I admitted myself into a hospital. I didn't know what was going on with me, but I was told that I was suffering from depression. So I had to make a decision, and my decision was not to go back to the job.

I stayed off work for probably about three years. During those three years I became pregnant again. Mind you, I'm still a single mother. I was forty-one at the time. Forty-one and pregnant and single: it was unbelievable. I said, "How in the *world* can I be doing this again?" But I carried the pregnancy through even though I knew that I didn't have to. I knew what to do. I prayed and I asked for guidance. I carried the pregnancy to term and had my baby girl, still not working.

That was a very difficult time in my life because I was poor for the first time in my life. All my life my daddy worked two full-time jobs so that we had everything that we needed. Then I started working and I made good money. So this time I lost just about everything. The only thing I kept was the house. I was very ill with the pregnancy. My thoughts were that I would never go back to a job again. I was going to become an entrepreneur because I didn't think I could handle a situation where I had a boss, someone over me, mistreating me.

I made a settlement with the union. I got a little bit of money and I started my own business. I got a computer and I started Anderson's Computer and Information Services. I worked it for a while, but I wasn't good at getting paid. It was very difficult for me to tell people, "Look, you owe me so much money."

I had this feeling that I had to give back. I felt that I was blessed, really. I wasn't working, but I felt blessed. I had this little bit of money and I started volunteering at a homeless shelter for girls. My job, as a volunteer, was to ride around in a van in some of the roughest areas in the city of Detroit. Our job was to service the prostitutes. We would take juice, sandwiches, and bleach kits. The bleach kits were because most of them were junkies and addicts. So we gave them the bleach kits so they could clean their works and wouldn't become infected with HIV or any other things.

I did that for about a year. That was the experience of a lifetime. I thought I knew the streets because I came from the streets, but I didn't know until I did this job just how it was. I saw young women. I remember one young lady who was probably about fifteen years old. She was probably about seven months pregnant and she was high as a kite. I remember giving her a sandwich. I said, "Here, take this sandwich." She took the bread and threw the bread to the side. She kept the meat and walked into some bushes. I'm just like, "What is she doing?" She went into the bushes and gave the meat to this kitten. I thought that was just something. That was just one of the many things I saw working on those streets.

Probably about a year after that I was asked to become a full-time staff person. I left the outreach portion and worked in the homeless shelter with these young women.

I stayed there for probably about six years. I was laid off. This was the first time I'd been laid off. This was something else I'd never experienced before. I was at my wits' end and didn't know what to do. My unemployment was running out. Then I heard that a friend of mine from back in my labor days was looking for an organizer. So I called her up and said, "Hey, I heard you were looking for an organizer." She said, "Yeah! Come on." So I worked for her for probably about three months as an environmental community organizer. This was new to me. I was used to labor organizing. You were organizing for specific things: workers bettering their wages and safety and things of that nature. This type of organizing was way different because the issues were broader. It was clean air, water— things that I had not really considered before for myself in my own personal life. I was a single mother. I never thought about the air. I never thought about the water.

I'd heard about environmentalists, and I thought that these people were doing nice work, but I really didn't have time to do it myself. Then when I learned that these environmental issues had an impact on my children and me. I learned that I couldn't ignore them. That's when I became a community organizer.

I worked for her for a little while. She recommended me to another organization as a community organizer, and I started working then for Warren/Conner Development Coalition. This is where I received my community organizing training. It wasn't titled that. It was just a job and you started doing the job. Just my interview alone was something I had never experienced before, because it was a mock community meeting. We were asked to sit in on this so that they could see how we would handle this situation. I was not used to a situation where real people—these were real people from the community—were cussing and yelling. What the hell? I simply wasn't used to that, even though I came from labor where they cuss and yell too.

Just getting that job was a difference. I learned different styles of organizing. Like if there's a community meeting you kind of staff the meeting. You situate people in the hall where you're having a meeting and you give them scripts to say. I thought that was a little dishonest, but sometimes it worked. So these were new organizing methods that I had not dealt with before. It was quite different.

The work that I did there was very intense. I had a huge area on the east side of Detroit where I had probably about thirty block clubs that I worked with. Their issues were just basic issues of city services, garbage, illegal dumping . . . it was just simply organizing to empower the people. That was the mission, to organize them [. . .] not so much that they would depend on me or the organization that I worked for, but so that they would become independent and empowered to work on these things for themselves and improve their own conditions.

I must say that it was some of the most challenging work that I've ever had, because a lot of the people felt that they didn't deserve anything better. So it was almost going out convincing people that you do deserve better, you deserve a cleaner community, you deserve city services that are on time. One of the major projects that we worked on was a shopping center that's on the corner of Warren and Conner. It is a nice large shopping center, but the conditions are horrible. The ceiling in the shopping center leaked. Doors were locked with chains. There were fumes, tiles missing, holes so large that your car would just fall into them in the parking lot. The owner did not feel responsible to improve those conditions; he felt that the people didn't deserve anything better. So here we were trying to tell the people, "Look, you *do* deserve better. Tell this man you're not going to shop here any longer." So that was my introduction to community organizing.

While I was working for Warren/Conner I was asked by the same young lady—her name was Donele Wilkins and she was the executive director of Detroit's Working for Environmental Justice—she said, "Rhonda, Sierra Club is looking for an environmental organizer. Why don't you apply?" I applied and did not hear anything. I pretty much forgot it.

I had also applied for a position at Wayne County Juvenile Detention Facility and had totally forgotten about it. They contacted me and asked me if I would come for my second interview. I went and interviewed for the second time, then for the third time, and then got the position. This job was something that changed my life again. I was locking up children and making sure that they stayed locked up. I worked there for about eight months. I'm working with children from the ages of nine to eighteen. These children are locked up for all kinds of things: murder, rape, carjacking, truancy . . . just all kinds of things.

I worked with the girls' unit as well as the boys' unit. It was one of the most difficult things I had ever done: locking up a child. I don't care what he or she was there for. Most of the children were there because of neglect. They had grown up in terribly abusive situations. These were things that were just totally not of their own making or control.

I saw fights while I was there that were just unbelievable. The anger that the children had was paralyzing. I had a situation when I was working on the girls' unit. It was time for them to go to bed and you had to lock them up. Three of them took off running. I was like, "Oh my God, where are these girls going?" They couldn't go anywhere because everything was locked up. They were running to the end of the hall. There's a window at the end of the hall that none of these children could see out of—there were no windows that they could actually look out of. But if they jumped they could look out of the window for just a brief second. When they came down, they were saying, "Ms. Anderson, it is so beautiful." That just tore at my heart.

Another time a girl was looking out of a window—the window was only about forty-five inches wide and probably a foot long—and she was screaming, "Ms. Anderson! Ms. Anderson! I love you, Ms. Anderson!" And you weren't supposed to show these children compassion, and it was just too hard for me.

This job that I had with the county was paying me the most I'd ever been able to make, but it was one of the hardest jobs I'd ever had to work. I would have to work three days out of the week with sixteen-hour shifts. I was neglecting my children. My children were going wild. I wasn't able to pick them up from school and drop them off because I was working these sixteen-hour shifts. So when I heard that Sierra Club wanted to interview me for a position as an organizer, I thought, "I'll just do this."

I showed up at my interview in African garb from head to toe, the whole nine yards. I'm really into African culture. My daughter goes to an African-centered school that a couple parents and myself organized probably about twelve years ago. So I show up at my interview with all this on. They interviewed me: John McCown, Allison Horton, Lydia Fisher, Anna Holden, and Donele Wilkins. I asked questions. Then they contacted me again about a month later and said, "Do you want the job?" And I said, "Yes." So I became this environmental justice organizer, doing the work that I do today. That was in 2000.

Remember how I said I hated organizing when I was with labor? I *love* organizing now. I absolutely love it. And I'm good at it. One of the things that's crucial to doing this job is being able to talk to people where they are. I don't have anything in my head that says, "You're supposed to be a certain way." So when I see people who are what other people would describe as uneducated, unemployed, and even homeless, I have no problems with it. I can talk to them straight to their face. I can sit down and engage them in conversation, and that's what it takes to organize. You have to be able to talk to people one-to-one, straight to their faces. You have to hold a conversation with them and gather, from what they say, what they need. Then you figure out how it is that you can assist them in getting it.

So the crucial part of my job today is doing just the basic organizing, which requires you to go door-to-door. It's not something where you tell somebody, "Come to this meeting." Most often you're going to have to knock on that door and say, "Hello, how are you? Can I talk to you?" And I can do it. It's easy. I've never experienced a situation where anyone was hostile. I'm just always so impressed and moved by how open people are. How many times have I knocked on a door and had someone say, "Come on in, baby. Sit down?" I go in, I look at the pictures and I hear the stories. When you make these personal, one-to-one connections, you gain the peoples' trust. Then it becomes easy to say, "This is something I can do to help you."

I'm not trying to help them in a way that they are going to be dependent on me: "Let's go back to Ms. Anderson and talk to her; she'll get it for us." Oh no. They have to become independent and stand on their own. My job is to not see them again, because they're now doing these things for themselves.

If you're going to meet people where they are, sometimes it's far away from what you actually want to work with them on. Say there's a polluting facility in a community and you know that this facility is making the people sick. But if that community is dealing with poverty where the women are trying to feed and shelter their children, then I have to talk to them where they are. That means that I have to steer them to places where they can get food, shelter, and clothes. Then we might be able to talk about that polluting facility down the street. But in the meantime you have to meet the people where they are.

The other thing I think it requires is that long-term commitment, because you have to keep going back. Even if we shut down that incinerator, they're not home free. There are other things that they need to be aware of too. There may be another incinerator across the road. There may be an expressway. There's this continuous educational thing that goes on.

It's hard work. It's labor-intense work. It also pays little money. There's no status to the position. I don't know how many times I've filled out a form that says, "What's your occupation?" "Organizer" is nowhere on there. I almost want to tell people, "Well, I'm an organizer." "An organizer? What is that?" It's not one of those status positions. It's nothing to get recognized for. The only ones that know what we're doing are us.

I stay because I like the work. I'm committed to the people, to the community. Sometimes I think of myself as having the spirit of Harriet Tubman. "You're going to be free, or else. You're not turning back now." This just has to be done. I also don't know how much longer I'll do this work. I'm fifty-three years old. Like I said, it's labor-intense and stressful and hard. But I enjoy myself too.

What Makes a Good Organizer?

So what makes a person a good organizer? What personality traits, what skills, what attitudes do you need to do this job well? These questions generated a lot of different kinds of answers.

"I think lots of different people can be good organizers, and be organizers in somewhat different ways," said Kim Fellner, who has written about and trained organizers across the country for many years. "It's hard to know what the defining characteristics are that you have to have. And while I think the organizing skills and techniques can be taught, I do think that there is also a gift to organizing. Often you see someone and you say, 'This person will just never be an organizer.' It's almost like pornography: you know it when you see it."

But there are some basic things that most organizers agree help a lot in doing this job. "I think there are two things that can't be taught and that you really need to figure out if you have them before you go into organizing," said Emily Gruszka. "One is a passion for social justice—that whole 'fire in the belly' slogan. The second is a real genuine love of people."

> There's got to be something inside a good organizer—a powerful drive to want to do this—that's more than just, "I want to do a job." . . . A good organizer is not afraid to challenge people. Someone who can think larger picture, strategically, who has a bigger vision of what's possible. Someone who's not afraid to engage with people; someone who is not afraid to talk, open up with people and build relationships with folks. Someone who is not afraid to make a mistake; someone who's not afraid to reflect on a mistake and learn from it. I think one of the key ingredients is action-reflection in organizing. And every situation is different, dealing with people is dealing with all kinds of personalities and every situation is going to be a little different. You have to go and do it, but smart organizers learn from each situation and build on that.
> —Patrick Sweeney

What is fire in the belly? Well, it's anger, but anger tempered
with purpose. It's passion, but passion directed at a goal,
and with a plan for getting there.

First of all, I think you have to have a lot of passion. You have to be a
passionate person. And I think that probably there is some passion in all of
us, it's just a matter of what irks us. But you have to be a person who cares
and is willing to go somewhere with that. I think most people care, but they
just tuck that away some place and don't know quite what to do with it.
    —Pennie Vance

You have to be really driven by that passion to be persistent and not give
up in spite of the many obstacles and challenges and frustrations and time
demands. I think you need a core fire-in-the-belly passion for justice and
social change. You need to have a vision for the world as it should be.
    —Robert Owens

Someone who's passionate about things and yet tempered. I think the
passion has to be tempered because of the role I see a community organizer
playing: motivating and encouraging people. You need to be able to reach
folks and appeal to them in the way you talk about issues and ask questions.
And yet it's the people in the organization that really need to be the
leaders and the movers and the pushers on things. So to have an organizer
be passionate but contained, so that there's space for other folks to feel
passionate and move to the front.
    —Brett Kelver

I don't think you can do this job and not care about what you're doing.
You can graduate from college with an English degree and go become a
computer programmer, and stay there for a couple years, and not care about
what you're doing. I don't think you can be a community organizer and
say, "Well, it's just a job for now. Something better will come along later."
Organizers tend to have a real passion for what they are working for.
    —Kelly (Corley) Pokharel

I think that a good community organizer must, above all, have a strong
sense of social justice and a commitment to try to fix some of the things that
are wrong in our society. I think that a community organizer has to have
the capability to put his or her own ambition at the service of the affected
people that he or she is working with. I think that someone who gets into
community work for the purpose of advancing their own status or career
inevitably will end up on the rocks.
    —Ben Thacker-Gwaltney

There is a level of anger and outrage tempered by patience that is very important. To stay in this work, you have to have a level of anger that can sustain you. Lots of people refer to that as "cold anger"—I find that a very effective metaphor. That is certainly a piece of it. But there also has to be a real ability to look hard at reality and see the potential and know that it's a long-term potential. There are lots of folks who have a lot of the skills, and want to do it, but simply can't temper their own anger at the world enough to stay in this work long-term.

And then there's this balance of caring enough about the details to make sure there's a key to the building when you need it to have a community meeting and caring enough about the big picture to really be able to talk to somebody effectively about a different vision for the world.
—Lisa Abbott

Anger does not mean rage; anger means a disciplined and controlled, calculated response to your own life experience. You don't want these things to happen again to you or particularly to your kids. So clarity about that is critical. In my own experience I think having to conquer fear is also crucial. You can't organize and you can't act on your anger and get people to react and respond in new ways if you're afraid. We all have fears from time to time and anxiety, but you can't be afraid to take a stance. You've got to be clear about your own weaknesses, but you can't feel like anybody, no matter how powerful or smart they might be, has anything on you. You've got to figure them out and then you can play in that ballpark. Deal with fear in such a way that you can be clear in any situation.
—Perry Perkins

But anger isn't enough.

To make organizing work as a way of channeling anger, you have to work with people. It's hard to be an organizer if you are a loner, if you don't like being with people, because community organizing is all about people. You have to like people and believe in people.

You must deeply love other human beings and be deeply disturbed by the condition that you find people in. That's number one. You've got to be a patient person, someone who can take time and watch a community come face to face with itself. Those would be the most important things: to genuinely care about people and their condition in the world and to have the patience to help them walk through it.
—John McCown

I think that a community organizer has to like people and has to be fascinated by people and willing to engage with people and listen to people and try to understand people. Because a community organizer is not always

Community organizing is all about people. You have to like people and believe in people. Virginia Organizing Project Organizer Jill Carson, left, works with a group of board members and staff at an annual planning retreat.

going to be working on issues that affect him or her, then it's essential to have that level of empathy and understanding that enable you to take those people's concerns and issues on, and come to care about them. You know, we're not talking about a mechanical skill here; you have to have an emotional starting point in order to do good organizing.

—Ben Thacker-Gwaltney

I think in organizing work you have to have empathy. You have to really be able to get into the other person's shoes. I think what kind of dovetails into empathy is the ability to listen, the ability to hear what people are saying and really see what their needs are. Once you see what their needs are, you can start talking about different approaches for it. I think that's what it takes. I think it's in the values that you hold and how they mesh with the work that you're doing. So if you're a community organizer who's working in an area, it's a matter of not only having empathy but in a way it's a love for that individual, that culture, those things that person represents. I think you have to have that connection.

—Brian Shields

People skills. That is the number one thing. I mean you need to be organized. You need to have computer skills. You need to be able to pick

up on the issues, but if you have poor people skills and you can't work with people, and sometimes some difficult people, you're not an effective organizer. If your members hate you, you're not doing your job. It may be that you're just not suited for it.
  —Robin Bagley

You have to be able to hear people. You have to respect what they need, whether it's going out to get a cigarette or perceiving them as Hispanic rather than Latino, whatever it is. You have to respect what they are. You don't always have to agree with them but you have to respect them.
  —Larry Yates

Certainly what I look for are people who are, most importantly, very relational people. We want people who like people, who are intrigued by people, people who are curious about people, and people who are tolerant of differences and have good insights about other people.
    The second piece is that I think good community organizers are people who have a passion about seeing justice done in communities. It really gets them on a gut level and they can't let it go. They get angry about the fact that there are such significant injustices in our local communities and our society at large and the world around us. I think those are two of the most important characteristics. Certainly having a good mind and being bright and having good writing and analytical skills helps a great deal. But I think it's those relational qualities and that passion for justice that are the two most essential elements.
  —Paul Cromwell

To organize well, you need to be able to build strong relationships with people—relationships based on acceptance, trust, shared purpose. The better you can do that, the better an organizer you will be.

I think an organizer is somebody who has the capacity to sustain a lot of productive, healthy relationships. Organizers understand that they have to invest in other people. But I also don't think that it's just about relationships. I think that out of relationships has to come some catalytic activity that allows people to get beyond their own individuality and begin to move as a collective. An organizer has that skill and can build relationships, but also has the ability to bring people into a room and help them balance their own ego needs so that the group can find the passion to take collective action around issues that they share.
  —Gary Sandusky

Relationships. You have to have relationships with the people that you're trying to organize. If you don't, people always see you as a stranger. One of the big things that was going on during the Civil Rights years in

Mississippi early on was that people initially looked at the SNCC [Student Nonviolent Coordinating Committee] organizers as outsiders. The White population definitely looked at them as outside agitators. But what the SNCC people did was they came in and became infused in the community. The Civil Rights movement didn't happen in a ballroom. This was the epitome of grassroots. You're talking about people who went in and lived in communities for six, seven months. They didn't have a per diem. They didn't have any housing. They lived with whoever was willing to put them up. They ate whatever someone was willing to cook for them. They didn't have any transportation. They rolled around with whoever was willing to drive them around.
　—Carlton Turner

You have to be able to communicate well. You have to be able to meet people where they are. You can't be judgmental about anything. You have to constantly be working to have an open mind. You can't be shy. You have to have an ability to talk to strangers. You have to be willing to get out in the community and meet people and put yourself in some not-so-comfortable places, both physically and emotionally. You can't be afraid of confrontation. You have to be shamelessly optimistic. And you have to have a good sense of humor to be a good organizer.
　—Karen Waters

One of the things about organizers is that they have to meet people where they are. They don't necessarily want to leave them there, but they have to be able to accept people where they are, at least for the most part, and not be terribly judgmental.
　—June Rostan

I think you have to have somebody who can connect with people. Someone who can relate. Someone who understands that if you show up in flip-flops, baggy pants, and a midriff, you're not going to convince farmers or ranchers that they should become members of the Northern Plains Resource Council and work towards responsible coal bed methane development.
　—Aaron Browning

You have to be at ease. You have to be genuine with people. If you don't really want to do this, don't do it. It will show up and it wouldn't serve you well in what you do. You should just be honest with people. My focus is on people in the community. Tell people the truth. In my growth as an organizer, I went through this stage when I would first go out and conduct meetings feeling like I did have to have all the answers and if they asked me a question I ought to be able to answer it. Finally I figured out that that's not really true. If they ask me a question and I don't know the answer, it's really okay to say, "Well, I don't know." People are okay with that. What I do tell them is, "We can find out." I learn more and more at the meetings I go to. You might not know, but the person next to you might. The settings you provide help that kind of thing to happen.

—Presdelane Harris

I think another characteristic of the organizer is being good at identifying and cultivating new leaders. I think that's the most challenging part. That always seems to slide away to a secondary priority. We pay for that, because we don't have enough leaders.

—Dennis Olson

I think an effective community organizer has to be able to build relationships with people. It's not therapeutic. It's not caretaking. It's not pastoral. They are relationships that somehow challenge people to take the next step to improve their community in a way that is different from charity ministries and service ministries. An effective organizer, for me, has to be someone that can teach people and give them tools to do what they need to do. I have to tell leaders, "I can't tell you why you need to do this. You have to tell me why. If you tell me why, then I can tell you how."

—Ray Higgins, Jr.

Facilitation is a whole skill set, but I think that's one of the most important pieces of being an organizer. You have to work with lots of different people from lots of different backgrounds and be able to work across race and class and gender and sexuality and age, despite wherever you are along that continuum.

—Leah Ottersbach

But developing relationships is only part of the picture.

An organizer has to help people move from where they are to where they want to be—to affect change in their community or in the world. To do that, an organizer must be able to think strategically and creatively.

I think that there are all kinds of personality types that make effective organizers. I think it is most important, and probably most lacking, that organizers be strategic thinkers, be able to analyze a situation and be able to understand how one activity or event affects another and affects another and affects another, and how and where you can influence those events and activities in order to create a different outcome. I'm amazed at how few people are natural strategic thinkers, not just in organizing, but in general. So a lot of times you see people acting on their rage in really counterproductive ways, and that's a failure called anger, but also a failure of strategic thinking.

—Burt Lauderdale

I think you need to know enough about policy issues to be able to provide guidance for people about what their options are for actually winning things and having enough experience and knowledge of that to give them good advice so that you're not spending a lot of time losing. You spend enough time losing when you do it right, and you don't have the luxury anymore to just fail continually forever.

    —Dennis Olson

I definitely want to add critical thinking to the list, as another characteristic, being able to strategize and think about issues. You need to be able to constantly ask yourself, with anything you read, "Whose voice am I hearing? What is their point of view? Where are they coming from? Are there alternatives?" Questions like that. I have to prompt myself to ask these questions all the time. It's easy to just be lazy. But I think strategic, critical thinking is really key to being an organizer.

    —Kevin Williams

Just like any other field or endeavor, an individual has strengths or weaknesses. There's a woman I know who is just excellent in building relationships and encouraging people to express themselves and gain a sense that they all share something collectively. But she doesn't have a sense of strategy. If an organizer is not strategic, then there's a limit to what he or she can do. Eventually people start to stumble into each other if there's nowhere to go. You can't just bring a bunch of people into a room and expect it to work out. Bad organizing is probably worse than no organizing at all. That's where this source of empowerment starts to come in. It's when folks can actually get together, work together, and struggle. They take risks and then gain. In my experience, it's a gain in moving a decision-maker to reach a decision that we'd been trying to get him to make. An organizer is someone who will transform the folks who are involved.

    —Gary Sandusky

I think a good organizer is curious and is intelligent. It's someone that can think strategically both internally and externally—internally, in terms of what will build the organization and develop leaders, and externally, in terms of the power we need to be effective in this region around the issues that are important to our people.

    —Ken Galdston

I think it helps to be able to thoughtfully integrate the universe. It helps to be able to put things together in a slightly different way. To help people see things in a different way. So you have to be able to do it and be able to communicate it. I think it takes a certain amount of intellectual, as opposed to academic, rigor. I think one needs to be able to understand how things work. There are lots of different ways to find out how things work. It isn't like the organizer has to already know how things work. The organizer has

to know how to find out how things work. It's the capacity to know what you don't know and find it out, whether that's the power analysis of the city, or how the employer does this or that, or where the money goes.
—Kim Fellner

You have to have a sense of strategy. You have to really think about how to do things. Different tactics and different approaches work in different places at different times. You can be too enamored of a tactic or you can be too afraid of a tactic. But you really should be making your decisions, if you're a good organizer, based on whether a tactic will work. Will it accomplish what needs to be accomplished? Part of it, of course, is will the people involved actually do this tactic? Does it make sense to them? You don't choose a tactic just because it's fun or it's exciting or somebody else did it. It's not because at some abstract level it should work. It's because there's really some evidence and a reason to think it will work and you've thought about it and strategized about it.
—Larry Yates

And it helps to be . . .

Organized

You have to be able to jump from one thing to another, juggle things a lot. I've worked with Pat Sweeney [director of the Western Organization of Resource Councils] for the whole time, and he's the most amazing person I've seen at being able to do that, being able to juggle different things. Being able to go from one real intense conversation with a leader or another staff person, to dealing with a funder, to dealing with a politician or a decision-maker or helping somebody else deal with that. To come up with a campaign strategy, then deal with the staff supervision question and not have either one spill over. That's a very important part of being a community organizer, because, like I said, there are so many different parts to it.
—John Smillie

I think one of the important things is being personally organized, having your stuff together and knowing how to find it. For me, I really like things written down. I'm a writer and a poet, so I really like things written down. I like to have a binder full of all the pieces of paperwork, all organized very carefully. But then I have friends and their offices are disasters. I can't imagine how they can find anything, but you ask them for something and they know exactly where it is. So everybody has their own style.
—Leah Ottersbach

I think if you don't have an organized personality, you can't be an effective community organizer. Different people have different perspectives on

this, and I respect that. I do. I've met some community organizers that I kind of felt weren't really that personally organized, but I have seen them do amazing work. But to me, I think one of the most important skills that I look for is somebody who can do the follow-up, because I think ninety percent of our work is follow-up. You know, you have a planning meeting, you have a strategy meeting, and you have to follow up tasks. You better not just file those away. If you don't type up that task list, and you don't get on the phone with people making sure that everyone's doing what they agreed to do, it's not going to come together. I think that's a very important skill.
—Aaron Browning

Optimistic

I think that organizers have to have optimism and hope, and they have to be able to act on it and convey it to other folks without coming across as cheesy. I think that organizers have to be inspired by small victories, perhaps inspired by small victories more than they are inspired by large victories, but have a faith that large victories come from small ones, and that you have to be strategic about those as well. That's what really has to charge your batteries, if you're going to be effective as an organizer, because it's a long-term approach, it's a long-term strategy.
—Burt Lauderdale

I think that organizers need to have faith. Even if you aren't a person of faith, per se, you need to be a person that believes in the best outcomes. You can't be a pessimist. You can't be one who will bad-talk yourself into failure. Organizers need to know how to buy the words they speak and the attitudes they demonstrate to make folks know that they can do it.
—Sheila Kingsberry-Burt

Patient

One quality you need would be patience. There's patience working with your members, patience working with leadership in different structures. Patience knowing that we're at the bottom of a social structure with all the weight of race, gender, and class on top of most of our members. With all that in mind, it just takes a lot of patience, knowing that you're going to have to weather anything from personal attacks to disputes, conflicts, and all that kind of stuff.

And a sense of humor: otherwise you'd have to jump out the window.
—Jon Liss

They really have to see beyond the immediate fight and be real committed to that. I think some people want to be organizers because they're angry.

Community groups, congregations, and unions join together to demand a living wage from their local government. Living wage campaigns can go on for years, and take a lot of patience.

Some people want to be organizers because it's cool. Or it's sort of an idealistic thing. Change the world. I think people have to understand that change happens slowly, that you really have to be committed to the long-term change and have some realization that it involves changing people.

It certainly takes hard work. It certainly takes a good—not sense of humor, but ability to roll with the punches. To know you're going to get beat up sometimes. And that's part of having a long-term view. You realize that you're in it for the long haul, and that sometimes setbacks are opportunities for strengthening the work. I think you have to be goal-focused, but not too goal-focused. You want to win this campaign, you want to create an organization that has power, you want to knock someone out of office or whatever—let's say you're so focused on that that you fail to see opportunities along the way that might not fit in with the straight and narrow strategy, but over the long run could help build something that's stronger and more lasting.
—Jerry Hardt

A good listener

You have to really be able to listen to people and to be able to set aside your own idea of what you want to see happen, and to be able to interpret success. It's never going to work out just the way you want it to work out. You're going to have to make compromises, but be able to find success.

You're grooming people like you're grooming a prize fighter—you find some things that they can get into and have some success at, to build some confidence. A lot of times, they won't even see it as success, but to be able to interpret it as success is an important quality in a community organizer, and in a leader.
    —Allen Cooper

I think the most important characteristic is being a good listener. For me it's not about being in power, but empowering, helping people get out there and solve their problems themselves. I think that you have to be willing to step back and not push your ideas, but help them see the options and help them choose good options. So you educate, you teach. I actually compare organizing a lot to being a mother. It's the part where, even though they don't make their bed the very best, you leave it alone because it's their bed and they get better at it.
    —Vickie Goodwin

The one characteristic that's probably most important is the ability to be a compassionate listener. Because this isn't really about the organizer yourself, it's really about working with people and understanding what people's needs are, or what we really need to do together to make positive change. I think maybe as with writing or with any other artistic endeavor—because I view being a community organizer as an artistic endeavor—that you really have to let yourself get out of the way and listen and learn from those around you. I think you need a real commitment—maybe a passion—for change, in a sense that when there's an injustice, you need to find a way to make it right.
    —Pamela Miller

To be effective you need to be able to listen a lot, and not just be a good listener in terms of being a sympathetic person who listens to other people's problems. You have to be an analytic listener. While you care about people as individuals, you're not there to solve their problems for them. You're listening for patterns among what a variety of people are saying. Effective community organizers try to come to a general understanding of what the community is like, as well as to identify any possibilities, any plausible kinds of things that people might want to work on together to make changes that would improve the life of the community in specific ways.
    —Ellen Ryan

If you are organizing you have to be part of the community. You have to be in the same place. No up, no down. You have to listen to the community. Because the community has many necessities. You don't have to think about your necessities; you have to think about the necessities of the community. When I go to the community maybe I say, "We have to do this. This is my necessity." But the community says, "No, we don't have to do this." We

have to listen to the people. What do they need? What do they want? In my experience from Bolivia and from here, the community has very good brains. Maybe the people, they cannot talk very good English. They cannot write in English, or even in Spanish. But they have brains. That's the more important thing.
　　—Alicia Ruiz

Many would say that it's the ability to convert fear into anger in order to make sure action happens. Others would know that it's the ability to listen to someone's anguish and connect the dots of that anguish to the anguish of others in order to understand that we can move from here to there together, that we're not alone. But there is a level of self-interest. Patience, I think, makes a great organizer, to be able to do those things. Good listening skills. The ability to change. And, even though many of us suffer from this ill, it's having as small of an ego as possible to understand that it's not about us. But I probably will say that the two biggest skills for me, as an organizer—regardless of the mechanics of organizing, because there are mechanics of organizing—are to be patient and to be a good listener, to understand.
　　—Lisbeth Meléndez Rivera

Fearless

I think a good organizer is a person that's sensitive to the needs of others. It's a person that's straightforward, aggressive, and won't take "no" for an answer. An organizer is a person that doesn't give up easily and a person that is not easily intimidated or threatened by opposition.
　　—Rochelle Ziyad

Or a combination of things

There are lots of traits that make a good organizer,
but different combinations work best in different people.

You've got to have the talent, but you also have to have the call and the ability to endure. If one of those three comes out, it's like a tripod: you're going to fall over.
　　—Ray Higgins, Jr.

Organizers have to be curious; they've got to have a good sense of humor; they've got to be incredibly patient; they've got to want to make something happen enough that they're willing to have a lot of conversations that don't go anywhere. They've got to have ego, enough confidence to have a lot of doors slammed in their faces.
　　You've got to have some anger or drive or just some deep-seated conviction to make something happen where nothing is happening.

Because organizing fundamentally is entrepreneurial; you're going against the grain, you're trying to organize power where at present there is no power. That means you're always playing against the odds. You're always trying to organize, whether you're pulling together African-Americans and Hispanics, or Chicano folks with recent immigrants, or whoever, you're pulling together people who aren't together now, and that's basically creative, and it's going upstream, and it just takes a lot of ego and a lot of drive to stick with it, to make something come together.
—Allen Cooper

I think it needs to be somebody who has had training and the opportunity to really learn. This is something that you learn. You are not born knowing what organizing is. You are socialized and you have experiences in your life that make you aware of unfair things in this world, of discrimination and injustice. I think, for me, that's the key piece. If you're enraged by the injustice in this world then that's a key piece. Everything else is something that you learn.

Obviously there are character issues. I think you need a certain level of energy for doing this work. But mainly you feel that you can make a difference, that this is something that can go beyond you. If you have that then it's also the willingness to learn. There are people who have tremendous experience and we can learn from that. It's having those opportunities and being willing to help.
—Guillermo Quinteros

I think that I look for someone who has the Burn. Who has a fire in their belly, who believes that they want to make change in this society and have a society that is more democratic and more just. It's really hard to articulate how that expresses itself—it expresses itself in different people in different ways. We ask all sorts of questions in our interview process that are trying to get at "What is this person's value system? How do they feel about corporations and how they treat people, and what the responsibilities of corporations are? How should government operate?" So having a congruent value system with the organization is important, I think.

But, beyond that, they have to be somebody who isn't looking for the spotlight themselves. If they think that perhaps they are going to be on television, that they are going to be the spokesperson for the organization, that they are trying to make a name for themselves, or start down that path, that's not somebody that we are looking for. We are looking for somebody who's willing to work behind the scenes, who's somewhat humble about that sort of thing, that does not need so much public recognition to feel like they are doing a good job, that they are being appreciated.

Somebody who's strategic, definitely. Someone who can understand the big picture of the issue, but who also can understand how you execute a strategy or a campaign plan, and I think that's a very important skill.

I think somebody who's a little bit sassy makes a good organizer. Who's willing to overcome what we call the Force of Politeness, which prevents, I think, more often than not, people from holding other people accountable, whether it's within our own organization or someone who is a decision maker or target. You have to be able to get over your Force of Politeness and be direct with people, and ask the difficult questions, both internally and externally.

—Aaron Browning

You can go down the traits of an organizer: relational, an ability to analyze power, an ability to challenge, an ability to be empathetic. To act in chaos and be able to make order out of chaos. To be able to move people collectively and move them individually. To be able to endure and persevere.

You have to get out. You have to make these direct phone calls and set up one-to-ones. You have to be willing to be challenged. You have to want to learn.

You have to be able to step into situations in which you don't know the answer. Be at peace with finding the question. Half the time I'm thinking, "I don't know what the hell we're supposed to do. I don't know where it's going to lead." It's a rabbit going down a hole and you're just following it.

I guess you have to be angry. You have to be hopeful and angry. You have to have some personal something coming from you that drives you. It can't be toxic or you'll just get eaten up.

—Ray Higgins, Jr.

Most of it you learn in the field. Everybody makes mistakes. Everybody says the wrong thing on a phone call to a county commissioner once in a while. You learn from that and you keep going. You get more politically smart as you go along. You figure out, when you're talking to people in the field, what's going to work, what's going to actually be effective in building this organization.

—Nicholas Graber-Grace

I think [good community organizers] have to have a sense of humor. Or maybe those are just the ones that I like to work with!

I think they have to be good listeners and good coaches, really, to support people where they need to be supported. They probably do need to be idealistic, or they'll just be too depressed all the time. You've gotta have a vision, and you've gotta really believe in it, and I think you do have to know why you want to do it.

It helps that you can keep track of many things at once, be able to multitask, and that you have a sense of respect and openness to thinking about things in different ways.

So you have to have your vision, but I think you also need to be flexible. I think a good community organizer is someone who's interested in

leadership development. That distinguishes a good community organizer from people who just do projects in their community, whether it's from a formal or informal process.
  —Kelley Weigel

You have to be courageous, but not so courageous that you forget that the people around you could be afraid. You have to be a good listener, and not just listen to what people say but to what they don't say and how people hold their bodies and how they interact with you. It's important to know the political landscape: who's in charge and how it works. You should know the processes and that kind of thing. If you know the process then you know how to disrupt the process.
  —Octavia Ware

I think a community organizer has to be smart in a strategic sense, though not necessarily possess a lot of information, although certain pieces of information are interesting to know and important to have. I think it's important for the community organizer to see information and intelligence and details and all of these things as a way of kicking ass, a way of winning on the issue, a way of beating the bad guys. So I think that the organizer has to be very, very smart about what to do with information, how to use it, because everything you do is about building power and winning the campaign. And an organizer needs to understand that.
  I guess another thing is, anyone who treats organizing as a job, as opposed to a passion, is probably not going to last.
  Let's see. Humility, people skills, strategic thinking, an ability to listen. You have to be able to cope with failure and compromise and all the rest. I think you have to have some ideological basis for why you're doing it. I think you have to have a political sense of why you're there and what you want to accomplish in terms of your goals. Unfortunately, the right wing has community organizers, too. You have to be able to know the difference between what we're trying to accomplish and what some of them are trying to accomplish.
  —Ben Thacker-Gwaltney

Faith. I stress that—having faith in the community. Being able to interpret the language and give it back to people. Being able to support decisions that may not be very wise and use them as an opportunity for learning. Looking for the learning moment. Rubén Núnez, the Lead Organizer for CDC [Colonias Development Council], and I always talk about the "learning moment"—how do you turn it around? Look for the positive impact. Never leave any holes.
  I think the organizer is the one who does not create dependency. Our motto is "If you're ready, let me know and I should be able to leave this community. If I did my job, then you don't need me."

You need someone who's passionate, someone who reads a lot and can understand research. Someone who can challenge research results and use that to describe to people their own world, a world that they may already know. Provide a different perspective on that.

—Diana Bustamante

I don't think there's one right answer. I've seen what I think are good organizers that fall into a couple different descriptions. I think all of them ought to be able to listen well to people's needs and not start from their own preconceived notions. I think all of them ought to be compassionate. All of them ought to have some sense of anger over injustices, but not uncontrollable anger.

Beyond that, I think some people are good because they're really, really persistent at finding those people that might make a difference because they have natural leadership qualities and seducing them into being involved.

I think some people are good at it because they're incredibly personable and it's so easy for others to like them. They easily relate to the aspirations and needs and desires of that particular group.

Then I think other people are good because they have a really keen strategic sense of how to win on an issue and what might work on a particular campaign. It's how to focus in on a specific, conceivable, tangible win.

I think there are an awful lot of bad community organizers out there. I think it comes when people don't listen, they bring in their preconceived notions, or they're very personable but not strategic enough.

—Janet Groat

I tell people that this is not brain surgery—fortunately. It's not rocket science; it's something that anybody can learn and that's how we practice the principles of community organizing and a number of the other trainings that we give. But there are personality traits that make it easier, certainly.

Somebody that is comfortable with people, obviously, that helps. Somebody that enjoys strategic thinking, someone that has a lot of patience. I think those things can be learned but it's certainly easier if you have those traits. There's got to be a sense of perseverance and there is nobody in that room [referring to people at a Western Organization of Resource Councils meeting in Montana] that is a quitter. I mean, when we all got into this work, we had to have known that it was going to be the most frustrating path that we could choose, and yet people are committed. They're spending their weekend in Billings, Montana, in December in a room for three days. Because they're committed. It's exciting.

—Matt Sura

Profile: Vivian Chang
Bridging Cultures

Vivian Chang is the Executive Director of the Asian Pacific Environmental Network in Oakland, California. She was interviewed in August 2002.

I am a second-generation child of Taiwanese parents. I was born and raised in the San Francisco Bay area. My grandmother survived by sewing clothes, and was widowed at a very young age. She made it on her own sheer power, and I draw a lot of my strength from her and from my great-grandmother and from my mother—all very, very strong women in their perspective on life and instinct to survive.

I spent most of my growing up in the outer suburbs of the Bay Area, actually in a very White community. My parents moved out there because of the public school system. But that meant that in a lot of ways we were living more out of our means than other people who lived around us. What it also meant was that I felt kind of severed from my own community when I was growing up. As soon as I could, at age eighteen, I moved away from the suburbs and cut my teeth doing some student activism work at the University of California, Berkeley, and that's really where my eyes opened to a lot of different things. One of them was community work and community organizing.

One particular event really shaped me deeply at that time. I had gone as part of a student-of-color group to the first Environmental People of Color Leadership Summit in Washington, D.C., in 1992. It was the first time I saw different communities, organized communities, coming together at that level, multi-racially. I think that was the first time that I really understood at a gut level what community organizing was.

After school I worked for a few years in the Bay Area and then went to southern California, where I spent five years as an organizer with AGENDA [Action for Grassroots Economic and Neighborhood Development] and the Los Angeles Metropolitan Alliance. It was hard for me to be separated from my family, and that was a big reason why I moved back. I spend a lot of time with my family. I go back to my parents' house, where my grandmother also lives, maybe once a week, to spend the day or a couple days with them. I also spend as much time as I can trying to get away into the mountains or to ride my bike. A bike is a great way to travel.

I really cut my teeth doing community organizing at an organization called the Asian Women Immigrant Advocates. It's an organization based in Oakland that does community-based organizing, worker organizing. It was organizing of Asian immigrant women workers, predominantly in the garment industry and the restaurant industry and hotel industry. At that time, the organization was engaged in a campaign targeting garment manufacturers. Due to the crazy laws in this country that are not by accident, garment manufacturers hold no liability for the working conditions and the pay and wage per hour conditions of their contractors. Most of the garment work in this country is done by contracting out labor. And so it was a campaign that targeted a particular manufacturer called Jessica McClintock to hold her liable. Completely illegal by labor law standards, but because we weren't a union, we were able to target her and boycott her and counter-organize against her. And that was kind of where I got my first formative experience, both in campaigns and in organizing.

The executive director at that time I definitely considered to be one of my mentors. Her name was Young Shin. I still think of her when I think about what a great leadership style means.

I went from there to spending five years with AGENDA and the Los Angeles Metropolitan Alliance, primarily organizing African-American and Latino communities in different parts of L.A. Until the day that I left, five years later, I still felt that the learning curve was just like a forty-five degree angle. I would say in terms of the crafting of what I really learned—those five years were incredibly formative for me in learning about the art, but also the discipline of community organizing.

I think in some ways my work in Los Angeles completely burnt me out in a physical way. Hours were crazy. But you know, I was never burnt out in that I never wanted to leave the work. And it continued to drive me. What sustained me was having a mentor—the director at that time, who was my boss, Anthony Thigpen, had twenty years of organizing experience in Los Angeles—who was always able to take whatever it is that we were doing and put it into context. When you're trying different things and you're learning, when organizing is a dynamic process, I just feel like you don't burn out from that. It's all about trying to figure out what works and taking the best of what you know and growing it. That's what really sustained me.

The one time in my life when I did burn out, I felt like I was plateauing. There was no one that was pushing me or challenging me or helping me deal with the challenges. I think about that now, because in my current position, part of what my job—really ninety percent of my job—is training and growing new organizers. I'm always trying to keep that in mind.

What makes a good community organizer?

One very important characteristic of a good community organizer is the ability to be able to connect with folks and the ability to move folks. That's baseline. Organizing is about relationships.

I would say the second one is actually discipline. That's really, really important, and it often goes unrecognized. To be a community organizer, you have to be persistent and you have to be systematic and disciplined. It's about following up on those leads after you do that door-knocking. It's about going back, and after you follow up with them, calling them again to make sure they turn out to the community meeting, and if they don't come to the community meeting, just following up with that person. "Hey, what's up?"

I would say the third combines perseverance and stamina and political vision. I guess what I mean by that is that you learn pretty quickly that the stuff that you're doing on a daily level is such a drop in the bucket in terms of what needs to happen to really, really fundamentally change power relations, to change the problems and conditions that our communities face and experience every day. It doesn't take you long to realize that, and once you hit that, you either quit and become burnt out and disillusioned, or you stay on. So it's not just stamina and perseverance; it's stamina and perseverance knowing that in your lifetime you may not get there. I think that's what carries me through the day-to-day kind of craziness.

—Vivian Chang

We recently started a new organizing project with APEN [Asian Pacific Environmental Network]. We started drawing people in on two different issues, education and housing. We had done this community survey asking people about both. At the first community meeting we broke down into small groups and people talked about housing and other people talked about education, and we had come to this place where we realized we needed to narrow now, to figure out really what we're going to work on first. And frankly, it's a scary moment as an organizer, because you realize, what happens if people disagree?

Let's draw the worst-case scenario: We have a discussion, people start disagreeing—no, we should do housing, no, we should do education, how dare you say that the problems that I'm experiencing or that my kids are experiencing are any less important than your housing issues, blah, blah, blah, blah, blah. All these bad scenarios around what could happen, right? So we were really concerned as the organizers, because these were very new folks. We had tried to tell people beforehand, in our calls and when we talked to folks, "Look, we're going to be making this decision at the community meeting, that's why it's so important that you come, but also we want you to keep in mind that who we are and what we're trying to build is a community organization that can take on any issue, be it education or housing. Yes, we need to choose something to work on now, but it's not just about that one issue." You try to prep folks, but you never quite know.

We get in the room, and we start the meeting talking about what we could really change in the city of Oakland. We started from that premise, and we talked about what our true goal was, which was to build a strong, powerful community organization. The first question, of course, that I got from the floor was, "What does that mean, strong powerful organization?" I was like, oh yeah, that's organizing lingo. "Think if we had 2,000 people in this room instead of twenty. What could we do?" So then we talked about the idea of building something that could take on any issue, about the long haul, and that whatever issue we pick now we need to think about that issue as a tool to organize our community and build our organization.

Then we get to the moment of truth. What should we work on? As staff, we had done some initial thinking, and so we wanted to be up front about that, that we also had opinions. So we said, "We've thought about this and here's what we think and we want to open it up to discussion." And we had as staff felt that housing made the most sense for us at this time for a bunch of different reasons. There was silence in the room. This was a mixed room, renters, homeowners, different folks, and one guy, Tony, got up, and he's like "You know what? I don't have to worry about housing. I own my own home. I've been there for twenty-five years. I don't need to worry about rent. It's not going to effect me." And I'm up there thinking, "Oh, no!" And he says, "But you know what? I think that makes sense, and waging this campaign, fighting this fight, it's not for me, it's for my children, it's for my grandchildren, for my neighbors, for folks that are trying to move into Oakland. I was just lucky to be here twenty-five years ago and to be in a place where I could buy this home." And I was like, this big relief, right? We were expecting to lose a couple folks, just people who were purely drawn by the issue; we didn't lose anyone. And it was really great.

• • • It's about seeing that spark that happens in people's eyes when you realize that something is possible, when you see someone just move from a place of "That's just the way it is, what can we do about it?" to "OK. Let's do something." • • •

There are disappointments, too. There are lots of examples I can think of trying to bring people into the organization and it's just not working, and it's because, actually, people have a lot going on in their lives. You know, you go over and do a home visit and you realize, someone's niece just died, or someone's son is in jail, or you realize that your member is in an abusive situation. Lots of stories like that. I would say actually it's not so much disappointment but a real sock-it-in-the-gut kind of feeling around how disempowered we are at this point in time.

I'm never so depressed about the state of where we're at than at the time of our victories. I think about this one campaign that the organization I was working with in Los Angeles was involved in, pushing the City Council to attach some conditions to welfare-to-work money that was coming down to the city. A lot of this welfare-to-work money goes into basically training people for temp jobs, or training them instead of real basic education that people need or vocational training for living wage jobs. It goes into kind of 'how to present yourself,' attitude, behavior—it's just ridiculous. So we had waged this campaign to attach conditions that this money can only be used to train people for jobs that exist, and for living wage jobs in the region, yada, yada, yada.

So it's a year-and-a-half campaign, and how the victory happened was through a City Council vote, so the City Council was the decision maker. We had to win a majority, so it was very much around pressuring certain City Council members, the City Council in general, to vote our way. And it was so anti-climactic when the victory happened. We were all there, 100 of us in the room, we had kind of said our piece, and when it came down to it, it was still just a vote. And it was never clearer to me than at that moment: when it comes down to it, it's still *them* voting. We could take over the meeting and all that kind of stuff, but there's a difference between confronting power—which is oftentimes what we do when we take over a particular City Council meeting, for example—and *having* power.

It was really depressing, actually. Even though we had "won," the depression came from the realization at that point for me just how disempowered we were. It came partly from a realization that I had a lot of doubts about how much of what we had won would really materialize, given the infrastructure that was there to implement the victory. I knew that what we had pushed for was a good first step, but it was nothing compared to where we need to get to really empower the lives of people.

In my current job, I'm thinking about how to train other organizers and figuring out a program, a training program, but also a support system to grow new organizers. I'm just starting down that road at APEN and I am just so lucky to be working with what I think are just some of the best organizers, really just thoughtful, kick-ass, humble, but incredibly smart, sharp, and skilled. Folks came at different places, and everybody's grown through the process. I think being able to provide a structure and a process and some guidance for that growth and development is definitely something that I feel good about.

In the communities that we're organizing in, the language capacity is a must. In the Laotian community there are five different languages. In our new organizing project we have a new organizer that speaks two different languages, three actually, including English, but finding organizers with language capacity is so hard.

The Asian Pacific Environmental Network brings together people from a wide variety of Asian communities in the Bay area.

The Laotian community in Richmond [California] is, according to the new census, and I know it's undercounted, less than 4,000 people, and there aren't a lot of folks just out there floating around speaking one of the five different Laotian languages.

There was one person who came to us who's just amazing. His name is Torm. Our organizers come with such incredible life experiences. Torm has thirteen kids. Torm left—ran—from Laos when he was about fourteen years old to escape the military, spent years in a refugee camp in Thailand, and ended up being one of the first Laotian families to move to the U.S.

The community here still very much has a social structure of the tribal, traditional village leadership. There are very, very clear hierarchical systems that were in place before they came here and they totally transferred over. And Torm is actually considered to be one of the folks that holds a lot of traditional leadership in that community and knows almost everyone, I would say. A lot of folks know him and look to him as a community leader.

May [another organizer] as well, just an incredible life experience, came to the U.S., had three kids at that time, worked, and somehow managed to get her GED. Anyway, just incredible life experiences. And each one of them has really transformed since coming to us.

At least for us, you're not going to find the perfect organizer walking in off the street. So when you look at an organizer, you draw up your ideal list. Often times you're not going to find that person. You can just continue looking for years; you're not going to find that person. The question is what are those baseline qualities that you're looking for and then it's on us to develop this person, develop together.

In my journey to where I am now, I've had different and deeper understandings of what a community organizer really does. What I found out when I began to actually do the organizing work is that it wasn't just about turnout numbers, that it wasn't just about the campaigns, but rather the challenges around leadership development and development of political consciousness and crafting it together—what it means to craft an alternative world view. In figuring out what are the ways you struggle with folks over that in a principled way.

A community organizer to me—and I know that there are very different definitions out there—but it's someone who has the ability to connect and motivate folks to come together and has the skills to lead a process by which people can come to agreement on something. It's about bringing people together to address the problems that the community experiences and the root causes of those problems, and then moving to a collective plan of action.

I've had several reactions, actually, when I say I'm a community organizer. I had one person say to me, "Oh, you must have really clean closets." I just tell folks it's about bringing communities together, about solving problems in that community and putting forward a proactive vision of what folks want to see happen in our communities and neighborhoods. It's about being able to affect the decisions that are made that impact that community.

Now, granted, you can play a lot of roles in the movement and not be a community organizer, and I do believe that what we need is a movement that really has places and niches and roles for everybody, so long as we agree on a vision and a strategy. There have been times in my life when I've done something that was one step removed—I was a trainer and facilitator working with community groups for a while, or I tried to venture for a little bit into being a researcher to support organizing—and every time that I did that, I just felt too removed, even though it was just one step removed, that wasn't what I wanted to do.

It's about seeing that spark that happens in people's eyes when you realize that something is possible, when you see someone just move from a place of "That's just the way it is, what can we do about it?" to "OK. Let's do something." Not only that but "It's wrong, and we need to do something about it." It's about seeing those small moments of transformation and that's what drives me. It's that moment that makes everything worth it.

6

Changing Lives
While Making Change

We asked the organizers to share stories of their proudest achievements in organizing. Many told stories of issue victories—battles won, laws passed, communities protected. But just as often, their stories told of more personal victories—
the transformation of individual lives. Leadership development is central to how
organizing enables people to effect change, and sometimes—not surprisingly—
the biggest change comes in the people themselves.

Transforming individuals

Individual transformations happen when people find
power in working together on issues that affect their lives.
Sometimes those transformations are sudden and life-changing.

> Proudest achievement? Art Stevens, Carol Frederick, Janie Hynes. If you
> met them and saw the fire in their eyes, you'd see that they get it. I had a
> hand in that and that makes me really proud. I guess I've saved and been
> a part of saving some land from some destructive practice and all that is
> great. I'm also proud of that, but it seems that the threat is always out there
> and that we've only saved it for a little while. When I look at Art or Carol
> or Janie, that's something that's going to last a lifetime for them. And so, I
> guess there's a permanence there that makes me proud.
> —Matt Sura

> One of the things that makes me really proud is seeing someone that I've
> recruited, either into membership or into leadership in our organization,
> blossom and discover their true gifts as a leader, and put those into the
> service of the campaign. There are some excellent examples of that within
> our organization right now. Standing and watching them give testimony, or
> talk to the press, or lead a meeting, or come in with a fistful of memberships
> of people they've gone out and recruited—nothing could make me happier

People find power in working together. They focus on their common goals rather than their individual problems, and have a lot of fun in the process. A local phone-a-thon gives members a chance to do something concrete to help the organization.

than that. And that's about building power. Because building power entails building leadership.
—Mark Trechock

I think I'm proudest of the internship program, where we actually teach public housing residents community organizing skills and leadership development skills. Right before I was hired, PHAR [Public Housing Association of Residents] got a grant to hire residents for five to ten hours a week for six months, for a living wage of ten dollars an hour, to learn community organizing and leadership development. This organization is about helping residents have a voice and to use that voice—for them to be able to use their voices and learn their rights, and change things. Because they're so used to feeling like they don't have any power. Lots of feelings of hopelessness. To see residents become empowered and start to get involved in the change is pretty remarkable.

Not everyone who comes to the internship program will stay involved with PHAR, per se, but they might stay leaders in their community. That's already happened. We have one resident that moved out of public housing shortly after completing the internship program, but now serves on the

board of a local social service agency. So now you have one seat on that board filled by someone who's felt and knows what it's like to be low-income; who's now setting the policy for a social service agency.
    —Holly Hatcher

One thing that I'm proud about is all the people who've become leaders over the years in our organizations, and seeing them move from a direct self-interest to becoming interested in other issues, and understanding how everything is connected. It does my heart good to work with these leaders and see them do a television interview for the first time, or speak at a public hearing, or lobby at the state legislature.
    —Kevin Williams

Alabama Arise is a coalition of 150 mostly church but also civic and community groups. We work on poverty issues in the state of Alabama. Each year the membership selects priority issues that we're going to address at the legislature. . . . I think the real excitement is when you talk to people and they make the connection; they get it. They become involved. We hear stories of people who previously had not thought about doing any of this kind of work. Because they had a chance to work with you, they say, "Oh yeah. I'm willing to do this, this, and this." That's good.
    —Presdalene Harris

During our third year of organizing we had heard a lot of people talking about living in deplorable rental housing conditions in our city [Springfield, Ohio]. There are a lot of older homes and they just weren't being kept up to code. We were hearing different people talk about living in houses that had holes in the floor. People were living without any running water or with backed-up sewage coming up in their yard. They would complain to their landlords and would be evicted. Or they wouldn't complain out of fear of being evicted. They would try to go to the city, but there was no system in place for them to try to hold those individuals accountable.
    JAM [Justice Action Mercy] was working with a core group of people, including some who had been living in some of these poor housing conditions. Folks were uncertain at first. They'd say, "I don't have a lot of money. There's nowhere else for me to go. This is it. I don't want to rock the boat and be without a home." But they gained confidence after doing some research and learning that there were other communities that had had the same problems and that different groups had put together plans to make decision-makers put in place rental registration and inspection processes. Our leaders began to say, "If other people are doing this, why can't we?" They really got fired up about it, saying, "It's not that we can't do it. Our community leaders have just chosen not to do it. They've turned a blind eye to this problem."
    We had one woman, Vanessa. Her house didn't have heat. There was a hole in her roof, so when it rained her living room got soaked. Her property

owner would not fix it. Vanessa got up at the action assembly in front of 600 people and she told her story. She looked at the county commissioners and she told them, "I'm holding you accountable to make sure this happens to no one else." At first, Vanessa didn't want to do that. She didn't want to be on the committee when we first started. She didn't want to let her story be known. She didn't want to be evicted. By the time we got to the action three months later, she was up in front of 600 with media and county commissioners, telling them, "I want you to change this. I want you to enact this new legislation that will give us rental inspections and registration in our city to hold irresponsible landlords accountable."
—Makiva Harper

I really like to see members go up the leadership ladder, see members really become good leaders. That's my favorite part, I think. I had one student when I worked for MASSPIRG [Massachusetts Public Interest Research Group] and she was kind of quiet, and she joined, and she was real passionate about people needing to vote. We had this youth vote campaign, working to get more youth voting and involved in the process so that they're not overlooked. And she really got involved, and started going to the board meetings and got involved with the campaign. I liked that a lot.
—Tiffany Hartung

The summer before last we had summer workers, and we had an intern over them. They were going to do the voter registration. There was one young lady who was terribly quiet and shy. The intern was like, "Well, we need to send her back." I was like, "No, you don't want to send her back. We want to help her overcome this." By the end of the summer she was one of our top producers because she was able to overcome her shyness. That's one of the things that I personally take pride in.
—Steve Bradberry

We just did a training in Grand Junction [Colorado]. Every year we do this four-day Principles of Community Organizers training with new leaders, new organizers. Every time I do this training I am proud of how much we can help people put in context issues of power and their own ability to see that they have skills. They have talents that, if they think about how to develop them, they can use to become leaders. I know this fellow from Native Action on the Northern Cheyenne, Tom Mexican Cheyenne. I can remember him coming to our trainings as a quiet, shy person, very little confidence about what he thought he could do. Seeing Tom Mexican Cheyenne stand up at a hearing down at Lame Deer one month after our training and deliver one of the most powerful pieces of testimony about why these coal companies shouldn't be here and just be this incredible voice of leadership—I mean those are things that you look for every week.
—Patrick Sweeney

Community organizers meet with people one-to-one, in small meetings, and in lots of other settings. In the process, many individual lives are transformed.

We've been working with some young people, and I'm proud just to see how they've developed, as young leaders—to see how much they've grown. And literally how they've grown, you know, physically. Because a lot of them I've known since they were children, and now they're teens and young adults. And so I think [those are some] of my proudest moments, seeing them speak at a meeting with the mayor or giving a presentation to another group of people. Or watching how they interact with one another. Different things like that, where you can see the fruits of the investment of time and resources.
  —Robby Rodriguez

On one level it's just watching one of our youth group members who wants to become an organizer, and other members really stepping to the plate, being elected to the board of directors and doing a lot of work. I find it very fulfilling to see these young folks stepping up and doing the work, and knowing that in some cases they're the children of current members or leaders. We're making generational change. I told some of them at the high school that they have to take my job. They can go to the university, then they've got one year to screw around, and then they've got to come in and take my job and let me retire.
  —Jon Liss

I helped start a youth chapter called WE CAN. We have eight different chapters in our organization, and each chapter chooses its own issues. We never had one for younger people, and that was something that I wanted to do when I first got involved. So I worked with a friend of mine at the college and together we created a youth chapter that was college and high school students. They chose their name. They drew their logo. They chose their campaign and did a campaign plan. They went to Washington, D.C. The first year was just amazing. They were just on fire, and they recruited more and more students. Some of them changed their career plans. I've given letters of reference to some of them. They just blossomed. There's one kid who was particularly awkward, and the other kids took him under their wing. He just changed so much. They did a press event. They put on a big event, Earth Day, with two thousand people in attendance. They were just amazing. So I was very proud of that.
  —DeAnna Woolston

Building bridges

Transformation often comes as a result of crossing into new territories— working with different kinds of people, discovering common interests with folks who used to seem foreign. Good organizing helps people bridge the gaps that keep them apart; only by working together can we effect real change.

The kickoff of my first affiliate, the Laramie Resource Council, was quite a moment because I remember the very first organizing meeting that I walked into with them. Right before the meeting I called my husband because I was scared to death. I had someone from the Peace and Justice movement, I had the wife of an Air Force colonel, I had a former Air Force sergeant who was very, very conservative but who really cared about the issues that we were working on. I had a vegetarian and a beef-grower. My husband said, "You sound upset," and I said, "I just don't think this is going to work." Well, I went in and they worked together. They were a great team. So the kickoff of that was really tremendous.
  —Vickie Goodwin

When I first came to Lexington, the chapter was maybe five or six people mainly working on environmental issues. It was some older, White men, a couple of college students, and Janet Tucker. That was the chapter. When I would talk to Janet she would tell me that she's really passionate about racial justice and economic justice, which in many ways are the same thing. She would talk to me about her vision and what she wanted to do with the chapter and what she wanted to do with KFTC [Kentuckians For The Commonwealth] and where she wanted it to go. What she was doing at the time was facilitating the meetings—which she hates doing—and pulling the agendas together. She was doing all the grunt work to make sure the chapter was sustained. She wasn't doing anything that was really feeding what she was truly passionate about. Those things weren't what she really wanted to be doing.

Fast-forward to where we are today. We had a chapter meeting Thursday before we came here. There were thirty people. One of our membership coordinators is a person of color, an African-American. Maybe two-thirds of the people who came to the chapter meeting were young people, college students as well as younger youth. We had people from the community, like transit workers. It was just an incredible mix. We've got three work teams in the chapter—environmental justice, economic justice, and anti-discrimination—in addition to the fundraising, publicity, and membership committees. All of those committees are working on issue campaigns and projects. It's an amazing transformation.

—Leah Ottersbach

Community organizing crosses the boundaries between races, ages and assumptions as people work together for change. People across the nation came out to support the Immigrant Freedom Riders in 2004.

I think it's the collective of leaders that are forging this effort in a very godforsaken part of this country, in northern and central Louisiana. In a very brief period of time in Monroe, Louisiana, Oucachita Parish, a place that David Duke carried twice, we have built a team of African-Americans, Whites, Asians, and others who want a community where we can struggle together to seek the common good.

We are at the center of political life in this city. We've done it with a deliberate attempt to cross, particularly, race and religion. You do that because there is a group of people that have an appetite for it and are willing to develop relationships that will sustain them. This work has expanded into northwest and central Louisiana. In each place we have developed a team of leaders who own the effort. These are people that three years ago would not believe they could shape decisions of community life but today they are coming to believe they can.

We had this assembly a few weeks ago where the Republican candidate for governor—who may very well be governor—came to our event. We were not concentrating on gubernatorial issues. We were concentrating on local concerns. In a period of (in terms of active work) two and a half years we were enough on the radar screen to get a guy that had been courting and was the darling of the religious right. He understood that it was a serious group and it was a group that really did want a relationship with him and took him seriously enough to pursue him. His coming wasn't an issue.

—Perry Perkins

I remember when the Lynchburg chapter came to the VOP [Virginia Organizing Project] board to petition for chapter status. Gene Tweedy is an extraordinary person. He's African-American, in his early thirties. He grew up in Lynchburg in the most notorious subsidized housing complex in the city. Tweedy was a juvenile probation officer. He describes himself as being able to straddle two worlds—the world of supposed law and order and the world of his street background and all that that entails. So he's a great guy. But in terms of gender, sexuality, and stuff like that he's fairly conservative.

So he's sitting at this table beside Jamie Michelle, who is a transgendered male-to-female, postoperative. She's the board representative from Virginians for Justice, which is the state gay/lesbian/bisexual/transgender lobby group. I could tell that Tweedy was totally freaked out by being that close to her. Nevertheless, they had this really fabulous conversation. I think they probably learned a lot from each other. That was exciting, to see people who were so totally different interacting in a way that they felt like they were on the same side. They felt like they were joined together, working for something.

—Ben Thacker-Gwaltney

One of the experiences that always comes to mind that was one of those moments where I just felt like, "Wow, this really does change people," was when we had a member who was doing a lot of work on a landfill waste-related issue. A lot of our members are fairly conservative; they come from small towns. We have people come to Washington who have never been on an airplane before, they've never eaten seafood before, they've never eaten in an ethnic restaurant, they've never been in a big city, they've never done lots of things. And so it's really a first for a lot of people, and I think it can be overwhelming in lots of ways, just the culture shock, being in Washington.

There was this one woman who came to town for a fly-in (which is a citizen lobby trip) and was working on a local landfill issue, and got involved to try to get legislation to give states and localities more control. She was an extremely conservative person, socially, and one of the things that I really enjoyed was during that fly-in was the day that the Supreme Court struck down the Colorado anti-gay initiative, and the entire D.C. gay community was out celebrating. She had gone with a friend to visit this friend's family, who was on the fly-in, and was caught in the middle of that on the subway. I remember the next day hearing the two of them talk about it to the other conservative ranch women, and how the incredible humanity of it struck them. I remember thinking, wow, that her experience through WORC [Western Organization of Resource Councils] with these fly-ins had just in this very unexpected way completely changed who she was and her outlook on people, and what their basic rights were. And her sort of willingness to open her eyes more and be a bit more understanding, and in a very personal way it was one of those times where I thought, "This is very worthwhile work to be doing."
—Sara Kendall

Transforming communities

And it's not just individuals who experience transformation in organizing; whole communities can change when they see the power of their collective action.

What makes me feel good is bringing in people from the community to become organizers, people who have been oppressed by those in power that see them as inferior. (In this border region, this usually translates into Euro-American and Mexican cultural, political, and economic clashes.) Mexican immigrants and their U.S.-born children have been able to develop and feel confident about themselves and about who they are in their community. They are able to understand that they do have a power to negotiate with the powers that be; in this case, it's the farmers negotiating with the White population. It's when people understand that they can make changes. They can call the county commissioner. They can call their representative or senator and get attention.
—Diana Bustamante

One of my proudest achievements would certainly be the work I did in 1995, 1996, and 1997 with a group of women in Prestonsburg, Kentucky, who were receiving public assistance and were watching as it began to be clear that federal welfare laws were going to change. They began to get involved at a very local level, a state level, and a national level. And that group of women involved folks who had never taken a step out of their front door without asking someone's permission. Suddenly, they found themselves leading the state, playing roles on a national level that they never imagined. The personal transformation in a very broad base of people was extraordinary. They were also able to do some interesting policy work at the state level and got the state to invest much, much more in opportunities for education for low-income parents on public assistance. So that set of experiences over those three years was very intense work. I would say that ninety percent of the group of women that I was working with were survivors of domestic violence experiences and so for them it was just a time of liberation and discovery on many, many fronts.

It's also one of my greatest disappointments to look at that group five years later and see what's happened to folks and how just devastating it is to not have resources or any support system in your life. So some folks have been able to overcome incredible odds, but many, many folks have found themselves back in very dire economic straits, family straits. So while I hold that as my source of greatest pride, it also has a tremendous amount of pain when you realize even with the extraordinary sense of confidence that people gained and real significant, tangible policy changes that they were able to win, in many cases it wasn't enough to make a difference in their own personal situations.
—Lisa Abbott

I've been at this for so little time that I don't feel like I have any achievements per se, but I think I'll feel a lot of satisfaction from seeing the organizing committee that I'm working with kick off its own local chapter. Being a part of starting a local chapter will be really satisfying. Seeing people get turned on to how they can have an impact or get excited about being part of a group that is trying to take action to make positive change. I think that's something that has been satisfying to me—seeing folks get excited and start to take charge, wanting to do things themselves and not looking so much to the organizer to start things. And there are times when for whatever reasons—preparation, subject matter—a meeting goes really well. It's really nice to be at the end of what feels like a good meeting, a successful meeting.
—Brett Kelver

I remember when in 1999 I started organizing the community in Culmore, it was so hard at the beginning. And then, a year later, when we did the evaluation, all these people really worked. At the beginning they weren't too comfortable with us as an organization, because there were a lot of individuals that would come there and lie to them . . . but when we did

Low-income people take to the streets to demand adequate health care services in the communities around Washington, D.C.

the evaluation, they said, "Well, we have learned how not to be afraid, we learned how to get along with the children, how to speak to others, and we learned other things that were going on in the county." And when you start listening to positive things coming from the community that was, in the beginning, rejecting you, not as an individual but as an organization, it makes you feel very proud. It made me feel very good.

—Edgar Rivera

There were some people in a small community that wanted us to help them. The water in the nearby river was being diverted into non-existence. It was, and is, a very, very small community, maybe 100 people. I was told the meeting was in the firehouse, so I went looking for the firehouse. It took me a while to realize that the firehouse was somebody's two-door garage.

Inside, there were two fire engines and people sitting on chairs and stools. There was just enough room between the door and the fire engines for the chairs. The people had brought little homemade snacks and coffee and tea. I'm looking at all these blank faces looking at me. I tell them what's possible. I tell them they have a right to put up a fight and there are tools they can use to win the fight. Faces start to light up. I continue with my presentation, detailing the possibilities, and I hang around for another two hours, talking to different individuals, hearing their stories and figuring things out. I remember that night vividly because of the hope in people's faces. There was something to be done and they did it.
　—Brian Shields

When I started in Austin, I inherited a school strategy where we were working with around fifteen schools to try to improve the quality of education and to organize for after-school programs. I worked to put together a collective of principals. I got the principals from each of the schools meeting on a monthly basis, and got one of the key principals, Al Mindez-Melton, to be a leader. He was getting bored. So he began thinking about applying for an area superintendent job. I went after him about that: "Why do you want to be an area superintendent? Why do you want to enter administration? What are you going to be giving up by leaving your school?" And then proposed to him to take that same kind of a leadership position with respect to the other fifteen schools in this network. I said, "Look, I want you to be the volunteer area superintendent for the fifteen schools we're working with, so that you would become the mentor of these other principals. You would become their superintendent, although you wouldn't have the bureaucratic power; as a leader, you would connect with their interests and they would follow you." So I did that meeting with him, and then we began working together putting together this principals' collective. They met on a monthly basis. They started collaborating with each other and they put together their own staff development day, where all of their staff, like 900 folks, came together and they identified their best teachers and asked them to put on workshops.

　Then they started running actions on the district. Their schools began putting together their own agenda for what they needed out of the budget. When budget time came around, they would have 150 parents at the school board. Class size was one of the issues. Fifth grade classes were way too big, so they made that one of their issues, and got the district to assign more teachers. They wanted a special science program, so there was an action where they had 150 parents there and got the school district to make that commitment.

　That's the achievement that I'm proudest of because I think I did the best organizing. I built a leadership collective that really had a life of its own. The principals began to mentor one another and take responsibility for the strategy, and they began developing these great leadership delegations on their campuses, and then they were winning all kinds of issues, left and

right. They got to where, if there was something going on at the central office that they didn't like, they would set a meeting with, like, the science coordinator, and would just scare the crap out of them.
— Allen Cooper

When we put together ICARE [Interchurch Coalition for Action, Reconciliation, and Empowerment] in Jacksonville, we spent about a year and a half laying the groundwork. I did one-to-ones with over 100 pastors. Out of that group, about thirty-five came together about four or five months later and began to form this organization. Then they identified lay leaders who started doing one-to-one visits with others in their congregations to listen for their concerns and visions. Then we identified those issues and researched those issues.

So we went for about a year before we went public. In February of 1997 we held our first public meeting. We invited the mayor, the sheriff, and the school superintendent to that meeting. We had about 750 people at Day Spring Baptist Church. We packed the place. The sheriff showed and he gave us everything we wanted. We applauded him loudly. Then we had the school superintendent stand up. He said, "I will work with you. We're going to create an in-school suspension program. We're going to figure out this literacy challenge." The place again erupted in applause.

The mayor had chosen not to come. He sent a lowly representative and our host pastor said, "Mr. Salem, are you here with the authority to speak on behalf of the mayor?" Mr. Salem said, "Yes, I am." Then he said, "Well, that's wonderful. Now will the mayor do this and this?" Mr. Salem said, "Well, I can't speak on behalf of the mayor. I'll have to speak to him tomorrow at the staff meeting." Our host pastor said, "Wait a minute. I thought you were speaking on behalf of the mayor."

The whole place erupted. The meeting went too late that night for it to get into the next day's paper, but the headline two days later was "Mayor Doesn't Show." The very next morning he called to apologize profusely to our two co-chairs. He was quoted in the newspaper as saying, "I blew it. I should have been there." Then three weeks later we had a follow-up meeting. We had about 100 of our leaders in the basement of one of our churches to meet with the mayor. The mayor brought eighteen of his top staff people to that meeting. The head of Public Works was there and the head of Parks and Rec. It was, "What can I do for you?" Our leaders were just thrilled.

If you have something like that happen, there is such energy in an organization. They are flying high and the sky is the limit. You're doing that in the context of people who have been told, forever and ever, "Your voice doesn't matter."
— Paul Cromwell

Profile:
Guillermo Quinteros
Urban Organizing in the Northeast

Guillermo Quinteros was the Executive Director of the Commonwealth Education Project/Commonwealth Coalition in Boston when he was interviewed in September 2003.

My father is from Peru. My mother is from Puerto Rico. The way that they met was that my mother won a Fulbright Fellowship to study in Peru. At that time Puerto Rico had been a colony for close to 100 years. When my mom grew up in Puerto Rico, there was almost no connection with the rest of Latin America. That was done on purpose.

Growing up she was very interested in trying to connect to the rest of Latin America. It was also a political statement. It was a nationalistic pro-independence statement. She wanted to study anthropology, so she ended up in Peru, where she met my father, who was also in anthropology.

I grew up as a child in Peru until I was twelve years old. During that time both my parents (especially my father) were very involved in university teaching. There was also a tradition in which the university was very engaged politically, especially with the unions and the shantytowns. It was very politicized and my parents were very involved.

When there was a military coup, we were on vacation. My mother and my siblings and I were on vacation in Puerto Rico, visiting my grandparents. After the coup my father was fired from the university. We could not return, but neither could my father come to Puerto Rico. My father ended up getting a job organizing a Latin American school of social work in Honduras. My father saw the map. Honduras and Puerto Rico—they are relatively close. So after almost seven months of not seeing my father, of not knowing what was going to happen, we ended up in Honduras. This was at the time, also, that the Nicaraguan revolution against Samosa was at its peak. We spent two years there. During that time the Sandinista revolution won, but Honduras also became the center of the American intervention.

People were thinking there was going to be an expansion of the revolution, so Honduras became militarized. We ended up moving to Mexico, which at that time had a very liberal international policy. There were a lot of people who were coming to Mexico from Latin America from all the dictatorships and military governments. Mexico was taking a lot of those people. At the same time, Mexico was internally extremely repressive. You were very limited about your political involvement. I spent close to six years there. I almost finished high school in Mexico. At that time we moved to Puerto Rico because of family reasons and because things were getting very tough, economically. Mexico was just about to go through the big crisis of the '80s.

We moved to Puerto Rico where I finished high school and did college. I went to college for economics. Coming from a tradition—from my parents and also from Latin America—of understanding things from the Left, political economy was a key analysis of understanding how our society works. But in Puerto Rico, as in the U.S., this was not the dominant approach in the economics departments.

I also spent that time really knowing Puerto Rico. That was the first time that I really spent a good chunk of my life in Puerto Rico besides just going for vacation. I was coming from this huge involvement in political movements. When I was in high school in Mexico we were extremely active in my school. We were organizing marches, remembering Allende in Chile, protesting against the military in Argentina, supporting strikes in Mexico, doing literacy projects in the mountains of Oaxaca . . . we were very politically active.

I arrived in Puerto Rico at a time in which there had been a huge university-student strike that was crushed three or four years before at the main university. As a result of that, people in general were very apolitical. So I not only got into a program—economics—that wasn't, as I thought, political economy, but it was also a university that was retreating and had expelled a lot of the students who were involved in the strike.

It was an environment which was extremely apolitical. So I ended up spending those four years in Puerto Rico really knowing more about Puerto Rico. It was very different. It's a colonial society. For me, coming from Latin America, where there is this pride about national identity, Puerto Rico was always seen as the sellout. They obviously had a more stable economy and all that, but people would make jokes that Puerto Ricans didn't really speak Spanish well because it was mixed with English. That time actually allowed me to understand a little better how tough it is to live in a colonial society. For the first twenty years of this last century they were not even allowed to be taught in their own language. They don't control their economy. It was a good way for me to start understanding.

As part of that I got very interested in understanding the United States better, especially because of immigration. There is huge immigration from Puerto Rico to the United States. There are almost more Puerto Ricans living in the United States than there are living on the island. So when

I finished college in Puerto Rico, I went to study history in New York. I studied Latin American history at Stony Brook in Long Island. It was a very interesting program in which there were a lot of students from Latin America.

So that's how I started working in New York. I started working with immigrant communities. I spent three years in New York and then I went back to Puerto Rico. I started doing more work around economic development projects. I was trying to understand the economic possibilities for Puerto Rico, in a society that is already extremely integrated in a global economy. I looked at the search for a national identity and the nation-state. I didn't understand yet how global it was already. Puerto Rico's experience with globalization was much more advanced than other countries in Latin America. Now we can take almost any economy in the world and it's just so interrelated.

From this experience, I decided that I needed to understand better what was happening. There were tools that I didn't have that could allow me to understand better where to direct my work. I thought about going to Boston for graduate school, but I decided before going back to school that I really wanted to work with Latino communities in the States.

So I came to Boston and started working in the South End in Boston, in a non-profit organization. That was a different experience for me, in terms of what the non-profits in this country and the whole culture around service provision were like and how apolitical they could be. I also taught in the public schools. That was an amazing experience. I have also been part of organizing a group that is working on Latino education at the statewide level. I'm still part of the board.

I taught in a middle school. It was a very interesting school that was a pilot project in social science. It was a school that was mixing three grades. Students were mixed. You developed research projects that were based on geographical areas. They would change every six weeks. During that time, working in teams around the continent, you would try to integrate all the different areas. So you would do math. You would do, obviously, geography. Language. Biology and science. It was an amazing school in a poor area of Worcester. It was just amazing to see kids getting the opportunity and the things they could do. At the same time the amount of work that good teachers spend is just amazing. It was something.

I did that for a couple years. Then I went to graduate school for two years to do urban planning, really focusing on governance and economic development. I focused a lot on decentralization and the role of local governments and NGOs. I was still looking at Latin America and how local governments and non-profits were working to provide services but also starting transformations and change. After finishing the program, I saw that there was a huge potential in the non-profit area to move beyond the service provision. Service is a huge part of what the communities need, but they could not stop there. How can we do it more politically, but also create a capacity within the community for having a critical and political understanding of their reality?

So that's how I started working in non-profits and doing more direct organizing. That work went from housing to education to combating discrimination. After working for some time in those areas, I started getting more into the political and electoral piece of those issues. How can we start relating these to civil engagement and electoral reform? It was through that work that I eventually started moving to where I am now. It was a very important realization during that time that this ethnic/racial work could not be done in isolation. It was easy for me to see that because of my background. It wasn't, "Oh, I'm Puerto Rican, so for all Puerto Ricans this is about us." It was much easier for me to see where the power is and why we needed to organize differently. It wasn't going to be just through organizing Latinos.

So I started doing some more coalition work and also working more closely with unions. I started working specifically around job conditions, because that was the other issue that I saw missing in the service provider community-based organizations in which clients were people who needed housing, education, or other services. With very few exceptions they were workers. The organization would not talk about working conditions or worker rights. Unions would do that, even though we knew that the majority of immigrants were not even unionized. There was a history of unions being anti-immigrant because of the whole discourse about immigrants taking Americans' jobs. The unions are changing now.

• • • This is what I like to do. I see it as a contribution. It's very exciting, in terms of where we are. It's part of what I believe. It's also because I've been challenged. I'm doing something different and at the same time I'm creating opportunities. I could get a job with better money, but this is providing me with what I need and doing exactly what I want. • • •

They have made it much easier to do this collaboration where unions and communities are working together. The organizations are starting to see their constituents also as workers. More unions are also working with the immigrant communities.

That's the kind of environment in which I was involved when I started working with the Commonwealth Coalition doing some electoral reform issues, working on a lawsuit on redistricting in Chelsea, and developing a statewide Latino political organization with the help of the Coalition. Eventually, when the opportunity came, I ended up working as Executive Director for the Commonwealth Coalition.

Chelsea is a very small city, but the area has the third largest Latino concentration in the state. The Latino population in Chelsea and in neighboring East Boston was being divided into three districts. Chelsea could be a single district on its own, or one of its two districts could include East Boston, instead of mostly White Revere or Charlestown.

In this case, there was no way to really explain in a simple way why we should focus on *this*, on why a district should be redrawn. So we needed to go into a discussion about how government works and how drawing the district influences who gets elected and who gets more influence in electing those people. Who has more leverage to make this elected representative accountable? Even more important, why is it that communities of color were disenfranchised by the current districts? People will say, "It's just a district," like it was created by God. They don't even think about it. Why is Chelsea divided in two? Why is it that those two representatives are not people who look like you? These people are not supporting issues that are important to you. They are elected. Who's electing them? They are representing the people who elect them. The drawing of the districts diminishes the power of particular communities. So that was a completely different level of analysis for people to engage in.

It's not like we're slaves on a plantation or in a place where they discriminate openly, where you could see it. People have a sense that there is something wrong here. Obviously our communities are being disenfranchised, but we don't know how it works. We go out and vote. We do all these things. That's supposed to mean that everything is fine, but it's not. So here you start looking at one issue that can really explain one of the ways it works. It's very eye-opening for people. People got extremely excited about it. Redistricting is a very difficult thing to understand, particularly because it happens only every ten years. It's very technical. We were the only organization in the state that organized community members to get educated before the redistricting. It was the only group in Massachusetts to propose an alternative map for a state rep seat. They didn't take our advice, so we, with the help of other organizations, did a lawsuit. We ended up losing it because of the issue of citizenship. But Boston also did a lawsuit, so there were two lawsuits in which we participated. The Boston one actually won. They had to redraw the districts.

The problem when you do something that gets sent to a legal court for so long is that the people just don't continue to engage at the same level. They lose control over the process. Some people actually testified, but then it became a legal-expertise discussion. So it was all about the lawyers and the experts in demographics and statistics in the court in downtown Boston.

One of the things I think about all the time is doing this kind of work in Puerto Rico, but I don't know. I have been in Boston for close to ten years already. My partner has been living in Boston even longer. She's from

Puerto Rico and she has already spent fifteen years in Boston. Now we have a child who was born in Boston. Puerto Rico is a tough place. There is nothing like the coalitions that we have in the States in terms of having unions and other groups at the same table. There is even less of that from a progressive perspective. So the possibilities are there.

I think my proudest achievement as an organizer is probably some of the work that I did in Chelsea with immigrant mothers, working on education. These were immigrants and refugees who had their kids in the public school that is run by a private university. There was no participation at all in the way the school was run. Parents can be completely marginalized. This is a system in which more than seventy percent of the kids are Latino. The schools don't have real PTOs. They choose who will be in the school councils and there were no Latinos.

Chelsea was the first public education system that was actually given to a private institution to manage and run, in this case Boston University. They still manage it. What happened was that there was a tremendous fight in which community people got in a very confrontational relationship with Boston University. Because of the tough relationship with the school system, parents and outside activists would get organized and demand their rights in the school committee or in the city council.

Boston University was the first system in Massachusetts to try to eliminate bilingual education. That was fought by organized people and eventually by lawsuits. That was what was happening. The problem was that, at the end of the day, we were not participating in improving the achievement of the students. So we decided that we needed to play an insider/outsider strategy in which we continued the pressure on the schools, but also, parents needed to be part of the system. They needed to take ownership of the PTOs. They needed to be part of fighting for the spaces in the school that would create a culture for open participation for teachers, parents, and students.

So that was extremely interesting because parents needed to learn about the school and how you want the school to be and what happens in the school. How could we help more of the students in academic achievement? That is a different approach than what we were doing before, which was mobilizing parents to go to City Hall to stop something. In one case it was a response to criticism from the schools that immigrant parents don't engage in their children's education. There are several barriers to that, because people have low education levels and little time. So that's what we engaged parents in, finding ways that they can help their kids. But how is it that they could also be part of the few spaces of governance of the school? For that, they also needed to learn about what happens there and how it works. Because it didn't help anybody to have parents sit in on discussions if they didn't know what was happening. They couldn't contribute to those discussions. That's part of the work that we did with Padres en Acción, Parents In Action. We brought different people and other organizations to help to build the capacity of parents.

It also required building a relationship with the school system. That was tough because other groups in the community were very critical of us. It was kind of talking to the enemy. But at the same time, we knew that we couldn't do this alone. We actually needed to bring them to the table if this was going to work. It needed to be a community engagement. So that's where we put a lot of our effort. There is currently a coalition, Chelsea Education Latino Group, which was born from this effort. That is still running. The school and different community-based organizations are part of it.

So we were working with a group of parents to try to move beyond simply being mobilized to protest the way the school was doing certain things. They were able to move from that to actually start understanding how the school works. Then they were able to sit at a table with the school and start taking the spaces where some power was—in the PTO and the school council. They were able to talk with an understanding and a vision of what they wanted for their school. That confirmed my belief that organizing is not about mobilizing. Mobilizing allows us to defend a lot of things, but this was about being at the table and being able to put together a proposal about how we wanted things to be done differently. For a group of woman immigrants to come to that realization was amazing. For me, it was a very satisfying experience.

This is what I like to do. I see it as a contribution. It's very exciting, in terms of where we are. It's part of what I believe. It's also because I've been challenged. I'm doing something different and at the same time I'm creating opportunities. I could get a job with better money, but this is providing me with what I need and doing exactly what I want.

Profile: Jana Adams
Faith in the City

Jana Adams is the Training Coordinator for the Direct Action and Research Training Center Network, a national network of grassroots, metropolitan, congregation-based, community organizations spread throughout the United States. She is based in Dayton, Ohio. She was interviewed in February 2006.

I grew up in suburban Dayton, Ohio, right outside the city. After years of schooling, I came home and taught for twelve years in suburban schools. During that time, I felt called to Christian education, so I went to Richmond, Virginia, and studied to be a Christian educator. When I came back to Dayton, I had used up all my resources, so I moved into what had been my grandmother's home because it was sitting, vacant, here in the inner city. That's when I first looked closely at the neighborhood around our church. My new home and my church were just a block away from each other.

I served my church as a Christian educator for six years. It was an historic African-American Baptist church, and it was the first time they'd ever had that position. I took like a $15,000 cut in salary to be a Christian educator, but it was something that really turned my life around. I loved Bethel Baptist Church and got more and more involved in my new neighborhood.

Right next door to me, there were two young boys, about four or six years of age. I used to get them snacks and give them some clothes from people in the community. Long story short, I found out that their mother was struggling with drugs. We took them in as a congregation. We gave them clothes, food, and a number of things. I soon found out that it was a whole community full of boys like Raymond and Trenell. There was no way our congregation could take care of all of them.

At that same time, an organizer had been trying to get our pastor engaged in congregation-based community organizing. Our pastor asked me, being a new person on staff, "Will you look into this?" It was the LEAD organization—Leaders for Equality and Action in Dayton. It was perfect timing, because I saw that we, as an organization, could not take care of all the children in the neighborhood, but perhaps we could work with other churches to get to the real reasons for what was happening in our community.

So somewhere in the first year, I was invited to come to a public action. I thought it was one of the most fantastic things I ever saw. Seeing a community come together in such a powerful, disciplined way was great. Not too long after that, I was sent to a five-day training for DART.

I remember our first action. We had children in our parking lot who were using our handicapped ramps as ramps for their bikes and playing all among our parked cars. Our pastor noticed that they even had some old mattresses and they were jumping on the mattresses. We were wondering, "My gosh! Why are they making a playground out of our parking lot?" Then we did some research and found out that there used to be some parks and playgrounds around, but they had been overrun and the equipment wasn't there. First of all, we were angry. We said, "They're doing this because there's nowhere for them to play around here. They have to cross some major streets to get to a playground." It took us a couple years to get something done. Our city commissioners said right away that they would develop a playground. We were excited because we were doing summer programs and we'd have somewhere other than the church parking lot to go. They said "yes" but then they offered us used equipment from a school. We were like, "No, we will not take that used equipment." It was a couple years before we were actually able to get them to put real equipment in a playground for our neighborhood. Then we celebrated by christening the playground. People came from all over the community. So many young people were touched by that playground over the years. It gave an opportunity for the church to really do some effective work.

When I was still working at the local level we had an action about community-based policing. We'd done some things for our neighborhood, like get the park built. But at this point we were asking on behalf of the larger community, to have some community-based police officers. I remember we had some kind of radical group that came in. We didn't know them; they just heard through the grapevine that we were doing this. We watched all those different people come together and allow one voice to be shared and say, "This is what we want." That's a proud moment, when I see people come to action and see results happen.

The biggest action I think I've seen was over a thousand people in Columbus, the state capital, to support our sister organization, BREAD. The whole auditorium was excited. People felt like they were, indeed, making a difference. Those are proud moments for me.

Of course, there've been disappointments. We've had city officials who have fought us and been against us and not seen that we are the people they are supposed to serve. We're just asking them to do what they really believe. That's what's disappointing to me, when we have to confront and fight against and struggle with people who don't have the bigger vision.

In the six years that I served as a Christian educator, I was often working with the community through the LEAD organization. It gave us an opportunity to do a number of things with the people in the community to effect some real change. I had been doing some work at the regional and national level with the DART organization. I had been doing some training with them and I was invited to be their national training coordinator. That was about six years ago. So I've served six years as a Christian educator in a church and then six years as a national training coordinator for the DART network. The DART network has about twenty-one different organizations now, in six states. It allows me the opportunity to travel around. I do training. I also do regional and national workshops.

It's really been on-the-job training: listening to people talk and then watching their procedures and trying to make sense of it. I was hired because organizers were so busy organizing that who has time to sit and write this down? One of my tasks has been to put this stuff into manuals and write it out for them.

I often ask myself why I do this work, and I really do feel like it's a calling. My heart just goes out to the people around me. I've been in this particular inner-city neighborhood for over twelve years now and I see it's not just about individual problems. It's systemic. I just feel called to see what I can do with the people to address these concerns. I think that congregation-based organizing links together with my religious beliefs. It gives a strategy for me to work with people to address some change. I do it because I just have to.

I think organizing is the only way for change. The only thing that I would pair it with is something like community development. But I think we shortchange the research part. We're always building power for change. I think we need to spend some more time thinking of strategies or demands we want to make. But in terms of change, I just don't trust some of those more traditional systems, like politics. We're nonpartisan because, regardless of whether Republicans or Democrats are in office, we hold them accountable for fairness and justice.

We spend a lot of time in the DART network showing people that justice is all throughout the Bible and most other faith traditions. We make that link for them continually. Matthew 23:23, where Jesus is talking to the Pharisees and says, "You've neglected the weightier matters of the law—justice, mercy and faithfulness," is almost a repeat of Micah 6:8. Micah asks, "What does the Lord require of you but to do justice, and to love kindness and to walk humbly with your God?" Doing justice is listed first in both those verses, but it isn't given top priority in many of our congregations. We do a great job of being faithful to God and to each other, we try to do kindness through charity, feeding, clothing, and tutoring programs, but the justice part often gets neglected. I love the quote from Pope Paul VI, "What is owed in justice should never be given in charity."

As a people, African-Americans feel and know injustice. What we try to do is to link that knowledge and that experience along with what the Bible says about injustice. I think it makes a nice tie, which is why we have a number of African-Americans and people who suffer injustice engaged in this work.

That's what I see as a good example of tapping the power of African-American churches. It's all within our scriptures. The question is, do we believe it? And perhaps we don't do it because we believe that we couldn't do it. We offer people vehicles through which they can live out their faith and act out their faith and make some real change.

We think in terms of being angry at the conditions in our community. I think that public outcry leads to the release of a new social imagination. You think of new ways. You don't just scream out that something's wrong. You do something about it and you do it in creative ways. As African-Americans, we often do the critiquing without doing the public processing. We definitely don't take that power and use that power and that anger. We don't channel it in ways that might, indeed, effect change. We talk about it and shout about it, but not enough people see this as the central ministry of the church. We African-Americans need to channel our anger and allow it to motivate us to build power for a greater degree of justice.

Let me explain a little how DART's congregation-based organizing works. We start out with listening. We listen to people's concerns. We do one-to-ones. We do house meetings where we listen to the concerns of our people. We also listen to what their self-interest happens to be. What do they want to work on? What do they want to get done that they have not been able to do individually?

Then you have to take a little bit of time for an assembly to figure out which, of all the problems you heard, are the two or three that you might address. So after listening we go into some research. Again, nothing is quite linear. Between listening and research we do some network building. You listen to people. You build relationships. We have what we call "Justice Ministry Network Teams." So as you're listening, the whole time you're doing the process, you're thinking, "Who else does this person know? Who might be in their network?" So when it's time, at the very end, for the big action, who might be able to turn out?

Research is a great process for our leaders. It's going and talking to people about what has already been done and understanding the problem. They figure out what the possible solutions are. Here are the demands we want to make of the powers that be.

We continue to build our networks and get the word out so that we can exercise our power. We call out all our people and they say, "This is what we want. Can you give it to us—yes or no?" That's our big assembly. It does not

DART trainer Kristina Fundora helps new staff and congregations make the links between their faith and organizing for justice.

stop there. A lot of times the decision-makers we're trying to reach say "yes" but we have to monitor and stay on top of them to hold them accountable for what they said they would do.

We have an action-reflection model. We take some time every meeting to reflect and think about what we've learned and what we've done with power in our community.

We confront and we're very serious about that, but we see it as the redeeming of a system, a calling back of a system. We're not just fighting to fight. We're asking them to come back and be what we believe God intended them to be. We try to make sure that we don't boo at our public assemblies. We're different because whatever we do is grounded in the Bible, not only in the content but also in the style and the way that we do things.

There is leadership development throughout the process. There are formal and informal trainings. The ideal would be that someone would begin with a one-to-one conversation with the organizer. That organizer helps that person uncover what some of their primary self-interests are and builds a relationship with them and offers them opportunities for training. We have a national training two times a year. It's a four and a half day orientation workshop of sorts. The idea would be to get that person to one of the national trainings as soon as possible. Before we do a listening process there are trainings at the local level about how to do one-to-ones and a reminder about how to do house meetings. Before research, there are trainings. At every kind of committee meeting we're trying to get more tips out. Training is integral. Maybe I'm biased because I'm a trainer. We even have advanced workshops once a year where we take particular topics and people get trained on them. And because everyone can't attend a national workshop, we have local orientation workshops so people can attend a four-hour session on a Saturday and they'll get the basics. We've trained our local leaders to actually lead those sessions so that organizers aren't always the ones doing the presenting.

In addition, we train our clergy. Once a year we have a big clergy conference where we bring in an outside speaker and we also prepare our people to talk about the clergy's role in congregation-based community organizing.

In addition, we have an organizing institute. It's not leadership development, but organizer development. We found out, as more and more DART organizations were being developed, that we had a problem. I think a number of networks have it. People weren't hearing, in college, that this was a field that they could enter. So the DART network worked to develop what we call organizer institutes, where there's extensive recruiting done. Even before the actual interview occurs we have staff who go around to campuses and talk to professors. They go around the nation as much as possible, talking and e-mailing and revving up the interest in the field of organizing with college students. We have five different interview weekends this year, where they have extensive training and interviewing. It's like a day-and-a-half process where we take them through learning how to do one-to-ones. We take them through a little research model. There are two days of interviews.

Then we select a number of candidates. It ends up being twenty or twenty-five who come to a seven-day, very intensive training. Then they have a three-month probationary period where they go into a particular organization. More experienced organizers mentor them and they have a particular responsibility. They have to prepare for a local orientation workshop. So their task is to first of all do one-to-ones and do the whole process. They go out and they meet people. They figure out who is going to do the training at this workshop. They have to work with clergy to form teams of people, to turn out a lot of people at this workshop. So their final test is their local orientation workshop. It's tested how many people they turned out. They don't know people and they have to build relationships, so they kind of start from zero from their point of view. But we give them churches where there's some potential.

At the end they are hired to be a part of our DART network based on their production, basically, at that last workshop. I should say, though, that they are paid all the way through. It's a training. I don't want them to think of it as an internship that they can leave. We've invested three months in them. It's our hope that they will feel called to it. At the beginning, after we hire them, they have trainings three times a year when they are about to go into other major processes—listening, research, or action. They come back together and they have trainings from DART staff or experienced organizers where they are trained in the processes.

I would advise anyone who wants to be an organizer—in any kind of organizing—first of all, to get as many different experiences as they possibly can. I'm not saying to fill a resume, but to really work in an organization and understand it fully. Then perhaps try various types of organization. So I'd say get as many different experiences as possible, but deep, full experiences. They should make sure that they try working out of their comfort zone and, again, with different types of people, and make sure that's what they enjoy. Then they've got to have some good skills. They've got to be able to write, they've got to be able to talk . . . whatever they happen to be studying, they've got to make sure that they've got the basics down well.

I think it's a calling. Those who stay determine that this is so important that they're going to make it work. They have a passion and a zeal for it. If you don't have that calling and that zeal, this work is unbelievable in terms of the time and commitment that it takes. The ones who stay in it stay because it's the right fit for them and they're willing to make the commitment it takes to do it.

Profile: Scott Douglas
Organizing in the South

Scott Douglas is Executive Director of Greater Birmingham Ministries in Birmingham, Alabama. He was interviewed in September 2003.

I was born in Nashville, Tennessee, on December 4, 1946. My nickname as a child was "Baby Douglas" because my father and mother could not agree on a name for me before we left the hospital. So I was signed out of the hospital as "Baby Douglas" and that stuck.

My mother was a lifetime maid who worked at other peoples' houses. I was often put down at school because my father was a deliveryman. He was the sole employee of what we then called a "feed store"—a hardware store with rabbit food, chicken feed, bales of hay, kindling—in the middle of urban Nashville. During the '40s and the '50s, before the health department came on, poor people still raised cows, chickens, and hogs in their backyards.

So I learned about the outside world through going down to my father's work place and watching customers come in, running my hands through rabbit food. I can still smell it now. My job as the oldest son was to take my father's boots off every day after work. I hated that job, but now I look back on it as our closest moments. I would take them off and all that hay and small seeds would come out. He worked seven days a week, twelve hours a day Monday through Saturday and up until about one or two p.m. on Sunday. We were still poor. We were the second poorest people on our street. Thank God for the Townsends; they were poorer than we were. They had like twelve children and we just had four, so it was probably based on that ratio.

I attended all-Black high schools and elementary schools. The integration wave came a little bit after I graduated.

As far as organizing goes, one relevant story is that I grew up in an all-Black environment, several blocks from Hubbard Hospital/Meharry

Medical School, which today is still the alma mater of nearly fifty percent of all Black doctors. I knew cab drivers who had almost finished medical school. Therefore, Nashville was a very literate town. We had Tennessee State University, Fisk University, and Hubbard Hospital. We had three Black higher education institutions on that side.

I felt the pangs of class superiority before I felt race superiority. I heard people talking about White people, but I never saw many. I never crossed the path of White folks in my life before high school, except for a few who would come by the house as insurance men. So my second-class identity thinking was framed around household income. The people I thought were rich were the Black people who tended to put my group of people with less money down. I couldn't stand it. I remember, in third grade, making a commitment to get rich enough to give all of my classmates $25,000.

I call it "income" more than class. We poorer kids formed what I would now call—but did not at that time—academic gangs. We helped each other study and tutored each other on homework so we could outperform the "rich" Black kids in class. We started that in about the fifth grade and we carried it all the way through twelfth grade. We did it to embarrass the rich people who thought that they were better than we were. We got a lot of awards, including president of the SGA [Student Government Association] and class president.

We didn't get the salutatorian and valedictorian for one major reason: there was an honors class that people on the fast track would always try to take. The English component was led by a Black teacher named Elizabeth K. Burgess. She was so tough that the valedictorian and the salutatorian took a regular English class curriculum in tenth grade so their grade scoring would be intact. But our being educated by Elizabeth K. Burgess meant that we got a much better education. We had 1,500 vocabulary words that we had to learn, and they weren't your usual words. We studied all the classic books. We did summer writing projects. I was the first African-American to win the "Youth Speaks Out" essay contest in Nashville. When I came back after tenth grade I was so proud to show it to Ms. Burgess. She went through there and graded the damn thing. Not one word did she say, like "I'm so proud of you." It was, "You can do better than this," [sounds of erasing].

But she set high standards for us in terms of language. I always remember what she said about communication and writing. She said, "The purpose of writing is to get what's in your head into the head of the other person with no loss."

Then I went to college. I got a scholarship to Fisk and I turned it down because I wanted to go into engineering. Fisk is a Black college in Nashville. I got accepted into the University of Tennessee in 1964, in a curriculum called Engineering Physics. That attracted me because at that time engineers in the United States couldn't dream and scientists couldn't build anything. They needed this interloper culture to really be a bridge between the scientific community and the engineering community.

It was a five-year curriculum, with lots of physics and engineering courses, but it was heavy on liberal arts. I liked that. One day during my freshman year, I was sitting in my dormitory room doing my homework and this White guy in my physics class came by and asked if I would tutor him in physics. One night we were working on a physics problem and he asked me what kind of scholarship I was on. I said, "I'm not on a scholarship, I'm on a loan."

He said, "What did you make on the ACT?"

I told him, and then said, "What did you make?" He had scored less than I did.

He said "Aren't you from Tennessee?"

I said, "Yes."

He said, "You're from Nashville, right?" In Tennessee at the time, scholarship preferences were to go to in-state students, all else being equal. He got upset before I did. He said, "You should have a scholarship. You got a higher score than I did. You did more extracurricular stuff in high school. And you're an in-state student." He was a White kid from Iowa. He was actually shocked that I wasn't on a scholarship. Then I got to be shocked.

So I went to the Dean of Physics to talk about it. She was a liberal professor from Oak Ridge. No, it wasn't the dean; she was the creator of this Engineering-Physics curriculum. She thought I was on a scholarship also. She said, "Well, there's nothing we can do about it now." That's when something very cold sank into me. What people had taught us young Black kids was that it's not Negroes that the White folks don't like. It's those "wild, crazy Negroes." If you get an education people will just forget what color you are. At the same time I was in my sophomore class at UT, Birmingham had happened just two years earlier. The 16th Street bomb had happened when I was in twelfth grade. 1964 was the Civil Rights Act, and the Voting Rights Act was '65; both happened in my freshman and sophomore years at UT.

There was some boiling social conscience at UT. My White allies and friends were mostly hippies and Appalachian beatniks. My first encounter with cohesive progressive thinking was at Highlander in '65. Somebody had told me about it. It was in Knoxville by the river bend. I was able to see Martin Luther King, Julian Bond, and other people I don't even remember now.

I began to hang around with a group called SSOC [Southern Student Organizing Committee] and the chapter at UT was not that advanced. By 1969 the racism had gotten so egregious at UT in terms of violent attacks and mistreatment of Blacks in classes that I spent a lot of my time as a junior helping freshman and sophomore Black kids do their class work. Especially English essays: I was the first Black student to be included in "Theme Vault" which is the volume of freshman essays that UT had.

One of my best friends there was named Aristo. His father was Italian and his mother was Yugoslavian and he was born in Chattanooga. He had the worst accent in the world. He had been a Tennessee golden-gloves champion boxer. Because he was not like the ordinary White, Protestant Southerner, he was ostracized by White kids. So he would come over and sit in the dorm's lounge with the Black kids. He came in very handy in the dorms when we had fights over which television show to watch. There was only one TV on each floor. When the White students wanted to watch *Batman*, the Black students would say, "Hey Aristo, we want to see *Star Trek*." He would go change it. In return we did his homework.

In 1964 my dormitory room was set on fire by some White students. The real danger wasn't that we would be burned. The danger was that we would suffocate. This was a brand-new dormitory, built in the '60s style of high-rise, slab-style, airtight, no windows. It was a monument to brick and glass. If you have the windows shut, the oxygen can be depleted. Later, another Black student and I got jumped on by some White kids. We eventually got them expelled from school. I don't know if that was good or not. They came back and founded the campus chapter of Young Americans for Freedom, a Barry Goldwater youth group, after they'd been away in the army for two years. They came back more militarized and more organized in their right-wing ideology.

So by 1967 myself and Jim Baxter—who's now a U.S. Attorney in Knoxville—formed the Black Students Union. I wrote the constitution. We recruited the first few members. This is the first thing I would call organizing, at least in terms of recruitment: there were Blacks who were afraid to join with us, Blacks who said there was no problem, Black students who said, "If you don't like it here, go someplace else." We had to deal with all that.

The political work kind of went down. There were some demands that we actually got. We wanted a Black counselor on campus at UT that Black kids could go to. We got one. He was Ralph Boston, the Olympic athlete. A decade later, he told me something at a conference at Fisk University that I'd suspected but couldn't prove. His real job was to monitor Black students and report to the administration. When you use the word "organizing" it kind of talks about that point where you have to be conscious. There is a kind of activity that's conscious, political, leadership building, cohesive, coherent, and that you have to build an agenda around. That was my first experience with that.

By the time I got past my sophomore year, I didn't last two years. I really got out because I couldn't get past the chemistry courses. You had to keep a B in all your science courses. I'd just pass them. I never liked chemistry. We had a class and I didn't realize it was the get-rid-of-sophomores course. Chemistry can be beautiful. But chemistry was being taught as if your goal in life was to build an industrial smokestack industry. All his reference was not to the exciting stuff that I would think about—what do crystals do and those kinds of pieces—but all about some damn refinery. I didn't want to know about refineries. That was smokestack stuff. I wanted to do rocket

What makes a good organizer?

I happen to believe that what makes an organizer good is what organization they're with. You're not going to be a good organizer in an ineffective organization. What makes organizers good is they relate to people in different walks of life. They can relate to people just like them. They listen very well. They consciously try to learn from their relationships and build on that learning. Somebody once said that the only experiences one learns from are the experiences one learns from. Having an experience is not necessarily a teaching moment. You have to choose to learn from experience. [Good organizers] consciously learn from experience and are consciously revisiting it. They're a friend of critical analysis and adopt it. They are a friend of popular education. If the facts alone, on paper, could do justice, we would have justice. The facts have been printed on the Vietnam War and on Civil Rights, on Housing and Health Care.

Organizing has to have some kind of relationship to popular education. It must have some sensitivity to place. Organizers have to have some respect for place. Place is not just the physical, but it's also respect for the experiences of others. Without that kind of respect you really can't do the best organizing. People may respect and seem to go along with your plans and strategies, but in many cases they do not respect you as a person. I've seen that happen. So you need respect for place, people, culture, and history. A good organizer realizes that learning is a process and not an endgame. They must also have a political analysis that incorporates the times. I think that's probably first and foremost. Is the organizing going on for just and fair distribution of physical resources like sidewalks and streetlights? If you're talking about getting involved in public schools—public schools are about two of the most important things in the world: children and budgets. You've got children and budgets on the same page. "This is just a budget. . . ." No, no, no. Show me your budget and I can see what your policy is.
—Scott Douglas

fuel. Of course you have to do science before you can do rocket fuel, like how stuff breaks down and that kind of stuff. But in those classes of 300 people you can't even read the board. So chemistry got it started. In my junior year I began to decline in my studies. I just didn't study.

In 1968 I was getting ready to go back to Nashville because I had something like a 2.2 GPA at the time. I wanted to drop out of school while

I still had a passing average so I could come back to it later. School and I were not getting along at all. I was sitting in a bar in Knoxville, Sam and Andy's Roman Room, when news came over the TV that Martin Luther King had been assassinated. That was the downest moment. I was sitting in a bar with all these crazy old White guys and news came that he had been shot. That was the nadir for me. I was thinking, "Anything can happen," in the irrational, chaotic sense of "anything." I went to Nashville and got a job in the aircraft industry, where race played into things. The only way I could get the job was I had to go through CETA, the Comprehensive Employment Training Act. It was a program designed to get industries to hire people of color and women, especially to get into industries that had not so readily absorbed people of color as employees.

I kept that job until I got laid off in '74. That was five years. I worked my way up to a sealer. We sealed the fuel tanks of large aircrafts, like C130s and C-5A's.

That was a good job. It was the second highest-paying industrial job in Nashville. It was union, but in many ways it wasn't the best of organized labor. The racism in that union was so strong that the company would have rules such as it was illegal to talk on the shop floor while you were working. Okay, I can do that. But White supervisors would start conversations with Black women. Then the Black men workers would get upset, because if a Black man was talking to a Black woman during the work shift he'd be reprimanded. So that caused a split between the Black men and Black women in the work force. Eventually we organized a Black caucus to address these and other grievances, such as Black workers not being promoted to certain jobs.

I would bring in the paper, *The Daily Worker*, and have workers reading it on the shop floor. I joined the Communist Party in 1972. I had told myself, "I'm going to work to free Angela Davis. If she gets freed I'll join. If she doesn't I won't." So she got freed in 1971 and I joined. In the locker room the White men would have pornographic pictures of White women in their lockers. The Black men, fighting for pornographic equity, I guessed, would have pictures of naked Black women in *their* lockers. People said I was a square because I told the Black workers, "You're not really showing that you're proud of your race here." So I put a picture of Angela behind bars in my locker. One by one other Black guys asked me for a copy. After a while, if they didn't have Angela Davis they had a Black musician or a poet or something. Then the White guys got embarrassed. So you started seeing Tammy Wynette and respectable pictures of people and stuff. If you ask about my greatest victory in the shop it was probably that.

There was another radicalizing event. I have a cousin, Deborah Johnson, in Chicago. She was the girlfriend of Fred Hampton, the powerful and influential Black Panther leader. December 4th is my birthday. That's the day Chicago's Red Squad and the FBI came in and assassinated Fred and wounded Deborah. She was pregnant with their child, Fred, Jr.

That was a big, big piece. The Chicago officials came out with the public story that there was an exchange of gunfire. They even showed a picture in the newspaper showing the bullet holes coming from inside. Some enterprising reporter went down and saw the house on his own and said, "There were no bullet holes. Those were nails." The reporter proved to be right. The police had gambled on a black and white picture in a grainy newspaper to cover up their murder. Deborah eventually received two million dollars in a settlement. That was years later. And of course it didn't replace the loss in her life or the loss in the community life. Fred Hampton was one of those charismatic people who also had great organizing abilities. So little is known of him today, but he was the one behind the Black Panthers' breakfast program in Chicago. He was the one who brought about a gang peace in Chicago. Crime went down under the community leadership of Fred Hampton. He was also mentioned in J. Edgar Hoover's papers as one of those people, like Dr. King, who was dangerous because he made people devout to an idea.

In '72 my job, in terms of working with the party, was largely writing stories from the South. I began to travel the South around different events. There was J.P. Stevens, a shipyard struggle, and paper workers. That was the lowest-ranking job in forestry. They were still doing it with wagons and pickups. It wasn't as mechanized as it is today. I would do interviews with Civil Rights veterans as well as current social justice campaigns. I know I got to go to North Carolina, Georgia, Mississippi, and Alabama. I was based in Tennessee. This was my first systematic contact with organizing as we know it in the South. Those were groups of people—some Black, some White, a few integrated—that were fighting visceral human rights issues, life or death issues.

The least visible movement to those outside of it may have been the public housing struggles. They had houses, but they were fighting for better housing policies. They were fighting against sexual exploitation of renters by management, which was a plague in public housing communities in those days. There were the Plaquemines Fishermen fighting for basic rights in Plaquemines Parish, Louisiana. The boss system still existed there, left over from pre-Reconstruction. They were all big exciting fights. I was organizing our group in Nashville. It got me to see all the different formations and structures and processes people took to make change. I don't know if I noticed it then, but I sure noticed it later: everybody had high degrees of passion and high degrees of knowledge about their issue. In some cases, they had a lot of experiences with the issues long before any organizing began to happen.

The travel got me exposed to a lot of different organizing forms that were happening in the South. A lot, but not all of them, were with people of color. I remember the miners from Harlan County, Kentucky, came through Alabama to tell their story to a majority Black audience. We had them tell their story, build some solidarity, and raise some money for the miner's campaign. So there were a lot of intersections going on. By 1974 I was working for Anne Braden and the Southern Organizing Committee [SOC] for Social and Economic Justice. That's what really took me in even deeper, in terms of talking, interviewing people, and writing stories about them. I still wrote some stories for *The Daily Worker,* but I also wrote stories for *The Southern Patriot,* the newsletter of SOC.

One thing about SOC was that it introduced me to at least the southern version of campaign organizing. Committed folks with a lot of information would spread the word and make those connections and bring in other folks. Someone once asked me, "What's the role of SOC in the whole scheme of things? What do you all do?" I said, "SOC brings national attention to local struggles with global significance." So many of our struggles never made the front pages because the stories never left the community. Isolation is the enemy of so many of our rural struggles. There was one case, in rural Mississippi, where the water companies are private. They started charging people like $1,000 a month for their water bill when it had been like $20. The people complained and thought it might be an error. They said, "Well, it might be an error but you pay the bill first. Then we'll get it straightened out." There was no way these people could pay those bills.

This was Leroy Johnson's group, ROCC [Rural Organizing and Cultural Center], which preceded Southern Echo. ROCC had young people organizing water brigades and bringing buckets of water to area citizens on their front porches so they could survive this fight. But this was SOC's solidarity campaign, and Fred Shuttlesworth came up with an idea. The water company would not yield to local organizing pressure in that county. We developed a nationwide postcard and phone-calling campaign. We got the home phone numbers of every member of this water company's board. We specified to people that the best time to call the board members was between two and four on Sundays. What are southern near-bourbon wannabes doing on Sundays between two and four? They're home; they're back from church. They're sitting at home with their families enjoying a quiet time. People called from California, New York, and Tennessee. They thought it was harassment. We said, "Your discomfort at every phone call during dinner on Sunday is nothing like the discomfort of an ninety-year-old woman who has no water. Let's not equate discomforts here."

They did something that was face-saving. The week following that call-in Sunday we heard from Leroy and Arnette Lewis that they had caved.

So that was up to '74. I still hadn't come across any systematic forms of organizing. The most natural organizing that was going on in that period—"natural" by being seamless—was the work that Pat Bryant was doing with the Gulf Coast Tenants Organization. He worked with public housing residents across the southeast to struggle for better housing policies. He came to my apartment in Birmingham in 1976 and said, "Scott, I had this dream."

I said, "What is it, Pat?"

Pat always had dreams. "I want to build this regional public housing organization."

I said, "Okay, go for it."

What he and the leaders who came after him were able to do was to put public housing residents squarely in the center of fights for important public policies. Jobs for Peace had just gotten started and Cheryl Christmas and others came down to visit our public housing regional meeting at the Federation of Southern Cooperatives. We told her about our dream of a "Build Houses, Not Bombs" company. It started with public housing residents talking about the need for housing and how much those needs are being put aside in this rush to build more weapons of war. She said, "That's impossible. You all can't do that." A year later Jobs for Peace made "Build Houses,

• • • There are some folks who try real hard, but the system beats them. The basic name of the game is to change people's relationships to their own self-governments from consumptive to productive. That transition can take place with effective, sustained organizing. • • •

Not Bombs" a national campaign. One thing they did do is show that you can put people on a path of broader struggle without betraying any of their convictions or commitments. That was the first deep organizing example I saw in the post civil rights movement era.

We had a southern tour of military bases. We witnessed public housing residents and allies going to the gates of military bases and kneeling in and praying to build houses, not bombs. We got some respect from the people who had housing in military bases. We had state representatives and preachers from the local areas. It was just like a caravan going from town to town. We would hook up with people in that town and then we would go out to the military base.

Bridging issues and crossing over issues is possible for the people at the "bottom" of capitalism's pecking order. The whole weight of capitalism is on them. Most of us can't see what's below us, only what's above us. But if you're on the bottom, *everything's* above you. It gives you some insight into what pressures look like and what they feel like. So that was 1984 and 1985. I experienced many different campaigns with different constituencies. I was in the peace movement; I was in the nuclear freeze movement. I was there when the Freeze joined with SANE and two wings of the peace movement came together. I was never very much in the environmental justice movement, although I was the Sierra Club's first organizer hired for environmental justice in the nation. That was in 1992. I stayed there just six months until my current position opened at Greater Birmingham Ministries.

I said, "I'm going to apply for that job. I've been on the board of GBM anyway. I'm going to apply for that job for one reason mainly. I know much of the work and I'm tired of traveling so much."

I became the executive director. This is my tenth year.

We had the "super sewer" campaign where Jefferson County had been ordered by the EPA to fix our broken storm sewers. The county said, "Well, you know that you all have to pay more for that." Everybody said, "Yeah, I guess so," because a girl had fallen into an open storm water sewer and drowned. So the community was behind it. An investigative reporter finds out that the sewer bills had already gone up, but the county hadn't quite gotten around to fixing the broken ones. They *had* gotten around to expanding new sewer lines to green areas of the county at the behest of the developers. They had built an infrastructure to give to the developers without even requiring a development fee. So if you build sewer lines you've got yourself a gated community and a mall and then you have suburban sprawl financed on the backs of urban rate-payers.

Greater Birmingham Ministries joined the environmentalists who'd been isolated by the county commissioners. They were called "tree lovers," "anti-growth," and all this kind of stuff. The environmentalists came to us and wanted to know if we'd join the coalition.

We at GBM said, "Yeah, but only if you add this item to the campaign."

"What?"

"Low-income residents should not be forced to subsidize the development of the outlying areas of the county where they won't benefit. They can't get there, can't work there, and they definitely won't live there." And we all agreed to that.

So we collected bill stubs from people whose bills had gone up. We did a demonstration at the county commission. We printed up some t-shirts saying "Stop the Super Sewer!" We had a large "demonstration in the rain;" it poured that day. It was about 100 people with these t-shirts on in the rain. The movement was so powerful that it un-elected the two greatest supporters of the sewer expansion. A federal investigation of bid processes for the super sewer is still going on. The super sewer was stopped dead in its trenches.

So that exhibited a campaign style too. We really didn't build an organized base of sewer consumers, but that work will continue. I wish the relationships had been built through this leadership development program. Matter of fact, my nickname for it was "Bebop 2K," the Better Birmingham Organizing Project 2000. Since that time we've elected one of our staff people to be a state legislator. But that was not out of strategic analysis. That was out of an accident of history, location and timing.

I guess I keep doing this work because there really isn't much of anything else to do. I've tried other stuff. The hardest thing in the world to see is human potential unrealized: things that should have been but will never be. To me, the greatest crime is to leave children behind. I think of J.R. In the fourth grade in Nashville, Jesse Rucker was just as smart as the rest of us, but he was not as slick in manipulating teachers as we were. So he came out as being slow and he was not slow. But once he got left behind he did slow in his appreciation of school and learning. He was a tall kid and he got left behind. He was embarrassed. He dropped out of school in the eighth grade. He came back a little later even farther behind. He played a little high school basketball and after that just had a life on the streets. I haven't seen him in a long time.

J.R. is one of the people who make this community as vital and lively as it is, but the system wouldn't fit J.R. There's room in it, but the thing about bureaucracy, especially educational bureaucracy, is that it's so arbitrary. The other thing that drives me—other than the J.R.'s getting left behind—is the cruelty and insanity of racism, which, to me, influences everything. A mentor of mine once wrote a small pamphlet: "Racism: The Nation's Most Dangerous Pollutant." I think of racism as a pollutant because it corrodes and corrupts everything it touches.

I'm thinking about moving in new directions, both within and outside of GBM. We just talked this weekend about leadership academies. I've been talking about that to myself for the last five years. Mainly I look at Highlander. I look at Southern Empowerment Project and Southern Echo. I said, "All these people travel some place for learnings and try like hell to bring it back. I want to build one just for Birmingham." Friends asked, "What does it look like?" I said, "Think of it as a night school for community leaders and the field work is civic action." There will be a local staff, mostly volunteer. We'll bring in organizers from around the country and the southeast—think of visiting professors. I think we can find the funds to do that. It will be an ongoing leadership development

Filmmakers Herb E. Smith and Shawn Lind interview Scott Douglas about community organizing in Birmingham.

cadre. The academy will engage residents of Birmingham and hopefully the entirety of Jefferson County.

Over ten years from now there will be some 1,500 folks who have been exposed to and tested on the values of critical analysis and power analysis, competing forms of power and control, and how to make the choices that are good for your community. Reliable forms of accountability, including your own accountability. We need to test these things over time, and you really can't test over time unless the sample doesn't change. The sample is the school board and its policies, the planning commission and its policies, and the implementation of those policies, the police and the criminal justice system. I am so convinced that Alabamians know less than five percent of the powers and responsibilities of the three major government mechanisms of municipal, county, and state. Mostly, they learn of them in crisis or in public scandal.

In Birmingham we had a terrible appointed school board. People said, "We want an elected school board."

"Why?"

"So we can hold them accountable."

I said, "How is the school board elected?"

"Well, it's appointed by the city council. That means they're accountable to them and not to us."

"What are you going to do?"

"We're going to elect a school board."

I said, "Wait a minute now. How do you feel about the city council?"

"We can't stand those crooks."

"How did they get there?"

"We elected them."

There are some folks who try real hard, but the system beats them. The basic name of the game is to change people's relationships to their own self-governments from consumptive to productive. That transition can take place with effective, sustained organizing.

Achievements and Victories

To stay in this work you have to have a proud achievement every week in my opinion, maybe every day. But certainly every week. Every month, you have to be able to say, "This was good; this worked."
    –Patrick Sweeney

We asked the organizers to tell us stories of their proudest achievements. The stories they tell represent a great cross-section of American organizing: a broad range of issues and constituencies using people power to get things changed.

There's not an incinerator

There was a medical waste incinerator we were fighting in Tennessee. It started with four people at a county commission meeting who got up and said, "We don't want this coming into our town." And six weeks later, there were 500 people out at things. It was on the front page of the paper. The incinerator proposal moved to eight different locations and got stopped at all of them. One of them was right at an interstate exit, and every time I drive by there, it's like "Yeah, right back there, there's ***not*** a medical waste incinerator."
    —Bob Becker

Power in numbers

I think it's exciting any time you have several hundred people in one room that are focused on the same agenda and confronting a powerful decision-maker and pinning them to make a commitment. We've done that in a lot of different issue campaigns over the past thirteen years. It's always exciting to see that and to see the power of people and to know that if there were five people in the room instead of 500 we would be treated completely differently. The result would be completely different. We've seen that time and again.

One time we had not gotten the kind of follow-through by the school district administration that we expected on a particular issue. So we decided to go to the school board meeting and engage the superintendent directly. This was after having had the superintendent out to a meeting of 600 people where he made some commitments but wasn't following through on them. So we went to the school board meeting to make that public. This was a meeting at which they were going to present the budget. Nobody was going to be there. It was going to be a very small meeting that they expected to be over very quickly. It was preceded by the superintendent presenting his strategic plan for the district in a press conference. Then there was going to be a break and then there was going to be this brief budget hearing.

We knew the media would be there because of the press conference. We decided that would be a good night to show up at the school board. So we mobilized at a church nearby and had a rally there. Then we went in buses over to the school district building where the school board meets. We arrived with about 200 people right as the superintendent was finishing the presentation of his strategic plan. In fact, as we arrived the media were packing up their cameras and getting ready to get back in their vans and go back to the station. But when they saw 200 people show up they set their cameras back up again because they knew they had an exciting story.

We packed this school board room, which has chairs for maybe fifty to seventy-five people. It was wall-to-wall people. When the budget meeting convened we requested to be on the agenda. The way the rules are for school board meetings, you can only speak for three minutes at a time and then they ring the bell. So we had about twenty people sign up for their three-minute speech. We had a lot of people prepared to say different things related to the same issue. The final demand was for the superintendent to consider a new reading program as a part of this overall strategic plan that he had just presented. We knew it was not in there, so we wanted to highlight that.

Whenever we'd show up at meetings before, the president of the school board had basically responded to public comment in a very perfunctory, obligatory way. Whenever the superintendent had an objection to what was being said by someone from the public, the school board president would just bow to whatever his response was. Usually it was just, "Thank you for your comment. We'll be sure to look into that." This particular night the school board president actually turned to the superintendent and said, "Due to the obvious large public interest in this issue we've seen here tonight, I believe that you ought to look into this one more time, Mr. Superintendent." And he sheepishly nodded his head.

That was a very empowering victory for our group. As a result of our action that night, and other actions that followed, we were able to move the school district to implement a new reading curriculum that made a big difference in some of the lowest performing schools. In fact, out of all eighty-eight elementary schools in the district, the top two in terms of improvement in reading scores are schools that are using this curriculum. And one of them had been the lowest performing school in reading in the whole state of Kentucky! This victory proved to our leadership that direct action works—that we have to demand change if we want it to happen. As Frederick Douglass said, "Power concedes nothing without a demand; it never has and never will."

—Robert Owens

Turning on the gas

There's this community called Salem [New Mexico]. Salem was one of the early communities with whom the CDC [Colonias Development Council] worked. They didn't have an infrastructure; there was no water or waste system. It had very, very inadequate housing. There was a time in Salem where people would bring in butane gas from Mexico. These are illegal tanks, and people were connecting their butane gas to their mobile homes. It was a very dangerous situation. There was no safety for anybody.

The people were able to say, "Look, this is a dangerous situation. Let's see what we can do." They mobilized. Someone from CDC could have called the gas company and said, "We need gas. We have the critical mass that you need to put this in. Do it." But the organizing effort was to prepare people to negotiate, to meet with the gas company and get the signatures themselves. It involved a process in which the community negotiated a payment plan on their own to be able to procure natural gas for ninety-eight percent of the population.

—Diana Bustamante

Not a drop to drink

There was a subdivision in Mingo County [West Virginia] that got all its water from a common well, and this coal company had done longwall mining underneath it, and sunk the well. There were fifty people out of water and man, they were pissed. They were all coal miners who'd just bought their new house or new modular home and moved it in and they were totally out of water. We had the state giving us the runaround and not doing anything.

So we put together this action where we went down to the state Division of Environmental Protection's Logan office with all these milk jugs and water bottles and everything. We said, "All right, guys, we're here to fill up. If you don't order that company to provide us water, then here we are to fill our jugs and we ain't leaving until we do." We handed them a letter to fax to whatever the name of that jerk was—David Callahan—he was head of the DEP [Department of Environmental Protection], saying, "These are our demands, and we want you to fax it to the coal company right now and tell them we ain't leaving until you write that order." And before we left, they had written the order. Everyone in the subdivision had the coal company delivering water to their doors.

—Allen Cooper

Making a stink (go away)

We had some great battles. In 1972 we won a big fight against Union Carbide, which was polluting the neighborhood with hydrogen sulfide, the smell of a fart. This is a smell that came from the manufacturing of Oscar Mayer hot dog casings. People had their doors and windows shut even on the hottest summer days. We organized in this very blue-collar community.

This was a time when women were not yet working, for the most part, outside the home. With ten days notice you could get fifty to a hundred people on a bus going down to Chicago to confront the chair of, say, a railroad corporation who happened to be on the Union Carbide board. You could take these people into a high-rise office building, to the thirtieth floor, with cameras from the TV stations, a hundred angry people ready to confront him.

We often used ridicule as a gimmick and humor. In this case Joanne Wilhelmy, the chair of the committee, confronted him and asked if he knew what it was like to live with this smell. And she then took out a bottle of trick perfume that smelled like a fart. And on the front page of the *Chicago Daily-News* the next day was a photo of Joanne holding a bottle up to this guy's nose. He had his eyes closed and his face scrunched up and his arms crossed. It was the height of [Saul] Alinsky's ideas about putting pressure on people who were indirectly, in some ways, connected with our issue or were on the board of a corporation like Union Carbide, and getting them to respond.

And we won that fight—forced them to put in a scrubber that cleaned up the smell and made the neighborhood livable. The leaders were very excited and proud of their win. It made a big difference in what it was like to live there.

—Ken Galdston

Sitting in at Woolworth's

On February 1, 1960, the sit-ins happened. Students in the North were organizing sympathy demonstrations at their local Woolworth's. I, along with two other students at Skidmore—an African-American student and a Jewish student from Chicago—organized these incredible meetings where we debated and discussed the issues of segregation and the sit-ins and what the Southern students were doing. There were 100, 150 people at our meetings debating and discussing. They got very wild and very heated, but it was very exhilarating. So we organized a demonstration at the Woolworth's. Two hundred women out of the 1,200 women that were students at Skidmore marched from campus to the Woolworth's. We marched around the shopping center a little bit and then came back to campus.

We get back to campus and a little knot of students formed on the corner outside the senior dorm. Thea, Ruby, and I were the leaders who were all seniors. The sophomores, juniors, and freshmen insisted, "We have to continue this! We have to do more!" So we figured out that we would send four students every hour, starting the next morning, to picket the Woolworth's. We sent four students down to picket on two-hour shifts. We were going to swap people out after every two hours to keep a presence up. They had signs saying things like "Segregation Unfair" and "Equal Rights For All."

The first four students who went down were arrested by the police and told that they were trespassing and in violation of a union-busting statute. We didn't know that it was a union-busting statute at the time, but it said that you could not carry a picket sign within a certain number of feet of an establishment. The four students were taken to the police station. They never were booked, because luckily one student's father was a lawyer and she knew that you had to be charged before you could be booked.

—Betty Garman Robinson

Saving the farm

One pretty exciting experience was when I was working for DRC [Dakota Resource Council] in North Dakota. We were organizing farmers who were getting foreclosed on, and we helped pass the 1987 Agriculture Credit Act that allowed for debt restructuring for FmHA [Farmers Home Administration] borrowers.

Reagan signed that on January 6, 1988, and within ten days of him signing it, FmHA burned this farmer's house down. It had been in foreclosure for years and had been run down. One of the provisions we had won, however, was the homestead exemption part of the bill that allowed farmers to keep their homestead and ten acres, so that they could maybe rent land and eventually get back to farming. It's kind of hard to do that if they burn it down.

We organized an action with this guy. We called the TV stations and went in with a dozen of our members to the FmHA office, and he applied to get his homestead back under this new act that had just been passed. The TV cameras were rolling and this poor secretary said, "I'll go back and see if the director's here." She comes back and says, "Well, he's not here right now." Somebody saw him; he was slinking around the back trying to escape. Somebody says, "There he goes!" and all of the cameras were on him as he slunk out of the FmHA office and ran away. That was the lead story on the news.

The next morning, Ralph Lee, the head of FmHA under Reagan, held a press conference saying, "The Reagan Administration does not have a scorched earth policy to burn farmers off the land." That was a pretty good story.

—Dennis Olson

Speaking truth to power

I was brand new on the job [at Kentuckians For The Commonwealth]. I think it was my first legislative session, and we were trying to pass an oil and gas bill. This same bill had been blocked the last three sessions of the last six years running because it had been sent to a hostile committee. This year we had finally gotten our bill into a good committee so we were really excited about its prospects. And the industry got the chair of the hostile committee to drop in a bill that mirrored our bill in terms of its structure. It had three main points of our bill but had absolutely zero substance. And so he dropped it in one night and it was up for a hearing in his committee the next day, and clearly their intention was to get a bill moving so that they could say, "Yea, we passed an oil and gas bill," and the issue would be dead.

It was a very snowy day, and lots of people had planned to come to Frankfort that day, but it ended up that little ol' me—brand new—and two of KFTC's star lobbyists, Patty Wallace and Ruth Colvin, were the only ones who could make it to Frankfort. The first thing we did was to go visit the chair of this hostile committee to at least ensure that he would allow us to testify that afternoon. We met and we strategized and we planned, and I was very earnest, trying to do everything right. I think Patty and Ruth sort of nodded and humored me and said, "Oh yes, that makes sense."

We went in to meet with him, and the meeting went pretty well. He agreed that we could testify and then Ruth Colvin—for those who are not familiar, these women are just the sweetest grandmothers you've ever seen in your life except they're as tough as nails—Ruth reached into her bag and she said, "There's just one more thing," and she pulled out a rope noose. And she said, "Years ago I told you we ought to string you up by your neck, and so I brought you this present as a reminder that you shouldn't be doing what you're doing."

I was about to crawl under the table. I was thinking, "Wait a minute, this was *not* in the script." And there was this awkward moment and then he laughed and brought all of his buddies into the room and showed them the noose and put it up on the wall. He started the hearing that afternoon several hours later by putting it around his neck and tightening up like a necktie and saying that he wanted to thank his friends from Kentuckians For The Commonwealth for this thoughtful gift.

Well the long and the short of it was, they testified, there were a couple of good folks on the committee and we won and the committee chair lost. At the end of the day, he had his rope noose around his neck and we went home. I had almost wet my pants. I was like, "This is not in the plan." It was just one of those moments when I realized that folks who have a direct stake in this have courage on levels I don't even know to really do some truth telling and to claim a voice that is their own and not feel like they have to play the game, with all the niceties.
    —Lisa Abbott

There's power in numbers

One of the biggest actions that I ever organized was a border rally in Sweetgrass [Montana] on the Canadian border in July of 1999. We had over a thousand people show up at the border. We actually did civil disobedience and stopped agricultural trucks coming in from Canada. At the same time, back at the coalition building, we had the president of National Farmers Union of Canada as one of the keynote speakers saying, "This isn't about American farmers hating Canadian farmers. This is about farmers on both sides of the border being screwed by this unjust system." That was one of the pinnacles of my career as an organizer.
    —Dennis Olson

Organizing for fair housing

The need for affordable housing is something that's been affecting the members of all of our congregations, so we had a big annual assembly. We had about 500 people come together. Affordable housing won by a landslide as the issue to work on this year. Now we've been doing

More than 1,000 people came to a rally on the U.S.-Canada border in Montana to protest free trade agreements.

research, and it's really been a fascinating process because we're all slowly becoming housing experts. You really have to be, to understand the issues here. This is very complex, but we've been able to bring in some experts from the Center For Community Change and other places that have been working with our folks to understand what it means to serve people at 100 percent median income or below that or above that.

When we get to the research, my role is to identify the right leaders who need to be a part of this committee and engage them. That's not based on who's an expert in housing; that's based on who's a real leader and is going to produce people for the action. I do one-to-ones with them to agitate them about why it's in their interest to be part of this housing committee.

Right now everybody has agreed that there's a housing crisis and the county has committed that they're going to do something about this problem. So that's great. The bad news is when you start to get into the details of what they're talking about. They want to set aside money for people who are at 120 percent of median income. That's people making about $60,000 to $70,000 a year. What about people making less than that? Most of the people who are being displaced from apartment complexes and mobile home parks are making a lot less than that. The county has not been very interested in those people; they are very focused on home ownership programs. That's nice, but people making $15,000 a year or less can't use any of those programs. You have to have some affordable rental options in our community.

We've been doing a lot of research meetings with experts in our community and we've been doing those as meetings to get information about the housing problem, but also as forums for really training our leaders and getting them ready for the type of actions coming up and getting them to understand more about the power dynamics in our community. It was very funny . . . one county official started off the meeting with, "Well, I just want you to treat me like family." At the end he was saying things like, "Don't call me Mr. Jones. Call me Anthony." So afterwards we had some really good discussions about why he was doing all that. He's trying to confuse us between public and personal. We're here to try to get public business done and act professionally. He's here trying to make this personal because he doesn't want us to hold him accountable. He's hoping that he can confuse us and have us leave saying, "Aw, he's such a nice guy." And he was a very personable guy. But then we'll get distracted by that and we won't notice that he's double-talking us here and saying that he'll do one thing but really not.

So there have been some really great learning opportunities to look at the dynamics in our community. We have leaders looking at the power dynamics of which county leaders are getting campaign funds from which developers. What are the relationships like here? In our initial discussions of approaching the idea of changing that, we're meeting with a lot of resistance. Recently the county released its Housing Trust Fund Ordinance that they're supposed to be voting on on March 14. We've had to very quickly become experts to really dissect that and understand the details of what it means. We've learned that when they say people at 120 percent or under can be served by the trust fund, that's nice, but in most communities, the money ends up going to the people at the very tippy-top of that grouping. So you do a mandate that it has to go to the people below. We've learned that when they say that it has to be given out in the form of loans, there are big repercussions in the terms of providing rental housing for folks. We're learning about what state law will or will not allow in terms of what becomes affordable. Leaders have been studying inclusionary zoning ordinances and what has worked well in different communities. We've learned about credit and that there's all sorts of credit issues involved in these housing programs.

—Haley Grossman

Going to jail

My first semester in college I organized a vanload of people to go to the School of Americas protest at Fort Benning, Georgia. That was really a turning point for me, because the whole first six months of college I felt sort of on my own. Even in the activist community I felt like I was more out there than anybody else. There wasn't much of a sense of community. I was looked at as a leader in the World Bank/IMF protests. Everyone expected me to be the one who was going to be arrested and spend all the time in jail. Nobody else was as decisive as to what their commitments were. When we went ahead of time, some people were saying, "Well, I have to get back for class," or "I can't stay for more than a couple of days." But as things went along everybody got really energized by what happened. We had a really great affinity group of people from the university and some high school kids from the area and a couple other folks. What wound up happening was that we had a very strong first day of protests [at Fort Benning]. Then the second day was the day that a lot of the arrests happened. I remember actually going ahead and getting arrested with a couple of different people from my affinity group even though we were in different places.

It was a very intense experience in terms of the standoff between the riot police and our group of demonstrators. We were very well organized and very nonviolent in tone the way we stepped forward to challenge that police line. When that happened we ultimately got arrested. I went into jail with a large group of people and it was an amazing experience being in the cell that night with a group of guys that I got to know really well. But at the same time I was concerned whether any of my group was going to be outside when I got out, or whether they had all packed up and gone home.

The next morning I had my arraignment and the government papered my case because they wanted to get people out of jail. I made my way back to the place where we were staying, knocked on the door and was very moved when I realized that everybody from my group was still there. Not only that, but two of the other people from our group were still in jail. Those two wound up staying in jail for a week of solidarity, which they hadn't planned on. I went from being concerned about being a leader and everybody else being finicky to being on the outside doing support work for people who actually were in jail. That was very good for me and I think for them. That week helped galvanize a much stronger sense of community and a more committed group of activists at the university. That wound up being the group that did a lot of work on a lot of other issues, in terms of violence and economic justice in Latin America.

—Nicholas Graber-Grace

Campaign for immigrant rights

In 1997 I coordinated a legislative campaign around immigrant rights where we were seeking to create a basic safety net of services and support for people who were going to lose SSI [Supplemental Social Security] and food stamps and health care as a result of the 1996 Federal Welfare Bill. For people that don't remember, the Federal Welfare Bill basically cut legally present immigrants from a variety of public services even though they had followed all the rules in coming to this country. They had green cards and everything. Many of them were on route to becoming citizens. Newt Gingrich and his pals said, "They're no longer eligible for a basic safety net."

We developed an agenda whereby we were trying to replace that with state-funded programs and extend those so that people would not be in as dire straits and would still be able to get food stamps and health care and some supplemental income (for disabled people). The reason that it was amazing work is that I was working for a coalition called the Massachusetts Immigrant and Refugee Coalition. They had about 103 member groups throughout the state that weren't particularly tightly tied to the coalition. They saw it as mostly a resource and information entity. It had never really engaged them in developing their leadership around organizing or grassroots lobbying because most of their legislative work had been on federal stuff. So when I was hired—in January, at the start of the legislative session—it was to really use this crisis as an opportunity to engage member groups in a more meaningful way at the state house and push to win the agenda.

It was a whirlwind few months because I had to think of those 103 groups and how I could prioritize. I couldn't involve all of them equally. Would we focus in certain parts of the state where we needed to impact certain legislators? Would we focus with the groups who had the most capacity? Would we focus on the groups that had the least capacity but [a great deal of] interest and therefore this was the moment to really cultivate that interest? We had to figure out how to create a structure that would build some new leadership and deal with the fact that we have a legislature in Massachusetts that is a very insider's game.

The groups were mainly service providers. Most of them were not organizing groups, but they wanted to get involved. In a fairly short period of time we had an Immigrant's Day at the statehouse, pulled together with a steering committee. We had somewhere between 500 and 700 people. It was fabulous. The end result was that we won a lot of what we set out to win. We didn't get everything. But we have a very conservative speaker who's very cautious about money, particularly about doing anything that might have long-term implications in the state budget. He was saying no to everything. We turned him around, basically, through a carefully-orchestrated campaign that focused on his inner circle of legislators that he trusted to push him.

There were people that it was their first time testifying in public. There were people who it was their first time at the statehouse. The experience of both building on that leadership as well as winning a lot of what we had set out to win—that was definitely my best work.

—Janet Groat

Laughing all the way to the bank

One of the finest organizing experiences I've had was in Duluth, Minnesota, where we were trying to negotiate with First Bank, which was the largest banking system in Minnesota. We had gotten them to agree to negotiate with us. We were all set to go to a meeting in the president's conference room to get the bank to negotiate more home mortgage and home improvement loans in the neighborhoods and community of Duluth. We get a call a half hour before the meeting and we are told that we are not going to be negotiating and that instead he had brought in some of his cronies to give us a lecture about economic development. At that point we were strategizing in our office. We quickly thought, "What should we do? We should not just back out of this meeting. We should go find out what we're going to do."

On our way over there, in the lobby of the bank, was this little concession stand that sold popcorn. Cindy Evanson, a single mom who was one of our leaders, grabbed a bag of popcorn and went upstairs. We all sit down. Right before the bank president speaks—he had also invited the media—Cindy Evanson stands up and says, "Well, we thought we were coming to this meeting in order to negotiate an agreement with Mr. Gelb, the president of the bank. Instead, it looks like we've been asked to come to a show. Whenever I go to a show I buy a bag of popcorn. We're here to listen. We figure that after all these people have spoken we'll start our meeting." His business buddies from the chamber of commerce and the local utilities couldn't laugh out loud, but you could see them kind of giggling under their breath. The media turned all their TV cameras toward us and then put them right back onto him. They were audibly laughing. That was so much fun.

—Paul Cromwell

Demanding safer schools

One of the most fun actions I ever had was an action in an elementary school in a blue-collar neighborhood in San Francisco, called Excelsior District. My director asked me to go there because she had met some parents. This school was mostly Hispanic and Asian. It was a very poor little elementary school. A large percentage of the classes were in trailers outside the school. So I did one-to-ones with members of a parent's group that met at the church. They would have a little group in one corner with a Chinese woman interpreting. Then there would be another large section that was Spanish. It was three languages.

It was all these parents, concerned about their kids, speeding traffic, potential gunshots, and stray bullets. They were worried about abductions because the property wasn't very secure. People could walk in and out. It was such an old school that some kids on the bottom floor had to go outside

Organizing helps community members learn how to negotiate with public officials on important public policy issues. Members of CLOUT (Citizens of Louisville Organized and United Together) meet with the Mayor of Louisville.

to go to the bathroom. There were no bathrooms in the trailers. There were these benches that were built into the wall at the playground. Kids could fall off on their heads. These teachers weren't doing well in this chaotic situation.

The school superintendent at that time was writing his Ph.D. and experimenting with school district work. He would take every single faculty and staff member out of the school if it didn't meet strict standards. He'd take all of them out and bring an all-new faculty in. This school was on the list because the scores were so bad. The teachers were working so hard, and the parents didn't want to see the teachers taken out. It was just this radical philosophy that this guy was doing. So that was the situation.

For that short spring, I went in and did visits and got to know people. It didn't take long for them to get a list of concerns. They got the interim principal comfortable enough to allow it to happen. Then we put pressure on the city because the superintendent hated the mayor. So that's the route we took, that the city has a responsibility. The school district is a public safety issue. We had this action. We had three months of work and like 200 parents and their kids packed into this cafeteria. There was this one Hispanic guy. I can't remember his name. He was one of the "pinners," so he was going to ask the mayor's assistant a question about having crossing guards. This guy [the mayor's assistant] was sharp. He was good. He was deflecting every question. He was very slick.

The stage had a set of stairs going down the hallway, so I grabbed this dad and took him aside. I said, "When you ask your question, you're going to have to be really tough." He didn't speak very good English. I said to him, "I want you to think about something. If you don't get that crossing guard, what could happen to your little girl?" He said, "Well, she could get run over." I said, "That's what I want you to think about when you're up there."

So he got up to the mic and he asked the mayor's assistant about this crossing guard. The mayor's assistant sort of glossed it over and said, "Well, we're doing the best we can, blah blah, blah." Then the guy, in his broken English, essentially said, "You didn't answer my question." He raised this tension. I saw the mayor's assistant just sit back in his seat and smile because he knew that he was being pinned. Then he said, "Are you going to tell the mayor to give us a crossing guard or not?" The guy said, "Yes."

I think that type of experience is what keeps me in the work. It's those moments like that.

—Ray Higgins, Jr.

Making schools safer for gay students too

I worked as an intern with the Virginia Organizing Project [VOP] during my third year at UVA [University of Virginia]. One day I come in and Joe Szakos says, "I have a project for you." And I'm thinking, "Well, this will be cool. I'll do something and then get to talk to someone on staff." But he tells me, "We've got a campaign we're thinking about doing." So two high school students—Lillian Ray and Nora Oberman— and I started meeting together. The city of Charlottesville school system did not have sexual orientation in their non-discrimination policies. This left the door open for a lot of harassment with no redress. So we decided to do this campaign and get sexual orientation added to the non-discrimination policies of the Charlottesville schools.

The three of us would meet with Ellen Ryan, the Lead Organizer for VOP, about the things that made sense in developing the campaign. We talked about how to meet with an official, how to write a letter to the editor effectively, how to talk to folks about this issue. We would role-play. We would sit down: "You're the mayor, this is so-and-so," for example.

In the second part of the meeting, the three of us and Joe and a number of folks who had worked on this issue in the past met to strategize. We'd come in and strategize in terms of what we needed to do to get this policy changed: letters to the editor, endorsements, and meetings with individual school board members. It was the first time I was held accountable for getting this stuff in: "All right Brian, you're going to get five letters to the editor on this issue. When you come back, we're going to ask you if you've got all five."

Seeing the role that strategy played in this process was a new piece for me. I had been involved in other things where stuff would happen that was very reactionary. We would go out—"We're really mad, this is really wrong"—and get a group of people together, but there was just no follow-up. There wasn't much thought into what we were doing and what the goal was. So this was the first time that I was beginning to see strategy as an integral part of this whole thing.

There are definite steps that will get you to the point where you can start meeting with officials and school board members. And that's what we ended up doing. We had a bunch of letters in the paper. We got to the point where we were getting letters in response, in the paper. People were getting involved. And then we prepared a couple of groups to go in and meet with key votes on that school board. There were seven on the school board, so we needed four. So we said, "We've got these two for sure, we need to check on this one and we need to swing some others." For the first time I was really thinking through this in a concrete "this is what needs to happen in order for this change to take place" kind of way.

They did change the school board policy as a result of this pressure from the group of citizens who had come together. And it wasn't just citizens who were working on sexual orientation issues. It was environmental groups. It was groups that had worked on living wage. It was groups that had worked on race issues. It was churches. It was a broad base of support to work on this change. That was the first campaign I got into.

—Brian Johns

The power of numbers (2)

When I came on staff at Family Matters, they had recently organized a community-built park; 600 people participated in the building of it, and that happened right before I started. There was a plan for a Chicago Park District field house to be built in this park, and the plan had been on the table since 1998. So when I came into the office and saw these plans, I wondered why it was 2001 and we still didn't have our field house. The answer to me was, "Well, the talks have been sort of stymied, and the Park District doesn't really want to build it anymore." They made this commitment to the community; they had a public meeting in 1998 where they presented the plans for this building. People in our neighborhood have a long history of broken promises that have been made to them, and this was just one more thing.

So, we restarted talks with the Chicago Park District. To begin with, we kept it on a leadership level, the leadership of different community organizations. I put together a coalition of organizations in the neighborhood who had been involved with this issue back three or four years when it was first going on. We had the leadership of those organizations, and then some of the key leaders from the parent groups that we run going to these meetings with the Park District. Finally, the Park District agreed in October that they'd build a field house, but they didn't want to build it in the park. They wanted to build it as an attachment to the school, which is about a block away and across a busy street, because then they could just build a small, little space in the parking lot and use all the school's facilities as a field house. And there are tremendous issues with that. The Chicago Park District is moving in that direction in the city of Chicago of using school facilities. They don't give the school any extra money for custodians or security purposes, which means the burden falls upon the schools to clean up, to keep it safe, and it means the community can't use a gymnasium or anything until the school is out of there, which on most days is 5:00 because there are sports programs. So we told them that was unacceptable, and they said, "Well, this is your option: take it or leave it."

So we went to the streets and did a petition campaign for the Park District to put it in the park; we collected over 1,000 signatures. That didn't go anywhere. We did a postcard campaign to the mayor because in Chicago, the mayor is king and the alderman are princes of fiefdoms, basically. We had over a thousand postcards sent to the mayor. He said to the Park District, "OK, these people are annoying me. What are we going to do about this?" The mayor had us go on this tour of school parks in the city so we could see how well these school-use facilities are going. We didn't see how well they were going.

I had been saying for a long time that the only way the Park District was going to agree that the building needed to be in the park was to see the community and to hear the community, beyond petitions. Our alderman was dead set against us having a community accountability session with the Park District because his experience of those types of meetings are that they only turn into screaming matches and nothing is ever accomplished from them. We decided to plan a community meeting in the spring. We did a lot of work out in the community talking to people so they were aware of the issue so when they came they were giving opinions and were informed rather than just reacting. We worked with people on communication skills, on how to stand up and say what you think without screaming and yelling.

We had 250 people attend this community meeting, and the Park District was sitting up there and the alderman was sitting up there. The Park District presented their little plan for why they thought it needed to be attached to the school and then we had the local school council give a rebuttal, because the local school council didn't want the building in their school. Then we opened up to community comments and over forty people stood up and spoke, and they just spoke so passionately and so articulately. No one yelled; no one called the Park District names. Everyone just said, "You know, these are kids; we don't want them crossing the street to the field house. We know what's best for our community. We know what's best for our school. Give us what we want."

The alderman had told me he wanted to speak last. He takes the mic, and he says, "Park District, you have listened to my community. Take this back downtown: give my community what it needs." That was much stronger than anything he had ever said. But he'd never seen 250 people present in a room. We had media there covering the meeting. The Park District said at the end of the meeting, "OK, we hear you. We'll come back with some different plans."

A week later we got a call, "OK, you win. We'll put it in the park." And then we worked with them that the community is going to be involved in the whole process so they're going to be able to vote on which design they like for the building, where they want the entrance to be, etc.

It's weird to be at the close of that now because that's been such a big part of my life for the last year. Not that we haven't been doing other stuff, because we have. But when you win something that you devoted all that time to, what do you do now?
—Emily Gruszka

Getting students involved

We had a situation in Alaska where we found out that the Anchorage school district was spraying pesticides throughout the schools. We did some research and found out that these were chemicals that were very harmful, particularly for children. I began working with an organization called Alaska Youth for Environmental Action. It was a relatively small group of young people and people from our organization that worked together for more than a year. We were able to convince the administration of the school district and the school board to implement a policy of least toxic pest management. So we were able to get the chemicals out of the schools.

Probably the most important thing, though, is that young people were involved in this over the course of time at teach-ins where we worked with them to learn techniques of organizing: how to research the health effects of the chemicals, how to do interviews with the media, how to write testimony, how to give public testimony—how to make the change that we actually created while we were doing it. That, to me was one of the most satisfying things, because the results were fairly apparent quickly, and it was really great to see the young people inspired to be able to take off and do some stuff on their own and then see them continuing in other areas of organizing because of their great success.

That was really fun. So many of the things we do, we may not see the results for . . . we may never see the results of what we do in our lifetimes. That was one example of something that had a fairly immediate and measurable success, and it was very satisfying.

—Pamela Miller

Starting young

I came into organizing very early, around the age of fourteen. I organized my fellow classmates to do a sit-in, civil disobedience, around the militarization of the island [Puerto Rico] and the Navy and what have you. We did it secretly. We actually told our parents that we were going to the bio center. There's a biology center that used to be at one of the sites on the islands. We were part of the advanced classes so we had all these classes that allowed us to do field trips and whatever. We told them that we were doing this field trip to Vieques.

—Lisbeth Meléndez Rivera

National People's Action

As a young organizer, I really got hooked on organizing at the National People's Action annual meeting in Washington, D.C., in 1976. National People's Action is a federation of local organizations around the country, with a home office and training center, the National Training and Information Center, in Chicago. In 1976, I was a twenty-one-year-old organizing apprentice put in charge of the logistics of getting several bus loads of people from Providence, Rhode Island, to Washington, D.C., for the National People's Action annual meeting.

We had a wonderful time. The logistics were a mess. But when we finally arrived in our Trailways buses, we spent three days running around Washington and the suburbs in little yellow school buses with hundreds

Puerto Ricans demand the demilitarization of the island of Vieques.

of people from all over the country. We went to visit government officials, usually unannounced and often at their homes, to talk about affordable housing, crime, utility rates, and all the other issues we were working on in our local neighborhoods at the time. It was exhilarating to do direct actions with specific, reasonable demands on so many issues with so many people at one time.

—Ellen Ryan

Demanding representation

I think one of PHAR's [Public Housing Association of Residents] finest hours was when we were in this struggle with Charlottesville City Council to get two public housing resident seats on the Housing Authority Board of Commissioners. One evening the group got itself together, turned out forty or fifty people to City Hall, big enough to make it look full. They made signs and brought their kids.

We had a lineup of speakers and they each said their piece to City Council, explaining why it was so important to have residents on this board which was making key decisions that would affect residents' lives. They were cheering for each other after each speaker and holding up signs. They had some of the leaders' kids in there holding up the signs. It was just high energy. It was good. And they won it. They got the seats. I think they got a sense, at that point, that they could really affect how the city works, at least the part of the city that directly governed them and their neighborhoods.

—Ben Thacker-Gwaltney

Keeping in touch

One campaign that I liked a lot was in Minnesota. Members of a small, rural, county organization were upset because after their school district was consolidated with another small school district nearby, parents suddenly started getting upwards of $200 in long distance charges on their telephone bills because their kids were calling each other. They were in separate local telephone exchanges even though they were only twelve miles apart from one another, and every call was an intrastate long distance call. It was cheaper to call New York or California than it was to place calls between the two local exchanges.

The parents thought it would be simple enough to get the state Public Utilities Commission to give them something called extended area service, which would combine the two exchanges into one local calling area. However, the Public Utilities Commission denied their request, saying, "Oh no! You don't have enough population to justify that."

Rather than give up, this small group of people managed to take on the major telephone companies and the state legislature and win. They did it primarily by talking to people in other school districts who were in the same situation. The most powerful conservative Republican legislator in the state happened to live in the same school district as the local group and happily introduced a bill to create local telephone dialing areas in consolidated school districts throughout the state. Rural legislators from around the state stood up with their phone bills in their hands in committee hearings, waving their phone bills around saying, "Yeah, my own kids need this! Look at this! It's a $125 phone bill!"

I think what I liked about it most was that the legislature offered to cut a deal with the group, to allow only their two local exchanges to be combined and leave the rest of the state the way it was. The group wouldn't go for it, and held out for statewide reform. I felt really proud to be working with people who cared about their own predicament, but weren't willing to leave out the rest of the rural communities in the state in order to get what they wanted.

Even though the telephone industry had thirty-two lobbyists in the legislature trying to kill the bill, it passed. Maybe twenty-five people in a town of 1,600 spearheaded a statewide effort to get the legislature to pass a new kind of extended area service in Minnesota called School District Extended Area Service.

—Ellen Ryan

Making neighborhoods safer

In 1983, I helped build a coalition that consisted of several disenfranchised neighborhoods in Denver. We pulled in Metropolitan Organizations for People, the institutionally based organizing group. We did original door-to-door organizing in neighborhoods north of the downtown area. Each neighborhood used to be a city itself absorbed by Denver during the early twentieth century. It's been a long time since I've been there so I don't know what the constituency of the neighborhoods looks like now, but at the time the older folks were Eastern Europeans who had settled to work in mine smelting and the industrial part of the city. Then there were newer Hispanic communities that had settled in the neighborhood more recently and even more recently, Southeast Asian new immigrant communities.

We were organizing around hazardous material transportation issues. There was this history of transportation planners just forcing all kinds of transportation corridors on the neighborhoods. The primary neighborhood, called Globeville, had literally been split by rail lines and two major interstate highways. One portion of the neighborhood was on one side of the highway and the other portion was on the other side of the highway. The intersection was nicknamed "the mousetrap" because instead of facilitating traffic it caught traffic. It was always a problem.

In 1982, a railroad car full of chemicals had been busted open. It filled the air with nitric acid fumes and a bunch of other stuff and forced everyone to evacuate. We were capitalizing on that. We had already done house meetings and were in the process of organizing. Then in August of 1984, a truck carrying military torpedoes overturned in the mousetrap—the intersection of Interstate 25 and Interstate 70. The containers were punctured and fuel was leaking into the road. One of the torpedoes was literally lying in the backyard of one of the people who ended up being a primary leader. It just spilled off the highway and rolled into the backyard. The accident prompted the evacuation of several neighborhoods, about 10,000–15,000 people. This ended up being a high profile campaign. We bought test bombs, which are empty shells that look like real bombs, at the surplus store. We invaded the mayor's office with these test bombs and said, "This is what it feels like."

We ended up working with a couple national groups to create a model nuclear and hazardous material transportation ordinance. We won the ordinance in Denver and then moved that into a couple of other cities in Colorado. Finally, the state intervened and we were able to influence some state legislation. That was one of the more fun campaigns I've been engaged in.
—Gary Sandusky

Protesting NAFTA

Our members in Montana and North Dakota had become very frustrated with the North American Free Trade Agreement and had gone through all the usual channels trying to get something accomplished. And so they decided to block the border with Canada for a day. It was a great action. A lot of work went into cultivating allies, so we had the churches there, the unions, rural small business people, farmers, and ranchers. We worked with the border guards and blocked truck traffic for about half a day. No one was arrested. One of the best visuals was of a member who had a wheelbarrow that was loaded with manure, and a sign stuck in it that said, "Free Trade and US farm policy." That photograph made all the papers in Montana and North Dakota, and some of the national press picked it up. It was a fun action; people enjoyed it.
   —Kevin Williams

Walking for justice

I participated less as an organizer and more as a participant, but this was kind of a formative thing for me: In the summer of 1992, before the Measure 9 vote, there was a two-week walk from Eugene, Oregon, to Portland, called the Walk for Love and Justice, which was a semi-interfaith effort instigated by the lesbian community of Portland, a group called the Lesbian Community Project. In each of the towns they stopped in, the goal

NAFTA opponents in Montana block the U.S.-Canada border to protest the trade agreement.

was to have a social event to talk to people about the situation and engage. I was really lucky in that I was the one who was picked to go from my organization.

Walking through the Willamette Valley and through lots of those little tiny towns, when this was still a very new issue and people were still very freaked out about it, there were times when it was pretty scary. It was the first time I think I truly felt at risk for standing up for what I believed in. We suffered vandalism and all kinds of insults and things. Sometimes, when we were near a bigger town, there'd be lots of people with us, but the core of the group was only twenty people, it was really small. One day, we were walking on some little back road, and it was very quiet, and this same pickup passed our group twice, with the gun rack and all that. It was one of those moments when you're thinking, "Okay, there's no one around. Here we are with our little flags." It was one of those moments when you start strategizing like, "Okay, where's the ditch? Where could I hide?" We were fine, nothing happened, I guess he was just curious. God only knows.
—Kelley Weigel

Controlling waste

I think one of the first victories I had was in 1996, with a group of people up in the Minot area that I had originally brought together to try to beat back an out-of-state waste dump. They lost on that issue, the dump came in, although they got some restrictions put on it, and then the organization broke up because of some internal conflicts. I went up [in 1996] and rebuilt the organization, person by person, and the first thing that they took on, they looked around themselves and said, "You know, in a way it's sort of too late for the present dump, but dumps draw dumps, and what we oughta do is go through and get municipal solid waste zoning in Ward County." And they set about to do that, with incredible leadership from people. We had one woman who basically wrote the ordinance, with a lot of help from other professionals and so on, but she just did that. She was good at it. We had another bunch of guys who were good at talking to people, I don't know how many meetings they had with different county commissioners, and they swung several votes around. And even though there was a big, multinational corporation that didn't want that zoning to happen, they got that zoning through the county commission, and there's never going to be another big, out-of-state waste dump in that county, I'll guarantee you. So that was a really proud moment. It was really the first time where I had that kind of experience where a group that I had built, members that I had recruited, leaders that I had helped to come into leadership had pulled together an effective campaign to get an important win for their community, and it was very elating, it really was.
—Mark Trechock

I got assigned to work on this massive national housing problem, which was the potential loss of subsidized housing units. A lot of people in Washington would have said, "Well, I've got to work on this problem so that means I have to talk to people on Capitol Hill and talk to experts and write papers and get op-eds placed." A lot of that never even occurred to me. What did occur to me was that I needed to get a bunch of tenants together. There were 400,000 tenants, or whatever—I knew the number then; I don't remember it now—who were potentially affected by this and none of them knew about it, except for a few in Chicago and I think some in Boston. Nobody else even knew this was coming at them and it was coming at them like a freight train. I figured, "Well, if there's a solution, the tenants have to be part of the solution." I got quite a bit of flack from Washington people for this.

I called a meeting. My boss, Barry Zigas, who was a real Washington insider, was very supportive of me. I called a meeting and I invited the experts and the advocates and the Legal Aid people and some tenants. The experts and Legal Aid people said, "Well, why should we go to that meeting? If there are tenants there it's going to be at such a low level. We can't really have a serious discussion on the issue because they don't understand the technical aspects of the issue." So basically it became a meeting of tenants and tenant organizers. There was a guy named Victor Bach from New York. There was a lawyer named Jim Grow from the National Housing Law Project and a couple other people who were experts and kept coming. They were great.

So we built a whole network of tenant groups that were working on this in Boston, Chicago, Dallas, San Francisco, L.A. These folks kept meeting together, mostly people of color, mostly African-American women. They decided that they wanted to form a national organization, a national alliance of HUD tenants. I wasn't sure that was a good idea. I had some sense of how difficult it would be to sustain an organization like that. At this point they were like a committee under the umbrella of the National Low-Income Housing Coalition. We could get them scholarships to conferences and all those kinds of things. I had a salary to staff them. But that's what they wanted to do. They were very clear-minded about it and it was their business, not mine. I was like, "We'll support you if you do it. Is it a good idea? I don't know. But it's not my decision." So they formed that organization that's been around now for eleven or twelve years. It's had quite an impact on HUD. A lot of the local groups have preserved a lot of housing. I don't know if anybody has a number, but I'm sure it's thousands of units. It never would have happened without those tenant groups and without some of the legislation that we got passed.
—Larry Yates

Marching for women's lives

It's funny because if you had asked me six months ago what my proudest achievement was, the answer would have been different, but today I can tell you that having every women's group on the Eastern Seaboard support low-income women and women of color and go to Washington, D.C., on April 25 [2004] for the March for Women's Lives was one instance of incredible pride. When I was working as a senior organizer our collective goal was 1.2 million people, and in fact the official number came out at 1.15 million. To stand at the Mall and see that number of people there. It was all of these people from many walks of life. For one moment we were all there understanding how important reproductive justice was and how important eliminating sexism was. It was incredibly anticlimactic at the end, when everybody went home. I think they should teach organizers about the adrenaline crash because we all go through it and it's hard.

—Lisbeth Meléndez Rivera

Addressing local needs

I am often reminded of an important organizing lesson I learned with the first group I was Lead Organizer for, in Absarokee, Montana. This community was actually the first hard-rock mining area that we organized. Prior to 1976 we had been organizing almost exclusively around coal issues. Most of our board members were farmers and ranchers and other community people who at that time cared about the expansion of strip mining from the East to the West and how to control it. We had an incredible discussion at a board meeting about whether we should expand to other issues. This was one of our first major organizational crossroads— should we go beyond coal and energy issues—it wasn't like coal and energy issues weren't complex and organizationally consuming enough.

Coal and energy involved water problems. We were engaged in a major campaign to institute the first water reservations system in the Yellowstone River. There were air pollution issues going on, and people were working to make sure that large coal-fired power plants associated with new strip mining would be clean. And we were working on the strip mining reclamation, so there were a lot of complicated pieces to this large campaign.

In the midst of all this comes this group that says, "Well, we're not working on coal mining. We're working on hard rock mining, but it's kind of the same thing. We really like the model that your outfit is using where you build a local affiliate, you build a local community group in the county, and the leaders in that county decide what they want to work on, pick their issue, and then you all get together and figure out how to lobby the state legislature collectively. We like this model, but you know we're not working on coal."

There were tensions around staffing and resources. Could the organization really cover all its current campaigns? Finally, I think it was probably Bob Tully, one of the leaders of the group who hadn't said a whole lot, who finally said, "You know, in the long-run, all of these issues are pretty much the same. It doesn't matter whether it's a coal company or a hard-rock mining company. This is all about whether we as Montana farmers, ranchers, citizens, or whatever, whether we're going to be in control and be able to decide our own future and destiny, or we're going to let these companies decide our future and destiny." Everybody said, "You're right, Bob," and they voted unanimously to expand the organizing to communities impacted by hard-rock mining. So they said, "All right, send the organizer out there to organize the affiliate."

So I go out to organize a new affiliate and I must say it really is one of the most rewarding and fun things you ever get to do as an organizer—to go meet new people, go door-to-door in a new community, be part of creating a new organization. One of the people I found in the Stillwater was Mary Donohoe. She was a rancher who we had known through family connections and was a member. I went up and sat down with Mary at her kitchen table, and I said, "Mary, who are some people in this community that you think would be interested in helping form an organization?" Mary pulls out the rural phone book. Under Absarokee and the surrounding community maybe, oh I don't know, 1,000 names in the phone book, something like that. And she started in the A's, and we sat there for four hours to get to the Z's, and she told me about everybody and who was there and who might be interested. I went out and talked to a bunch of the names on that list to build our organizing committee.

We called the first organizing committee meeting in town, and we had it at the community center, which is always a great place to have a meeting. We had about twelve members there. The community center was right on the main street of this little town, and the highway is the main street, like in many little towns. The traffic goes right through town, and the community center is right on the corner, and it was the summertime, a hot day, and the doors were open, so you could hear the traffic.

One of the things we were talking about in this agenda was, what would be a good first local issue for the group to organize on, what are some local problems that you think a organization could address and deal with in this community? People were struggling with this question. Then this rumbling, huge truck goes by and it's so loud we had to stop the meeting. So everybody stops for a couple seconds; truck drives by. And then the organizer, me, I'm prodding people again, "Well what are some local issues; what are some local problems that we could address here?" About ten minutes later another truck drives by, and we have to stop the meeting again, right? So we're still struggling away; we're about twenty minutes, thirty minutes into this conversation, and the third truck comes by. And we stop the meeting, and I finally turn to somebody and said, "Well, what are these trucks?"

The meeting just erupted into a discussion about all these trucks going down the road from this old mine. They're dangerous as heck, and our kids are at our bus stops, and they're running twenty-four hours a day, and the bridges are wrecked and the roads are terrible. All of a sudden there's this incredible conversation about the problem of these trucks hauling chromite, a surplus mineral that was stored at the top of this old mine at the top of this farming community. They had to haul this chromite, a very heavy ore, in these huge trucks. So that night people said, "Can we do anything about this? If this is a problem, what can we do about it?"

People said, "Well, we could ask them to only go during the daylight hours. They shouldn't be hauling at night, and they shouldn't be hauling when the kids are on the school bus. You know the school buses are out at 6:30 in the morning picking up kids. And they shouldn't be hauling when kids are getting dropped by the school buses."

"Okay, that's a good idea. What else could we do?"

"They should be paying the county to fix these bridges and maintain the roads because of all these potholes."

"Okay, that's a good idea."

They came up with a whole bunch of things they thought they could do to make this trucking company solve the problem. So that was the organizing issue. They went on to have their first great action with the head of the trucking company, who came to a town meeting that they called. This is a little town again, so when you turn out 125 people at the community center for a town meeting, and you figure out the percentage of community people you turn out to this meeting, it's like, if you were doing this in New York City, you'd have a million people at your meeting. The members were organized—they placed their essential demands in front of this truck company who, of course, did not capitulate at all.

So they did a petition drive, ended up collecting up and down the road, over eighty miles, and talking to every single neighbor, every single person on the road. The petition eventually went to the county commissioner. They had a county commissioner meeting and successfully limited the truck traffic hours and got more money for the road maintenance and building fund and that sort of thing and got the road fixed. They won this issue, and they won it because they were tenacious, and they got out there and talked to every single neighbor and friend they had up and down this road.

With this first issue we started the first hard rock chapter, the affiliate called the Stillwater Protective Association. That affiliate was built in 1976, and they are still a chapter of Northern Plains Resource Council nearly thirty years later.

—Patrick Sweeney

Profile: Dave Mann
Consulting
(Life After Organizing)

Dave Mann is the former Director of the Minnesota Alliance for Progressive Action. He now works as an independent consultant to community organizations. He lives in Minneapolis and was interviewed in February 2003.

I grew up in central Pennsylvania, right outside of Harrisburg—a very white-bread environment. My upbringing was a middle class and working class mix. Later in life my dad started doing better, he became the president of Pennsylvania Blue Shield after I left, but he was sort of working his way up. I had three sisters, so we were just getting by for my early years.

I worked pretty hard as a kid. I had a job starting from age eleven, and then I went to college about an hour and a half north of there, Bucknell University. I was in school from '68-'72. It was interesting because being in school for me—and this is not something I am particularly proud of—was largely a social experience. I had been in a pretty restricted environment at home and this was my chance to get out, so I experienced the cultural aspects of that period more than the political aspects, but I was certainly touched by the political aspects. I realized that I could be sent off to war, and so I was sort of involved in the anti-war stuff, but not a lot.

When I got out of school, I was working in computers, first for the university and then in the private sector. Then about '78, someone invited me to a meeting of a local anti-nuclear group—there was a power plant being built about an hour away. We were also about an hour and half north of Three Mile Island. I must have been ready, because I went to this one meeting and someone gave a talk, and I bought four books and went home and started reading, and I just was consumed. I started volunteering and being involved with this local alliance.

And then in March, 1979, the accident at Three Mile Island happened, and it just catapulted me into a whole different path. I was, for about a year and a half, working a full-time job doing computer work, and then doing full-time volunteer organizing. I didn't actually get out of computers as a way to make a living until '87, but I increasingly worked part-time jobs so that I would have time to do this.

My work got involved with a range of things—it went from anti-nuclear/safe energy to utility rate reform. We were a small town. I was still living in the town where I went to school, and we were doing Central America solidarity work, labor solidarity work, all that kind of stuff. It's interesting, we just kind of plunged into it. None of us had any training. A lot of what we were doing, when I look back on it, was much more community education, and what I would call issue organizing as opposed to community organizing where you are really trying to build leadership and power. I think we accidentally built some leadership, and if I look back I can think of some great lessons.

But you know, probably the most interesting experience in that for me was not one that I would do again; for about a year I ended up representing our grassroots alliance in front of the state utility commission, opposing the rate increase that the utility company was trying to get for this nuclear power plant that basically was excess capacity—they didn't need it. It was a pretty interesting experience of being, essentially, a lay lawyer and getting to figure out how to use the system.

That period from '78 to '85 was really my introduction to this arena of work, and I loved it. The labor solidarity stuff opened my eyes about labor unions. The thing I realized during that period was how connected all the issues I worked with seemed to be, and how disconnected the various groups of people working on them were. I think that's what really led me down the path to coalition work. I did go to some conferences and I took some workshops, but I still wasn't learning a methodology or anything.

In '85 I went through a divorce and spent a couple of years just pulling back from everything and realized that I was really ready to make my passion also be my occupation. It was interesting, because during that time I had friends who taught at the university, and they would try and offer alternative career days for the students, and they would often bring me in. Even though I was doing computer work, I was coming in to talk about the other work, the organizing, and it was sort of interesting because I had to listen to my own advice in '85: This is what you care about, find a way to do it.

I think we all have things in our lives that influence how we deal with issues of justice. Mine was really an internal family dynamic. I had a mom who was overbearing and emotionally unstable, and I experienced a lot of abuse of power, is the way I would characterize it now. Now that I'm a dad, I realize what I should have gotten. I think that at some level, it tapped into my need for justice. The injustice that I experienced—and I couldn't have expressed it that way then, when I went through it as a kid—there was nothing I could do but figure out how to survive. But as an adult there was an opportunity to actually *do* something. It tapped a need in me.

I knew that I wanted to be involved in coalition work. My only real awareness of coalition work was the '84 Jesse Jackson presidential campaign, and so I initially set out to figure out a way to plug into the '88 Jackson campaign. I couldn't do it in this small town in central Pennsylvania and make money—at least, I didn't know how to do it at the time—and so through a friend and happenstance I landed in Minnesota. I spent a summer going around and looking, and found that there was going to be a Jackson campaign there, but there also was this group of people who were talking about forming something a little more permanent and institutionally based. And it just seemed right up my alley.

I volunteered my time trying to pull this coalition together. It was pretty interesting, because I didn't know anything about Minnesota politics or the players. I didn't really know anything about setting up a formal organization and running it. The thing that I had run in Pennsylvania was unincorporated, and I didn't have to deal with the IRS and foundation proposals and all that. So there was this one-year period of learning just a whole bunch of stuff. It was probably one of the most exciting periods of my life, professionally.

> • • • [W]e were trying to create something that no one had really—they didn't know what we were trying to create. We were trying to create this multi-constituency coalition that didn't have an issue. And people were really just boggled by this. It was fascinating. It was like a puzzle, trying to figure out how to put it together. • • •

Working with another guy who was from Minnesota, I helped to found this organization which became the Minnesota Alliance for Progressive Action in '87, and I worked there until 2000. For the first time I got involved in legislative issues, for the first time I got involved in electoral activities. I ended up running our electoral program. I didn't do a lot of lobbying, but a lot of my role was trying to figure out how to bring the legislative process to the grassroots, and then bring them back to the legislative process. I really had very little interest in being a lobbyist, and fortunately, one of our folks did.

I realize that having worked in the private sector I had a set of skills that were rare in an organization like this—organizational management skills. Setting up systems was my thing. It was an opportunity to apply things I knew to stuff I cared about. But the exciting part was more just meeting all the different people I got to meet.

It was also pretty interesting because we were trying to create something that no one had really—they didn't know what we were trying to create. We were trying to create this multi-constituency coalition that didn't have an issue. And people were really just boggled by this. It was fascinating. It was like a puzzle, trying to figure out how to put it together. The most dramatic piece of the year for us was when we got about six months into a planning process, we're all set, like a month away from launching something, and had this awakening one day that we were totally on the wrong track. And that we had to step back and start over. Not to start over in terms of relationships, but start over in terms of how we were approaching this. It made it a much better organization. There were some people who really had a lot of ownership about that strategy. But we recognized that it was going to be gone in a year if we did the first strategy. I guess just learning, for me, learning a lot more about politics in the more formal sense, both electoral and legislative, was exciting. And just understanding—the one thing that I really learned from Mel [Duncan, then the Executive Director of the Minnesota Alliance for Progressive Action]— was that so many times what you see is not what's going on. And learning to constantly figure out what really is going on.

I also thought a lot about how you build organizational capacity during that time. I remember pretty early on realizing that, while the issues all seemed important, what got me was the concept of how you learn to do work so that you can win on a consistent basis—whatever the issue was. Over time what I began to realize was that, even when we won, we sort of started over on the next campaign.

At one point, there was a guy we were supporting for governor, and there was a chance of my going to work with him if he won. I realized that was not what I wanted to do. I think part of it is that I believe that even when our friends get elected, there needs to be someone outside, pushing and holding them accountable. Maybe that's why I don't want to be a part of that; I don't want to run the risk of being inside and losing my vision.

A lot of my upbringing was about conforming. That's the message I got a lot. And I don't think I wanted to conform any more. Going to the governor's office would have been conforming, whereas staying outside and building power is not. It's weird, because it's not like I'm this totally alternative person. But there's a piece of me that wants to have just a foot outside the norm.

In the early '90s, we were dealing with much smaller budget shortfalls than now, and at the same time they were talking about cutting all these programs, the business community was in there asking for tax cuts—not unlike today—and we did this action. We actually had a meeting of our coalition where, as the organizers said, "We don't know what to do here, this is just a swamp."

It was one of those moments where, instead of having a proposal, we just said, "Blecchh," and the people in the room just kind of picked it up, and we developed this action, where—it was the year after the Twins had won the World Series, and they had these Homer hankies—so we developed our own hanky, on the top ten executive salary compensation packages in the state. Their name, their organization, and how much they got. And it

What makes a good community organizer?

In my mind, the primary role of a community organizer is to help people figure out how to address the concerns in their lives and build their own capacity for addressing those concerns in a way that alters power structures.

Organizers have to be good listeners. They have the ability to build trust with people. They have integrity; they can be counted on to do what they say they are going to do.

You've got to like people. I don't think you necessarily have to be an extrovert, but you need to like people. And there's a certain level—there's a weird balance of being empathetic but not getting caught up in empathy. Being empathetic but turning that empathy into a plan to help people deal with whatever's going on with them. I'm talking about the relationship to individuals, but obviously my belief is that those individuals come together into an organization of some kind. It doesn't have to be a formal organization, but people acting collectively. That's part of community organizing.

Over the years of interviewing people for jobs, the thing I look most for is instincts. I'm less concerned with their knowledge base and their theories and I'm much more concerned with, "What's your passion?" and "What are your instincts?" If you have those two things you can learn the rest. I don't think you can learn organizing if you don't have the passion and the instincts. And those instincts are a function of the things I said earlier: listening, liking people, those kinds of things. To some extent, you can teach some of that, but I think there's something in your core that has to be there. And that's not true for all social justice jobs, but it is true for organizing, I think.

You have to be willing to live outside the culture to some extent to do this. I'm in a strange position with my son now. The day he starts asking, "What do you do, Daddy?" it's like, all I can do is take him along and let him see. I've talked to a lot of organizers whose kids don't understand what they do. It's not like seeing a fireman on TV, or whatever.

I think one of the challenges, and that's something I might tell someone who's getting into organizing, is that, if you want to be a good organizer, you need to *plan* on how you're going to have time for reflection. Acting is only part—is probably the least important part—of the organizing game. It's where you see the culmination of what you've done, but the real important part is laying the groundwork and then reflecting on it afterwards.

I guess the other thing is, anyone who treats organizing as a job, as opposed to a passion, is probably not going to last.

—Dave Mann

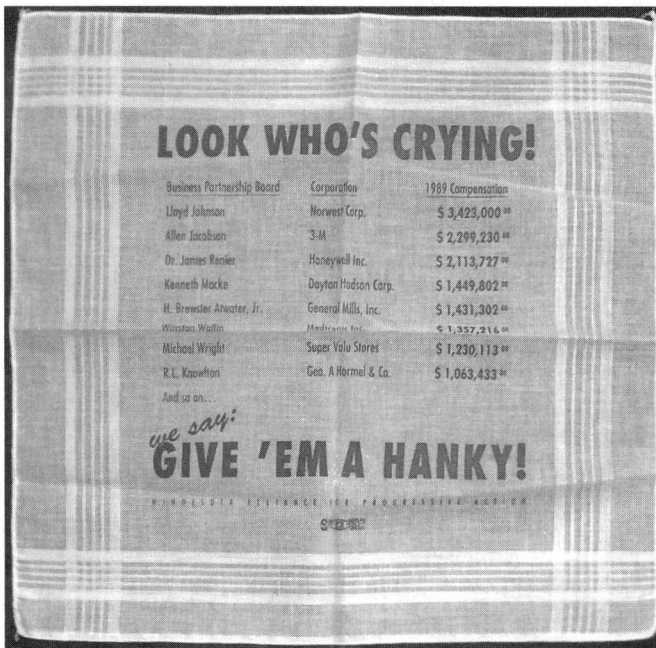

Community groups often use creative ways to make their points. At rallies and hearings, a group in Minnesota used a hanky that listed the top ten executive salary compensation packages in the state.

said, "Look who's crying!" listed their names, their organizations, and their compensations, and said, "Give 'em a hanky."

We did this whole rally that was sort of a mockery of tax cuts for the rich. You know, we need a tax break on our yachts, that kind of stuff. A very fun, creative thing, just to try to change the spirit. Well, we gave one of those hankies to every legislator, and for the rest of the session, every time the lackeys for the business community started talking about this stuff, a handful of people would just start waving these hankies on the floor—didn't say a word, they'd just wave them. It's really weird because we were pushing for an increase in taxes on the wealthy, and we didn't win that—but what we *did* do was change the tenor of the thing. We said, "Look, there is another aspect to this. These guys can't say, 'Cut the budget *and* give us tax cuts at the same time.'" It was a moment of realizing that you can, out of despair, create something, that being creative and fun can help change the dynamic, and that a symbol like that has a longer life than just the rally.

It became a collector's item, actually.

When I left MAPA it was with some sadness, but also recognizing that thirteen years was a long time for me to be with one organization, and it seemed particularly long because I had either been co-directing or directing for the last five years. I had at that point a three-year old. And my wife did social justice organizing, and it just was too much. So I took a break and came back as one of the dreaded consultants. And actually it was a pretty interesting process—I'm trying to remake what it means to be a consultant, not be the expert, but more of a collaborator. My real focus right now is on how we build power. What does it mean to build power, and how do we use issues as a tool, and not just as ends in themselves?

I facilitated a meeting recently where we were talking about the political climate and how do you really build power over the long term? And this woman had this to say, "Well, it seems to me we have to learn to realize that a loss can be a victory." And we're so accustomed to saying that we passed a piece of legislation, or we won a campaign, and sometimes losing it can actually be the best thing. But that's hard, because especially when you're fresh at organizing, you want that win. That's why I think the mentoring is so important. And the other piece of it is, if you're really organizing for systemic change, then what you're asking for is probably not going to be winnable on a short-term basis. You may figure out short-term wins that are building towards that, but ultimately—I mean, we can learn from the Right: how many times have they put stuff out there and we said, "You guys are crazy," and ten years later, it was law?

Disappointments Are Inevitable

We asked the organizers to recall their moments of greatest disappointment. What failures or defeats were the hardest to take?

Disappointment comes from a variety of sources

> Part of being in organizing is that you lose a lot. Early on I remember this article, "What do you do when you win?" Organizations are so used to losing that when they win they're kind of caught off guard. "Oh my God, what do we do now?"
> —Steve Bradberry

Some disappointments come from the nature of the work—
organizing doesn't always lead to the kind of change we had hoped for.

> Kind of a big, general frustration is that work at the grassroots level is so intense and involved, and it can be so painstakingly slow to achieve what seem like really small victories, when people with a lot of power, money, and influence can walk into an office and pretty much get exactly what they want in one visit. It seems like a real uphill battle for the purpose of making positive change.
> —Brett Kelver

> These are not easy fights. Certainly, I think the mood of this country over the past couple of years has become much more anti-democratic and much more greedy. I'm finding that the work is becoming more difficult. This is not easy work and you do run into defeats. You get knocked down, you get the wind knocked out of you, and you let that disappointment turn to anger. Then you figure out, "Okay, that's the reaction. They're making us react. What are we going to do next?"
> —Paul Cromwell

Some frustrations are with the organizers themselves:
if only I had done a better job. . . .

Most of my disappointments are stuff that I've failed to do. I put on an
energy conference and didn't do follow-through. And then it's too late, and
you've got to start all over again because the follow-through wasn't done. I
had excuses of being too busy or whatever, but that's always a threat, that
you're not going to follow through. That was huge.
    —DeAnna Woolston

My biggest disappointment was not building an organization in West
Virginia. I basically spent three years being a campaign director, pulling
people together and running a series of campaigns. But then realizing that
in fact, I had pulled together a group of people and we'd won some things,
and we'd raised some money, but I'd not built an organization. There wasn't
a group of leaders at the center of the organization.
    —Allen Cooper

In the very beginning, I had a bad experience, which we all had to learn
from. This was in regard to the tailings pit nearby the wild and scenic Rio
Grande [in New Mexico]. We started proposing some solutions to the
issue. One of the solutions we [Amigos Bravos] proposed was to increase
the size of the existing tailings facility. Quite a number of the activists in
the community didn't like that solution. They were the very people who
we needed to be in alliance with in order to win the fight. Although we
managed to work through our differences and ended up winning the larger
fight, which is to say we saved the Guadalupe Mountains, the incident really
wounded us as an organization in that community.
    We had to admit that we'd made a mistake. About five years later
we had a strategic planning session for the organization and some
representatives from that community came back and said, "Look, we need
your help, we want you to come back." We had done a great deal of outreach
work in the interim years. We respectfully avoided the community where
we'd run into trouble but slowly made friends with some of the individuals
and sought out their counsel and advice on other issues, and provided them
with public opportunities to speak about the issues that mattered to them.
When the community came to us asking for assistance, it was tremendously
gratifying. We came back a lot wiser and able to be a lot more effective.
    —Brian Shields

And sometimes you just plain get beat.

This is tough work. We have been pushing for a living wage ordinance here
in Jacksonville [Florida] to ensure that city workers and workers contracted
with the city are paid—not a minimum wage—but a living wage, which

the Living Wage Coalition here in Jacksonville determined would be $9.19 an hour with health insurance, $10.19 an hour without health insurance. We have a city that is in a frenzy right now of greed and deal-making and city incentives in order to get ready for the 2005 Super Bowl. Politicians are stepping all over themselves to make sure that businesses in town are getting tax breaks and government handouts. And yet they are ignoring, in my mind, the lowest paid workers.

On Friday, there was a special subcommittee that had been set up to examine this living wage ordinance. They had heard from not only people who were extremely familiar with all the research but we also had forty people testify on behalf of the ordinance, representing over twenty different organizations in town. Only five people spoke against it. The researchers, including the city council's own researcher, brought in reports that said the post-studies have shown none of the dire predictions about living wage ordinances around the country before they were passed have come true. Not only have these living wage ordinances directly benefited the workers

Living wage campaigns across the country face obstacles, yet keep rising up.

involved, but they have also made very good business sense in terms of increased worker productivity and morale. It's good business sense in terms of worker absenteeism and turnover.

We had all of those testimonials and the City Council committee voted three to one not to recommend it [the living wage ordinance]. It has to do with ideology, certainly not with a price tag.

—Paul Cromwell

In Alabama, the failure of the tax reform plan in 1992 was devastating. I mean it was one of those where the members had to pick me back up and say, "Look, we knew we were in this for the long haul." I still had hopes on the last night of the legislature up until 8:00. I thought we were still going to be able to get it through the Senate. And it ultimately fell apart. We had a lot invested in that. I was the only staffer at the time. I had driven 4,000 miles in January doing workshops. I did twenty-eight workshops on tax reform that winter in church basements and such.

Our role in that effort was to address how this comprehensive tax-reform package was going to affect poor people. Business had its reasons for being at the table, and education had its reasons for being at the table, but that was our role. Nobody below the poverty line was going to pay income taxes, if that plan had passed. And to this day we have the highest income tax burden in the country on a family of three at the poverty line. It's about $333 a year. You multiply that by the number of years since 1992 and that's how much money we've taken out of the pockets of low-income people because it didn't pass. So it's going to be hard to rest until we pass something to fix that.

—Kimble Forrister

The Living Wage Campaign got struck down by the state supreme court [in Louisiana]. Certainly that was a disappointment, because it was a great campaign. What happened was we had an election in the city of New Orleans to raise the minimum wage because we are home-rule chartered. People have the right to vote this type of thing into being.

We had a coalition that was really great. We got all these organizations for a meeting we were having. We had people come out and they were speaking out on behalf of the minimum wage. "Why is the minimum wage a good thing?" You had labor, community people, and churches. We split everybody up in small groups; there were people who wanted to work strictly with the churches and people who wanted to work strictly with the students. The members led the conversations. Then the people came back and said, "This is what we're going to do." They had the whole list with names. That was a tremendous thing.

The Living Wage Campaign, as a whole, just had so many pieces to it. You couldn't open your mouth without us shoving living wage down it. When the electoral thing started out we had one city council person, one mayoral candidate, and everyone else who was running for office was against the living wage. By the time it was over all the city council candidates were for the living wage and there was only one mayoral candidate who was against it. We turned that whole thing around.

So we won at the election almost two to one, an overwhelming victory. Then it went to court because businesses were saying, "It's unconstitutional," because there was a law that had been passed saying local municipalities could not raise their minimum wage above the federal level.

The first judge agreed with us, that we had the right to vote into effect a higher minimum wage. Then it went to the state supreme court. At the state supreme court one judge ruled in our favor. The rest of the judges were all over the board. They were not in unison. They had various reasons to overturn it. So that was a disappointment.

—Steve Bradberry

The issue that I worked the hardest on and was probably the most passionate about was trying to change the makeup of our Oil and Gas Commission. In Colorado, our Oil and Gas Commission is made up of seven members appointed by the governor, and six of them are currently working for the industry they're regulating. And so their mandate to protect public health, safety, welfare, and the environment is often times overlooked because they want to benefit the industry and get the resources out of the ground as quickly as possible, as economically as possible.

We've been trying to pass this conflict-of-interest legislation that bans them from working for the industry they're regulating. It was exciting this year just because the speaker of the house happened to be the representative from the area that was being most impacted. We had a great person to introduce the bill, high profile. And we made it more high profile by going to Denver, which, for us, is a little bit of a hike—it's a four-hour drive. We did some events on the capitol steps to bring attention to the fact that gas and oil drilling wasn't without impact and was truly affecting people in their homes. Wells can be built 150 feet from your house, and so we set up a mock rig 150 feet from the State House, big fanfare, big signs: how do you enjoy having a well 150 feet from your house? Got a lot of press around that!

We also did some other things like had a tour with some street theater with a hen-house theme to it. I was running around in a chicken suit with people that I care about and that are passionate but still laughing a lot. That combined pretty much most of the things that I love: humor and passion and friendship and working for something you believe in.

We ended up getting it passed through the House on first and second reading and they decided somehow to do a third reading. In the meantime, the oil and gas industry flew in thirteen different people who were CEOs and had a lot of influence and money, and hired an additional nine lobbyists. So pretty soon you couldn't even walk in the hallways because it was so filled with suits. They defeated it by one vote. They were able to turn just enough people. It was disheartening to have our democracy so easily sold out and have what was clearly an issue of public interest so easily manipulated by money.

But that was also a victory because we really did get a huge amount of media and really pushed the issue from something that a handful of folks understood to something that people had at least heard about.

—Matt Sura

One of the first campaigns that I was involved in taking the lead on was a campaign that we were working with our young people on. I had just started at SWOP [Southwest Organizing Project in New Mexico]. It was about getting a policy changed, but the bigger issue was about how young people—particularly young people of color—are being criminalized and stereotyped and scapegoated.

One of the ways that we were addressing this was to get this policy changed at the local mall that said that young people aged twenty-one and under could not walk in groups of five or more during the week or three or more during the weekends. So we thought, that's something that we ought to be able to get changed. We did all this research, and we had actions, and we got cards signed, and we did a boycott. We did all this stuff, and at some point we filed a lawsuit, because our feeling was that it was being enforced in a discriminatory manner. Only young people of color were being targeted by this particular policy—like ninety-five percent. What would happen was they'd get taken into the hallways of the mall, back into the offices that they have kind of hidden. They'd get photographed, and patted down, and often cited with criminal trespassing, and all this kind of stuff. So ninety-five percent of the people who had that done to them were Hispanic.

We filed the suit in federal court, lost, and then appealed, and the court of appeals basically said that Hispanics don't exist as a class. We were at the point where we could go to the Supreme Court, where the chances aren't good and we could get our case hurt. And then I got a letter from the mall, and it was like, "Okay, we're about to sue *you* for all this money. But we won't, if you agree that you won't appeal this." So we had to agree not to. That was a tough one.

Well, the policy didn't end up getting changed with regards to the mall thing, but the practice of detaining young people and photographing them and citing them with criminal trespassing has stopped. That was part of the settlement. So that was a victory.

—Robby Rodriguez

Sometimes failure comes when victory seems closest.

There've been a lot of disappointments, of course, and most of the disappointments have to do with the inability to gain enough power to push an issue over the top. And it seems like they are more bitter when you actually come close, because if you really get nowhere, you don't raise that hope within yourself that you're actually going to win.

I remember the first year I was here, out-of-state waste was a big issue, because North Dakota had a number of proposals for out-of-state waste landfills that had surfaced. And we were trying to get a federal bill that would give our states and communities the ability to regulate out-of-state waste. A federal judge had decided that this is interstate commerce, and that states can't regulate it unless Congress gives them the authority. It was a pretty big issue in the '93–'94 Congress.

The first time I went to Washington to lobby, in the spring of 1994, was on this issue with a bunch of wonderful people from all over with the Western Organization of Resource Councils, including two of my own members. And we managed, by the end of 1994, to get bills passed in both the House and the Senate, but it was late in the session, the bills were quite different, and we couldn't get a concurrence, and at the last minute, we failed to get that bill passed. That fall, then, leadership of both houses changed. The new chair of the House committee which would deal with it had something like thirteen out-of-state waste dumps in his district, and we've never been able to get anywhere with this bill since then. So, it was a very bitter disappointment that we could get a bill through both houses of Congress, but not get it passed.

—Mark Trechock

One of the frustrations with organizing and trying to create long-term change is that many people come with this impression that the government somehow is going to solve the problem. That if we just either ask them or we pass a law that somehow that will be enough to make it better. I have long-term frustration with the fact that we passed the national Surface Mining and Reclamation Act. Citizens from all over the country, including out here in the West, came together and lobbied their Congressional people and others to try to control the coal industry and the damage they had created both in Appalachia and the Midwest and other states, and were attempting to do it out here in the West. That was an incredible effort, when you think about citizens taking on a powerful industry like that, to actually get the Congress to pass an act to regulate it. It took many, many years to get that done and a lot of perseverance—our members working in concert with people from Kentucky and Tennessee and West Virginia, Indiana, Pennsylvania, all these other states.

I think it was an incredible experience for our folks. When President Carter signed the Surface Mining Act in 1977, people were very proud of that. But it's not over with when you pass this law that says, "You will reclaim; you will not leave high walls; you will not have acid mine drainage." Well, guess what? Twenty-five, thirty years later we have mountain-top removal, which is one of the most disgusting practices on the face of the

earth, and you still have acid mine drainage, and you still have companies that are not complying with the law. People have to recognize that in order to make this happen you have to stay at it, which is one of the reasons why I think community organizations are so important, because it's not just passing a law, it's implementing it. It's the demand that they enforce this with the companies—and that goes on to this day in terms of the frustration of enforcement of the Surface Mining Act. It also reminds me that for long-term change we must work to build power to the point of governance. That is, until our leaders who remain accountable to their communities are part of the governance of their communities, we will not completely succeed.
—Patrick Sweeney

And other times, opportunities can be snatched from the jaws of defeat. That's where real organizing comes in.

Losing is always disappointing. We just lost a huge campaign yesterday. But I think I learn the most from losing, so I am actually excited. I'm like, "Now we have an opportunity, especially because our members are upset, to take that energy and focus it into something constructive—into a more aggressive and more assertive campaign that challenges people a little bit more than we have in the past." Because, as you know, it's really hard to get people to hold a sign, even, and to become a little more radical in their thinking about strategy. And when they're dealt a blow like this, I think it presents us with a window of opportunity to help people think about some strategies that they normally wouldn't think about that will help us win. So I'm excited about that.
—Aaron Browning

Profile: Jerome Scott
Educating a Movement

Jerome Scott is the Executive Director of Project South in Atlanta. He was interviewed in May 2003.

I grew up in Detroit, Michigan. Soon after graduating from high school I enlisted in the military. Soon after that I found myself in Vietnam.

Vietnam was the place that totally changed my life. Before going to Vietnam I was basically just a person that didn't really think. But while I was in Vietnam someone asked me, "Why are you here?" And I couldn't answer that question. Ever since that point, I determined that no matter what I was doing or where I was, if anybody ever asked me what am I doing this for, I will have a reason for it. It was that situation in Vietnam that sent me out on the course of becoming an activist.

When I got back I worked in the auto plant for Chrysler and was a founding member of the League of Revolutionary Black Workers. The League started in the middle '60s and lasted to 1974. During that period of time we used to have workers come to a Sunday meeting. Up to 300 or 400 workers would come to a Sunday meeting. We had to meet on Sunday because back then everyone was working at least six days a week. So not only was it a Sunday, it was their only day off.

Just about everybody in the League had to learn how to organize. You have to emerge as a leader or what good are you? So I think that process forced me to learn how to organize and how to develop other leaders.

I was involved in a wildcat strike in the early '70s, and was fired as a result of that wildcat strike. I was basically blacklisted from the auto industry.

Then I moved to Chicago for three years, working on some housing stuff on the west side of Chicago. Then I got an opportunity to move south because I was working for a printing company in Chicago that opened up an office here in Atlanta. I'd always wanted to move south. I'd never lived here, and I knew that being an activist in the South would probably be the best place in the country to be because the rules were so clear.

I moved here in '79. I worked for that printing company for about five or six years, and in 1986 we started Project South, the Institute for the Elimination of Poverty and Genocide. It evolved, over the past sixteen years, into a popular education and action research organization. That's what we do now.

In 1985 and 1986 there was this campaign going on in Alabama called "I'll Vote On." It came out of this whole process of the federal government prosecuting seven civil rights workers for vote fraud. What they had done was figured out that if they were going to win elections in rural Alabama, where Black folks were a majority, they had to develop an understanding of the absentee ballot boxes. Historically, what would happen is they would win the regular voting election, and then by the next morning, by the time the absentee ballots were counted, they would lose. So they mastered the skill of the absentee ballots and began to win elections straight across Alabama, from Mississippi to Georgia.

One of the national representatives from Alabama called in the federal government and said, "These people have to be cheating. They can't be winning like that." The federal government picked up about 100 elderly people in the middle of the night and took them from the Black Belt of Alabama down to Mobile to interrogate them about who voted for them.

What was happening was that the civil rights workers would come to their house, help them with this complicated process of doing the voting absentee. They would vote for themselves, but they needed to know how to do the process. After interrogating almost 100 elderly people, they came down and decided that they were going to prosecute these civil rights workers. By the time they all got to court, these elderly people said, "No, no, no, I voted for myself. But I can't read and I need help." So they all got acquitted. But one of the things that happened during that process was that we had freedom rides come from all over the country to do door-to-door knocking in rural Alabama to make sure that this didn't intimidate these elderly people from not voting again. That's why it was called "I'll Vote On."

Doing that process, we realized that a lot of people who came back on that freedom ride didn't know a lot of the history of the South. They didn't know the strategic importance of the South. We decided that we needed to rekindle that history. That was the basis for starting Project South.

My frame of reference used to be, when I first started in the '60s, that we were going to fundamentally change this country in the next five years. We were going to win, and that's what kept us involved.

But after the early '70s and going into the '80s, my frame of reference totally changed because we didn't win. We were sure then that it wasn't going to be a victory soon. So then my frame of reference went to being the long distance runner. It was the long haul. I was choosing my battles strategically rather than just going on battle to battle.

I chose a battle that was long-term and that would lead into another one. Keep that long distance runner mentality. You don't have to go fast, you just have to be steady. So I think it's the frame of reference. A lot of people left after the early '70s because we didn't win. They didn't change their frame of reference. They said, "We didn't win. I'm going. I'm going to go be the lawyer that I wanted to be in the first place."

I think it all depends on whether or not you have enough understanding of the movement process that you can take the attitude of a long distance runner instead of a sprinter.

The main thing that we do right now is educate people. That's our central thing. The world has changed so drastically over the past thirty years. When you look at organizing, many people are trying to organize in the same way that they organized in the '60s and '70s.

In fact, this world is really different. We have to have a global movement because the world is one global marketplace. There has emerged a global elite, the corporate elite that basically pulls the strings of everything. We need to model our movement on that basis. We have to be doing the networking globally while other people concentrate on doing the networking statewide and nationally. We have to have those kinds of hookups.

We chose education because we want to change the model of organizing to fit the way this world has evolved. Education is key to that. We know that you have to do mobilizing and organizing. What we try to do is partner up with organizations that are doing mobilizing and organizing, and we handle the education within that process.

• • • Vietnam was the place that totally changed my life. Before going to Vietnam I was basically just a person that didn't really think. But while I was in Vietnam someone asked me, "Why are you here?" And I couldn't answer that question. Ever since that point, I determined that no matter what I was doing or where I was, if anybody ever asked me what am I doing this for, I will have a reason for it. • • •

We're now doing a living wage campaign in Atlanta. Connected with that campaign is an LDI [Leadership Development Initiative]. So everybody that comes through the living wage campaign has an opportunity to be a part of an education opportunity. In Atlanta, about twelve to fifteen people have taken that opportunity. There are hundreds of people involved in that campaign, so it's a small percentage of people that take that opportunity.

We have workshops once a month for the LDI and they go around various issues. At first it was just understanding the living wage. Then it was understanding the bigger picture and how the living wage hooks up to the bigger picture and the bigger movement. How do we organize our campaign in such a way that we want it to hook up to the bigger picture and not be just a victory in Atlanta?

Now we're getting ready to go statewide, which means it will be operating in at least three other cities, as well as having the state legislative campaign. We'll follow the same process in those three cities. As a matter of fact, the three cities that are being picked already have LDIs. That LDI will be expanded on the basis of living wage.

I think this education process only works if you hook it up with an organizing project or a campaign project. You've got people coming in that you can give the opportunity for education. That, to me, is the main tenet of the process. It's a long-term thing. Our LDIs have been working for about three years now. If anybody out there wants to learn more about us you could call us or check our Web site. We've got education materials that people can use: books and various workshops and things that people can start over all kinds of issues.

Project South had a major breakthrough in Florida inasmuch as we were able to partner up with a labor union, 1199 SEIU [Service Employees International Union] Florida. They organize nursing home workers. In Florida the nursing home industry is huge. We've been working with them for about three or four years now, and the same thing has happened. We go down there once a month, and do our leadership development initiatives. We usually send two people to do an educational workshop. Now we only have to send one because we have established people in the various groups of Florida where they can partner with us and do the education. So the model works.

There are two big obstacles. The biggest one is convincing people to give it a chance. With a trade union you're talking about time demands. They don't see any necessity for taking time off of organizing for doing any kind of education. But this particular trade union, because of a history that we shared, said, "Okay, let's try it." Even with that it took a year of negotiations before we could try it.

Then the second biggest obstacle is to say, "Okay, it's not going to be quick. It's not like I'm going to come here and do a workshop and you're going to understand the world. We have to have a long commitment to partnerships with each other." Our first commitment with them was three years and now we're on our second three years. So those are the two things. But the model works.

I think we [organizing in the South] went on a respite after the middle '70s. We went on that respite for many reasons. The Civil Rights Movement had gained a lot of victories. We got the Voting Rights Act passed. Some people retreated because what they wanted to see done was done. Others retreated because they were forced to retreat. Think about all the Panthers that are in prison or killed. A lot of the leadership was in prison or killed off. A lot of people went on to do something else.

I think the reason why the movement is not as broad today as it needs to be is because we're just coming out of that slumber. I think about it in terms of that last ten years. When I think about ten years ago and today, I'm amazed that so much has gone on. Think about all these living wage campaigns. Ten years ago today, none of them were going on. Now there's over 100.

I think about the whole movement around welfare reform. It's a national movement now. They're trying to restore and get rid of the time limits and all that stuff. That wasn't here ten years ago. So if I think about it from the last ten years, I am happy that we've got as much as we've got.

If I think about what we need to do, then I'm saying, "Man, we have to get some more. Some leaders have got to emerge and the movement has got to get broader and we have got to be more communicative with each other so that we can develop a strategy."

I'm of the opinion that the reason we don't have a strategy or a real national movement is because we don't have that critical mass of people who are talking to each other and thinking about their vision for the future. What do we build? We talk a lot about how bad things are, but we never talk about what we want to build. I think that conversation around our vision for the future is going to be the basis of developing a national movement.

9

Advice to Aspiring Organizers

Each of the organizers was asked what advice they would give to someone who wanted to become a community organizer. Some of the advice is directed at high school or college students, some to people considering a mid-career change to organizing. Altogether, their advice draws on a great wealth of experience shared with those who might join them one day.

All encourage someone considering the field to give it a try. Just jump in!

Just jump in!

Jump in. Test it out. There's nothing that replaces experience. I would also say find yourself a mentor or a few mentors. For me, that was critical, because at the times when I was having struggles and challenges, my mentors were able to put it in a bigger perspective and to offer some guidance. No one person is going to have everything that you're going to need, so build yourself like a little kitchen cabinet of folks that can mentor and develop you.

There are some schools that are out there, training programs, kind of organizer boot camps—the Center for Third World Organizing's Minority Apprenticeship Program, Union Summer, and all that. Those are great in the sense that you feel a little more confident when you walk out of there, you know some structure, training, all that kind of stuff.

I would also say take your time and look at a bunch of different community organizations. Everyone does their organizing in a different way. If you have a situation where you work with a community organization in an internship for three months, and then another one and another one, it's a great chance to see different models of organizing: union organizing, community organizing, faith-based organizing. It's a great opportunity to try and think about the pros and cons of each approach.

—Vivian Chang

One thing I would say is you can absolutely do it. There are great organizations all over the country. It is a real commitment and life-long choice and career option. So don't see it as the thing you will do until you find out what you really want to do, but really challenge yourself to say, "Is this a life that I could pursue?" Another is to be willing to really apprentice yourself, for lack of a better word, to go somewhere to learn and not worry that you don't get it all. I think organizing takes years and years to know how much you don't know but certainly to gain any sense of confidence. Oftentimes people arrive at their second year of organizing and think, "I don't quite know what my job is yet, I don't really feel confident in this, I must not be able to do it." And the truth is, they're sort of right on track. So, to have patience with yourself and to really see yourself as a lifelong learner and to look for the organizations, the people, the mentors who will support you in that lifelong development.
    —Lisa Abbott

I would tell them most definitely to go to college. That is the number one thing, and it's a great experience.
    I think for someone who is just out of college, it doesn't pay great, but neither does teaching, and neither does law enforcement and some other very worthy jobs.
    I would tell them it would develop their people skills and give them a tremendous amount of experience in various areas.
    —Robin Bagley

If they were really serious and wanted to make a career of it, I'd probably suggest going to college at one of these alternative kind of places, to get a feel of alternative cultural process stuff, something like a Warren Wilson or Oberlin where they'll be steeped in a culture that's one side of organizing. You'd learn by doing all the process stuff. And by being involved in a lot of the extracurricular activities.
    Go to Oberlin and be on the Central American Solidarity Organizing Committee that I'm sure they have there. You would learn a lot of the process stuff by doing it. You'd also learn about being a member, about not running the meetings but seeing other people run them. And then go do it.
    —Bob Becker

Volunteer with an organization. See if you can get a summer job so you can get in and see what's involved. There's nothing in school that's really going to prepare you. ACORN is in a lot of books. People say, "Yeah, I read about it in class." But the books don't get into the day-to-day and the nitty-gritty.
    For instance, voter registration is some boring work. We get summer youth workers and we like to have them do the voter registration. It's never just go out and register these voters. It's helping them understand that how this act of getting someone to register to vote moves a bigger campaign.

How does your getting someone out here to register to vote tie into raising wages a dollar an hour? How does that tie into fighting against a predatory lending campaign?

Until people can understand that these small, boring details tie into the bigger issue, they won't understand organizing. The book might talk about Civil Rights. You hear about Martin Luther King and you hear about Malcolm X, all the dynamic speakers or the dynamic personalities. But then you had people who were in communities like Bob Moses. He used to go out and get beat up in Mississippi just to walk people down to the courthouse to register to vote. That's what changes things. The speakers were fine and well, but the work was done by the people who were out there doing the little stuff that nobody saw.

—Steve Bradberry

Find another community organizer and beg them to let you follow them around. And just tag along. Just sit in the back and listen, watch, take it all in, and keep a journal, reflect on what it is that you've learned. And beg them to let you do even the most menial task.

Try to get an internship with a group that does community organizing, and just ask them if you can do whatever, but stay out of their way, too. Don't expect that they are going to be able to pay so much attention to you, because they're so busy, and have so much work to do, that it's really hard to be able to invest in interns and stuff like that. The advice I would give to a high school student is find an internship if you can, or just find a group that does organizing. Start going to their meetings. Become a member and start with whatever free time you have, volunteering for the organization as a member, maybe. With some menial tasks. I don't think you should start taking a leadership position in the organization, but we have tons of meetings all the time that we invite our members to, and the best way to start understanding how the organization functions as a community organization is by going to those. So I would encourage that.

I'd go see Howard Berger at the College of Idaho in Caldwell and see if you can sit through his history class. I'm sure there are other college professors around the country who teach people about organizing, especially around the civil rights movement, or labor organizing, or even some of the good organizing that's going on right now, you can learn as much as you can about it.

—Aaron Browning

I don't think there's any way to learn it other than finding somebody who knows what they're doing, but who is also at a point in their life where they're willing to make an investment in another person, take another person's development seriously. Figure out a way to work with them, figure out a way that they can mentor you and teach you.

I mean, if you're into something, then go do it, but if you've got a choice, where I learned the most is when I was working with other organizers who were able to run with me on individual meetings, who were able to come to an action that I did, and give me very specific, very concrete critiques about what I'd done. Those were far and away the most valuable experiences. In Austin I was supervised by Willie Bennett, and I could watch him run a meeting, watch him do a training session, and then have him run with me and then meet with me and talk with me on a regular basis about what I was doing. I could raise very specific questions. For example, if I was at a meeting, and somebody blew up at me or didn't react well, I could describe that meeting, and he could give me some perspective on it, or I could ask him to come with me to the next meeting. That kind of hands-on mentoring is indispensable.

Other than that, I think you have to invest in yourself—reading and learning about the world.

—Allen Cooper

Learn about the world

Based on what I've seen, the most important thing to do (and probably the most easily rejected, but I will make no presumptions) is read. There's a book out looking at ethnic differences by Miroslav Volf. He's Croat. He's talking about the United States, but he's looking at Croatia as the model. He talks about how now he's not welcome in Croatia. He talked about—kind of like a theological piece—how important it is to forgive but not forget. How do you forgive and not forget? He's got some South African experience stuff in there. It's important to read for a young organizer in the United States of America today and read first about liberation struggles and organizing drives of people around the country and the world.

The other task is to un-educate yourself on what you think you know about this country. It's probably wrong anyway. It's not wrong that people have these ideas; it's just that they need to be measured against new realities. Read about cultures and struggles, preferably in the last half of the twentieth century. I think you have to read about stuff in the era of the dominance of U.S. imperialism to catch up to this moment. You can go back and quote the Greek warriors and Roman warriors and all that stuff. That's good. But catch up to what's going on now. This is just me, but I would ask folks to be in touch with your own spirituality. I didn't say religion. That will keep you on course to a destination you haven't seen yet.

—Scott Douglas

Get all your running around out of your system first. Go out and see the world and work at a for-profit job for a while. Go wait tables; go clean some motel rooms; go do some things that we undervalue in this world. Go do some job that's menial and hard and where you'll meet other people that maybe don't like their jobs at all. Get an education I think, although

I'm not totally sold that that's a necessary thing to do, but get a lot of your lighthearted experiences. Go do it. Go do it and revel in it and have fun and at some point, your natural internal clock will tell you this is not enough. Fun is great, but it's not enough. I need something else. And then you're ready to organize, I think.
—Teresa Erickson

Come hang out with us for a little bit. We work with young people at SWOP [Southwest Organizing Project], and one of the things that I always try to communicate to them is, "Learn about the world first." That's not to say that if you want to start working with us we'll turn you away, but get a sense of some place outside of where you are comfortable. Meet other people. If you have the opportunity, go places. If you want to and it's right for you, go to school. Unless you've got a really good reason not to, go to school. Maybe you won't get your degree—although I do encourage that—but at least go, because it's going to open your eyes to different things. The same with traveling and going other places, things like that. I think that's real important in terms of just getting some perspective that's outside of what you're used to and what you're real familiar with. And then be connected with an organization. Learn about what it is that they do. Then you can determine for yourself if that's something you want to continue. What we do at SWOP is we have internships, we do a lot of that. So they have an idea of what it is and if they want to do it or not.
—Robby Rodriguez

Learn about the process—government, civics, and history. Sometimes people ask, "How did this issue get so bad in our state?" When you understand the history it makes perfect sense why it is the way it is. When you have the historical background, it's like, "Oh, that's why that is like this. It serves somebody well to have it like this." So the historical pieces are important. There are things you can do in school that I didn't do, like reading the newspapers. Read and find out what's going on. Connect with organizations that may connect with issues that you care about. Just go and talk to them. First get information from that organization and read it and make sure that their take on the issue is in line with what you think and feel in your personal worldview.

Understand who you are. I took the Myers-Briggs personality test, and I'm an ISTJ [introvert, sensing, thinking, judging]. I've learned over time how to be more extroverted. I've had to, because of my job. If you tend to be more to yourself, push yourself to break out of that mold and go connect with people in other places. Join some club or group that does something that you care about. Put yourself out there. That helps you connect with people, learn more about people, and maybe start to build a base for some issues that are important to you.
—Presdelane Harris

I know a lot of organizers who are really random majors that you wouldn't think. They might've been English majors or math majors. I took a lot of science classes and international development classes, but I know a lot of people who have also taken a lot of political science classes. I took a grant-writing class, which was kind of unique for a college class. I think maybe a communications class, which I didn't take. There are classes that give you opportunities to get out and work with community groups, leaning more towards those kinds of classes. But that depends on the college or the department you're in. Learn how to use a Mac!

—Tiffany Hartung

I think informational interviewing was good. When you finish doing an informational interview with someone, you should always say, "Who else do you think I should meet with?" My circle wasn't that big. I had to continually think about who else I could meet with. You have to push yourself to do that. You have to be aggressive and value yourself enough to think they're going to say "Yes." That's hard. I know that not everyone can do that.

I think volunteering on a campaign is a really, really good way to do it, because people want volunteers. It just so happens that electoral campaigns are the ones that need it most. Think about what skills you have to offer in a campaign. Be present. Don't take a volunteer position that has you making calls from home. Take a position that puts you in contact with other people. Certainly issue campaigns can do that too.

Use the informational interviews to ferret out what might be a good place to volunteer. That's usually what I have advised the few people that have asked me. Maybe people in mid-career can take an income cut without jumping ship altogether.

—Janet Groat

I would say, "Do it." I would say that the lifeblood of this country requires organizing. It requires people's engagement and involvement. Why does fascism set in? Fascism sets in because people are automatons. They're not thinking. They don't question authority. They don't have their own critical thinking skills. Organizing is not an easy profession. You've always got contradictions. You've always got complexity. You're going by the seat of your pants sometimes. It's no straight line. You can't just study your job and then go do it, because there are all these unknown qualities that enter into it. I just think it's fun. It gives you the possibility of being creative. It puts you in relationships with many people. It's exhilarating and it does offer hope for the future. It keeps you optimistic and not pessimistic.

—Betty Garman Robinson

Get involved in issues you care about! March on Washington or rally at your local city hall.

Do what makes your heart beat faster.

Once, when I was trying to pick a job, I was saying, "I don't know if I want to do this. I don't know if it's the right job." One of my friends looked at me and said, "Do what makes your heart beat faster." It was absolutely the best advice. That's really what I tell people. "What is it that makes your heart beat faster?" There's almost always something.

Then I say, "Well, let's think about who is doing that work. What do you see around you?" Then you try to figure out who is doing that and where one might start if one wanted to do that. It's harder if you have people wanting to start their own organizations. Then you do want to make sure that they have a mentor.

I urge people to go interview the people doing the work, rather than considering it a job interview. I say, "Here are four people you can start with who are doing something kind of along those lines. Check them out and pick someone you like, who inspires you, whose work inspires you. One where you want to see what that's like. Then convince them to hire you."

Lots of times people will go in looking for work, and I say, "The trick is not really to go job hunting but for you to think about what it is that you want to do. Then find a way to do that." And if that doesn't work, you can

have a fallback and look for a job. But the first thing you should do is really think about, "What do I have the hots for?" and try and make that happen.
  —Kim Fellner

I would say, first of all, get involved first-hand in community work.

Get a broad education, read the newspaper. Keep up with politics to some degree, enough to understand how that world works.

In school, I think a general liberal arts education is useful. I wish I had taken a couple of economics courses, so that I would at least understand what the people who have studied economics think about economics. And political science and history, you know, because folks in Alabama don't understand the roots of our 1901 state constitution and how it was a backlash against progressive movements. That in the 1890s, they were working on reforms that weren't accomplished for thirty, fifty, and seventy years after that. They were working on women's suffrage and a progressive income tax back then.

And then keep involved in volunteer efforts so that you have a connection with the real world to test out what you're learning from the books.
  —Kimble Forrister

Go to college. You can have fun in college. Take the courses that you want to take, that you enjoy. If you want to become an organizer then you have to have some desire to see change. And if you want to see change then you have to understand that it takes power to create change. You have to understand that without values undergirding the pursuit of power, it can corrupt. It can be a yucky thing. You'll just be some political operative and you'll wonder why.

As an organizer you have to feel pain or you wouldn't want to change anything. To effectively do that at that age you have to allow yourself to be invested in the relationships you build with other students and teachers.

Create the vision of the world that you want to see and let your teachers teach you how to get there. Demand that they teach you. Have a good time and be open to that journey through college. After college, put it to form. Go wherever you can go. Do volunteer programs, if you can afford it.
  -Ray Higgins, Jr.

I would say get a good education, no matter what field you study. Expose yourself to communities that you might not have been raised in or might not be familiar with. Be curious. Find a mentor. Find somebody who can guide you. I haven't come across very many high school students who even have an inkling that there is such a profession. At least in my experience, it's coming across folks who are headed in the social work direction or in the legal direction or into ministry, like myself. I knew I wanted to do

Participants at a Dismantling Racism workshop do a small group exercise to learn about similarities and differences among people.

something in the world that had to do with improving the community. The traditional avenues for that were becoming a minister in the church or running for office or something like that. So I think it's exposing people to this kind of work initially. Then if they're interested in this kind of work, really encourage them to find a mentor, somebody who they can work under and really learn the tools of the trade. Get themselves involved with a formal or informal network of people who are also doing this work so that they can learn from a variety of people.

—Paul Cromwell

Read a lot of whatever you're interested in, especially accounts of organizing. Hang out with organizers. It's something that's not really put out there as a profession that people can go into a whole lot. It's not, "Oh, I'll be a doctor or an organizer. I'm still figuring it out." You have to seek it out. Talk to people who do it. For me, the choice was between organizing and direct service, or advocacy, or education, and organizing seemed to do the most to effect change.

Talk to people in similar professions about how they go about working for change. I had a friend who went into advocacy full steam, and that's just great. But I'd say talk to as many people as possible in similar professions. Just find out about it. Ride-alongs [with an organizer] were huge for me, in terms of just hearing conversations. Or just going into a chapter meeting and just being able to hear how that went.

—Brian Johns

Change perspective.

I think that the best experience that a student interested in community organizing could have is to spend some time, especially if they've grown up in privilege, outside of that privilege. They really need to get beyond the book knowledge and the head knowledge to a heart knowledge of what people are going through. It's very easy for young people who grow up in privilege to believe the very same things that their parents believed about why people are poor or why people are being exploited or whatever.

I think that somehow they have to connect. They need to connect to the people that they want to organize to really understand what's going on. The only way you're going to do that is to spend some time with those folks. It would be great if they could have an exchange program where they actually live in a housing project with a family. Or sleep on the couch because you couldn't pay the rent and you got put out and you had to bring all your children and your husband, if you had one, to your Mama's house to stay until you can pull it together again.

There are different ways that they can experience those problems, not having grown up in them. It's not that I don't respect the academic position, but there's just more to understanding the plight of people than the academics of it. I think that they have to be open to using some non-traditional learning methods themselves to gain knowledge about how to become better organizers.

—Sheila Kingsberry-Burt

I guess it would depend on who you are. Me, I really had to immerse myself in the harsh realities of the world because I didn't know that stuff. I see a lot of younger people who do want to be organizers who also come from backgrounds not that different from mine. They've got a lot to learn. I think organizing is a pragmatic profession. If you're too idealistic you're not going to make it. You're going to get too disillusioned. You have to be able to cope with failure and compromise and all the rest. You learn how to do that by coming to grips with the realities of peoples' lives, especially people who are getting put down and worked over and taken advantage of on a regular basis. Just listening to their stories will teach you a lot.

—Ben Thacker-Gwaltney

I would advise that they study people and study process, how people interact in order to do things, to make decisions, carry out activities. So study people and study process. I would advise them to learn history, and in particular to learn people's history, but to avoid dogma. A well-rounded understanding of the American Revolution, for example, as opposed to just the real simple, short, clichéd version. I think most people need to get outraged about that history, but if someone really wants to be an organizer, I would advise them to learn that history. I think it affects a lot in terms of how we can move forward.

And then I would suggest that they get in the field somehow, maybe that is an internship—probably a good idea, but it really has to be in the right place. They should do some sort of a landscape, start to kind of study themselves, some interviews, or whatever they are really serious about, and then see if there is a way that they can do some work in a place where there is good organizing going on, where they can learn.
—Burt Lauderdale

I guess the main thing is to find—more than the issues—to find someone you want to be your mentor. That feels to me to be the most important piece. Do a bunch of interviews with people who are doing different kinds of organizing. I guess I'm a believer that there's not a right and a wrong school of organizing, that if there was, we'd all be doing the right one. So I'm less concerned about the model of organizing, for someone that's new, than I am about someone they feel can really help them develop and that they can trust, and that they can have a good experience with.
—Dave Mann

The first thing I would say to them is, "Do it because you love it." It certainly isn't the money that attracts you. Do it because you love it. And as you do it, take care of yourself. As you work for communities you have a tendency to get attached to the people in a community. You can't hear about all this struggling and help people to navigate these problems without getting attached to them. But you can't get too attached, because if you get too attached you can't turn it loose. You find yourself lying in bed awake at night, long after it's over. You can't last that way. That's my advice. I don't know how anyone would take it. I don't take it.
—John McCown

Find out what makes your passions flare and follow it. I think so many times young folks are told not to do something, not to go into organizing because they're troublemakers and because this is going to make people not like them. The reality is that that's a fallacy. If this is what you feel you want to do, then you see yourself already doing it. Go to school. Study what interests you, anything from biology to art to what have you. Everything in this life has the capacity to become an area and a skill for you to create a more equitable society.
—Lisbeth Meléndez Rivera

Learn about organizing.

First of all, it's important to know the great history of community organizing, not only in this country but around the world, to understand what happened with labor organizing and the history of that. They do not have that in schools. Understand what happened with the Civil Rights Movement, because again, it really gets cheated. It really was a part of our history, so important and so critical. So to understand that and to be inspired by leaders, not just famous ones, but people who did organize for change throughout this country for so many years. I think adding that historical perspective is really important. I also think it's important for young people to work with the organizing community. We've been very fortunate to have high school students working with us, just working side by side with people, not just to have a one-way kind of what is often referred to as a mentorship, but a two-way kind of thing, where there's a dialogue going on, an exchange of information about how to do it and sharing ideas about what organizing entails on a day-to-day basis. Maybe spend some time, maybe a two- or three-month stint during the summer or after school. I think that's really the way to learn not only the nuts and bolts of it, but also to be inspired by what it can achieve.
—Pamela Miller

Try it out. If possible get into one of the stipend programs or raise the money or do it for free. High school and college kids have summers off. If someone's not in school it's a little harder. There's so much youth organizing going on. They could go be a leader, which I think is just as good for them as learning how to be an organizer, being part of a campaign. A lot of young organizers come at it from an issue perspective or a constituency: "I want to organize youth," "I want to work on housing." Over time I've tried to dissuade them from that completely. You want to get to the point where the constituency and the issue don't matter. It's about power and people and development. It's getting them to go in and do it.
—James Mumm

Find a mentor. Find someone you trust, someone who's got a hell of a lot more—not just organizing experience, but life experience. I think if I were to do it over again I would just want to be in an organization for two or three years and not be on staff, just kind of watch first. Learn to think. You have to have the capacity to imagine a community differently. That is a thought process that is both reflective upon action but also requires the capacity to think abstractly and take the things that you're thinking about and reading about and play them out and how they might work themselves out in a given community. Another thing I would say besides mentors is just

What should an organizer read?

Several organizers made suggestions of reading they thought would be useful to an aspiring—or experienced—organizer:

> Someone used to say, "You should read Saul Alinsky's writing about organizing before you start and again three years later. If you read it in between you'll get all balled up and try to do it his way." I think the Alinsky writing is very interesting and it's a snapshot of a particular kind of organizing at a particular time in history. It's not the only kind and it's not the only time.
>
> I'd much rather read the Dalai Lama talking about how to live a good life and have that get me through how to live my life well than read somebody telling me how to do my organizing work. But that's not for everybody.
>
> I think we're working with human beings and how we work individually and in groups. I don't think that has changed. I think our understanding of it has changed. I don't always think that one leader's understanding is more right than the previous one. So Cicero talking about The People is pretty important for us to understand. We don't need to necessarily adopt it, but we should think about values and politics and how they interact and the location of wisdom, power, and authority. That's what we do all day. Cicero had something to say about that. So did Thomas Jefferson.
>
> — Dave Beckwith

be curious about people. Learn to ask people about themselves. In doing so, begin to recover and know and learn to tell your own story.
—Perry Perkins

The advice I'd give them would be to get some experience and do some organizing themselves to see if they've got the stomach for it. It takes a little bit of stomach, I think. You can't be afraid of conflict. Nobody in their right mind loves conflict, but you have to be prepared if tempers flare. If you take on someone in power they may not like what you're doing. You have to be able to not run from the conflict.

I'd also say learn to write, learn to communicate. If that means going to school, go do that. If you think you can learn to write and communicate some other way by an internship or on your own, go do that. I think that's an important part of the job. You have to be able to write, at least some. Your verbal communication skills have to be very good.
—June Rostan

What should an organizer read?

Anything about another person's struggle or another person's story, whether it has anything to do with community organizing or not, is good. Especially something outside of your own perspective. If you're White and middle class, read a book about someone who's poor and Latino growing up in the inner city. Read something about a Chinese immigrant, or growing up in Africa, just to familiarize yourself with what's going on out there.

— Kelly (Corley) Pokharel

Sometimes there is not one particular handbook on how to organize. All of them have some of the same things and very different things. It's about what you see when people actually apply it and learning the histories of it. Study history, because you'll always see organizers in it. It doesn't matter if it is the American Revolution or the French Revolution. It doesn't matter if it's the Russian Revolution of 1710 or 1917. People talk about civil war "breaking out" but you always notice that it was someone out there talking and bringing people together. At the end of the day organizers are the ones who make history. We make history.

— Lisbeth Melendez-Rivera

More books recommended by interviewees are listed in "What Organizers Read and Watch," page 233.

If they're planning to go to college I would encourage them to do that, and be active in student or community organizations while they're in school. I'd ask them to check in with me every once in awhile to talk about what they're doing and thinking about. I'd ask them to look for internship opportunities with a variety of organizations they're interested in. I might ask them to attend workshops and training sessions related to organizing from time to time.

If they're not planning to go to college I'd probably encourage them to get some kind of technical or business education beyond high school. I might not have said that twenty-five years ago, but I know that coming directly out of high school doesn't prepare most people very well for the demands of organizing today. Being able to read critically, write clearly, interpret statistics and financial data, and handle a variety of computer software programs are pretty basic skills needed in organizing in most parts of the United States. A background in things like history, communications, economics, plus demonstrated ability to do research and write clearly, would help make someone more attractive as a potential employee of a community organization. Another option would be to get a one-year internship in organizing after high school and then go back for additional education.

One reason I recommend going to college while being active in organizing as a student and seeking out internship opportunities is that if you stay in organizing, as you get into more senior positions, being able to write well makes a lot of difference. It doesn't matter quite as much when you're first starting out, but you'll still have to be able to put together agendas, fact sheets, notices about meetings, press releases. You'll also need to be able to teach people in the groups you work with how to do these things.

Beyond internships, I'd ask them to go out of their way to meet other organizers, read, and visit organizations of interest to them. I'd hope they don't get distracted into some other career, or decide they want to earn a lot of money, or something like that. I think internships make the most sense. It gives a potential organizer the opportunity to work in several organizations and sample the options.
—Ellen Ryan

It's good to learn from people that have been doing it, but also you have things to offer. You have new ideas. It's a lot about training. Some people say everything is theory. That's not everything. It's about doing the work. This is a two-way thing. You learn—but you also have to teach.
—Wanda Salaman

Frankly, I don't think our arena of community organizing has very many good entry points. There are a lot of ways to get your feet wet in organizing and walk away disenchanted. There are organizations with a culture of "You don't matter. You're young, you're fodder. We're going to chew you up, give you a bad experience, abuse you, and if you leave, who the fuck cares?" That's probably why we don't hold people. I think there are a lot of organizers that are really good to their leadership and abysmal to green staff. I actually don't think there are very many good avenues for a high school student to get involved in organizing.

You have to have a protector and a mentor. As a green organizer, you're more likely to have a bad experience than to have a good experience. I'd look for a situation where I really felt like someone was going to provide care and nurturing and give you a good experience.
—Gary Sandusky

I would advise anybody who wants to be an organizer to find out what's going on in your community and pick something you feel passionate about and start working on it. Try to link up with other people who feel the same way and start brainstorming. See what you think could be done, starting on a local level.

I think the best way to learn is just by doing it and experimenting with what works. Other things have helped: going to trainings, working with professors who agreed with the issues and were willing to take a stand on it. Linking up with national student organizations like STARC [Students Transforming and Resisting Corporations]. There's a bunch of groups like that: SEAC [Student Environmental Action Coalition], SPAN [Student Peace Action Network]. It was good to link up with other folks from around the country to hear about what's working on their campuses and what's not, which issues people are working on and how to link those issues together.

Also going to big mass actions against WTO [World Trade Organization] and IMF [International Monetary Fund] and the Democratic Convention in Los Angeles helped, maybe not so much on nuts and bolts of organizing, but just in terms of building the movement. It was inspiring to be there for those.

—Abigail Singer

To me it's hooking up with a good outfit that has quality leadership and organizers, senior organizers, that you could learn from. I think organizing is something you have to do, it's not something you learn in a textbook necessarily. You have to go out and do it.

I think if I were doing this, if I were young now and I were looking at and thinking about organizing as a career, I would want to find a group, an institution that had really quality leadership in their organizing corps that I could mentor with, that I could shadow, that I could learn from as I was developing my set of experiences and my ability to reflect on what happened. Because I'd have somebody else to talk to and help me out. I think the best people that we have developed are those that we've spent the quality time to help mentor through this and to think through their situations just like somebody helped us think through ours.

—Patrick Sweeney

One piece of advice I'd give students is to get involved in a community group right away so that they can understand how it ticks from the inside out. I wouldn't advise the student to go find a degree in community organizing and then go out and try to find a job and hang up his or her shingle because, frankly, there aren't a lot of academic programs out there that will prepare you to do it. Obviously, people may want to get a degree, finish their degrees. I encourage them to do it, but while they're doing it, they ought to be spending their free time getting involved with organizing.

—Mark Trechock

Start organizing *now*. Don't wait for anybody to tell you. If you see something that you want corrected, if you see something that you don't like, start organizing around that issue now. Organize it the best way you see how. There is no manual for community organizing. . . it's about the outcome. If you're effective about getting the goal accomplished then you've organized. I think it's important that you start now and not wait to have an adult show you how, because if you do that you're going to get sucked into doing things the same way we've been doing them, and apparently the way we've been doing it has not been working.

There need to be new ideas and new ways of connecting people and getting people mobilized and enthusiastic about work. I think young people can do that on their own without seeking leadership or seeking someone to tell them how to organize. Youth so often feel like, "I don't know how to do that. I'll go find an old person to tell me." Then they do exactly what we do. That doesn't work, so they get frustrated and they don't want to do it any more. But if they feel like they want to organize, begin to organize. Do it the best way that you know how.

. . . You've got to have hope. If you don't have any hope then you're doomed from the beginning.

—Carlton Turner

Talk to people who are doing it. But more than that, talk to people who have been influenced by it. I've seen people do exactly what I did: walk into an office and suddenly they're traveling around, they're speaking, making a difference. There's a sense of empowerment, a really wonderful feeling. You don't feel like this helpless person who can't do anything. So I think that if people were thinking about doing this, I'd want them to talk to people who are helped by organizers. And find an organization that they can get involved with, even if all they do is listen. Then I think you'd begin to get a picture of what this is all about.

—Pennie Vance

Get to know as many different people as you can. Get comfortable around different kinds of people. Get comfortable going into different environments. I would definitely encourage them to learn how to challenge authority and to learn how to speak, preferably in more than one language. I think that's always a good thing, to not be afraid to get up in front of a crowd and speak.

Learn about the issues of the day. Read the newspaper. Be aware of public events and question current events. Learn not to take things at face value.

One of the things that I think is a misconception about organizing is that it's just about getting a bunch of people to rally about a cause. There's so much more than that. There's follow-up. There's documenting and writing. There's one-to-one conversations that you have with people in power that make a huge difference. Don't be afraid to do that.

What you really have to have, especially as a young person—and what we really need to imbue our young organizers with—is the ability to be fearless. That's what it comes down to. You have to know, at the end of the day, that you might get taken to jail. You might get anything. You have to be able to have high principles and say, "This is where I'm taking my stand."

You also can't be stupid. You have to know when to back down, too. Fearlessness and integrity: people have to know that your word is your word and that you mean what you say. You have to learn to make what you say match what you do.

—Karen Waters

I would say take the leap. If you invest the time and effort, you're going to be richly rewarded. If you're interested, organizing is a very worthwhile vocation. If you like working with people and have a sense that we need to change the world, organizing is something you ought to try. It's a heck of a lot better than flipping burgers at McDonald's, or working at Wal-Mart, which is now the number one employer in the world.

—Kevin Williams

The most important thing is to not get discouraged easily. To recognize that there's a tremendous number of people in this country and in this world working for social change. At high school age, I was so idealistic and cynical. I saw a lot of things in stark black and white. There's a lot of power in that, and it made for interesting and heated discussions with my friends. But in terms of active involvement at that age, I know that I lacked the confidence to be seriously involved, and most of all I didn't know how to plug in.

I wish there was some way to communicate just how much power one person has to make a difference, and to communicate that in a way that could wipe out the cynicism, fear, embarrassment, etc. that haunts many teenagers. And that it's possible to make a living, working for things you believe.

—Christina Wulf

Profile: Abigail Singer
A Young Organizer in Appalachia

Abigail Singer was interviewed six months into her first full-time job as an organizer. She was the Coordinator of Organizing for the Oak Ridge Environmental Peace Alliance in Tennessee. As the book goes to press, she is still an organizer, now with Katuah Earth First!, a campaign to stop mountaintop removal coal mining in Appalachia.

I grew up in a suburb just north of Chicago, in Winnetka. I lived there until I left for college. I went to Pitzer College in Claremont, in southern California. I majored in social justice and sustainable development. I designed my own major. After I graduated, I stuck around in the Los Angeles area for a while and then did some traveling. Then I moved to Knoxville to take an organizing job with the Oak Ridge Environmental Peace Alliance.

If you know Winnetka, you know that it's a fairly White, conservative, uneventful place. I didn't really know what activism was, growing up, until I went away to school. I'd always been an environmentalist, but that is about it. The college I went to was pretty progressive, so the professors would teach things like critical thinking. My freshman year I took a class called Resistance to Monoculture. So I had things like that to facilitate the direction that I was going in.

There were a bunch of things going on in Claremont while I was there. There was a lot of police brutality. The dining hall workers were organizing to have their union be recognized by the contractor at our college. I was working on a campaign to save a biological field station that was indigenous land and an endangered ecosystem. It was also some of the last open space left in Los Angeles County. It was being threatened by development, by a corporate-backed biotechnology institute. So I started working on that my sophomore year. I probably put more time into that campaign than into my schoolwork.

Most of my friends from school are in organizing in some way. I went to a pretty progressive school, so it's probably not representative of most colleges. I'd say a good percentage. Maybe not organizing specifically, but lots of people went into some kind of non-profit work. You know, working with media or education.

We had a lot of internships with communities in our area and non-profits. For most people it takes doing research on your own to really find out what's out there. I guess you have to be clued in to some extent already in order to find out about all those opportunities.

It helped to go to a private school that could afford to give its student organizations money to pay for stuff like that. For me it wasn't as big an issue as it probably is for other folks. It's definitely an issue. I was lucky. I got my school to fly me to protests. I got flown to the Hague to be part of the Greenpeace Student Climate Summit. I think it's great that there are schools that are willing to do that kind of thing. Travel is a huge expense. If organizations that are trying to be conscious of racism, classism, and all kinds of oppression really make an effort to provide scholarships for travel and make their fees not so expensive that helps people gain access.

I got linked up to STARC [Students Transforming and Resisting Corporations] by chance. I was visiting a friend in Eugene, Oregon over the summer and STARC was having their national conference there. I ran into someone I had met at one of the mass actions. She said, "Oh, we're having this conference. Are you coming?" and I said, "Oh yeah, that's this week. I guess I could stay in Eugene another week." So I did, and it was a really great conference. So I got involved with STARC that way.

With my major, I didn't have very many marketable skills other than organizing, and I guess in a more general sense, organizing to me is one of the most effective ways to confront the crisis we're facing on a global level and all the crises that make up the situation we're facing now. It seemed the only appropriate response for me. It's something I know I can do, and at least be somewhat effective, hopefully.

After I graduated I moved into a co-op in Pomona, which is a town just east of LA. I was just looking for a summer job. I was applying for organizing jobs online, and I saw an opening at OREPA [Oak Ridge Environmental Peace Alliance] at www.idealist.org. I'd never heard of them before. I didn't have any experience on nuclear issues, but it sounded like an interesting campaign. So I applied for it, not really expecting to hear back. I just e-mailed a resume. I was visiting friends on the east coast when they called me for a phone interview. Then they ended up flying me down there for an interview in Knoxville. It was pretty random. They offered me the job so I took it. I knew I could learn a lot at this job. From what they said about OREPA's group process it sounded like I shared a lot of their strategies and values, like consensus.

There are two of us on staff, me and the coordinator of the organization, Ralph Hutchison, who has been there probably about ten years. It would help me to work with other organizers. Ralph doesn't really organize. He does more administrative stuff. I'm a really group-oriented person, so I would like to work more with other people. I would like to come up with a strategy and have other people around to bounce ideas off of. Trainings are always good. You know, networking.

It's really easy to burn out doing this kind of work. It's hard. It takes a lot of time, and one thing that I find really difficult is the fact that there's always too much to do and there's never enough time to do it. There's never enough people to get the work done. A lot of times you feel like you can either stay up until all hours and try to do as much as you can to really be effective, or you can try to take some time for yourself and lead a more sustainable lifestyle. It seems like this unattainable balance that you need to reach in order to be effective in the long term. I think some people are just better at getting that balance than others.

I don't know that organizing is what I'm going to do. I really don't know what I'm going to do, but it's what I'm doing for now.

I think we need to be working on all levels. Media is really critical in terms of reaching people. Art and culture and theater are also great ways to reach people. I feel like what really needs to happen is that mainstream Americans need to realize what's going on in the world and how our lifestyles are perpetuating all this oppression and environmental destruction. To me, the challenge is how to get through to those people who get their news from watching Fox at 6:00 and who read the paper. Your average American goes to work, comes home, watches TV, goes to bed, and gets up for work the next day. It's that whole routine. Any mechanism to break that cycle is a way to organize.

Profile: Dave Beckwith
Funding Community Organizing

Dave Beckwith is a long-time organizer who now works as Executive Director of the Needmor Fund, a foundation that funds community organizing across the country. He lives in Toledo, Ohio, and was interviewed in June 2003.

I'm an organizer. I'm a foundation director because I'm an organizer.

I got my values from my dad and from my family. My dad's a pastor. He was active in civil rights and peace work, even in the '50s and '60s. He's an American Baptist minister. In some ways, the model of what it is to be a man was created in my mind, very early. A man believes in something. His work is about that. His life revolves around his work. His family and his relationships are all one piece. A key piece of that is what you believe in. So that was the model.

I looked for ways to carry it out. I never thought of what career I might have. I thought of what I care about and how I could do something about it.

A few years back, I saw a video of a community group in Boston that started off with a clip of Dr. Martin Luther King speaking in Boston. It reminded me that my dad had taken me to that march. I was probably thirteen. We were marshals. I got to wear the orange vest. We marched from Roxbury, the African-American community outside Boston, to south Boston, where the White people who were angry about desegregation lived, to the Boston Common. We went to the non-violence training, we went to the march preparation meetings, we got our orange vests, we reported to the special area, we took our assignments, and we marched. We participated in the whole thing. At the end, we circled around the gazebo where he was speaking from, so I was fifteen yards from him.

Seeing the video reminded me how powerful that experience was. It wasn't just seeing Martin Luther King speak, or seeing the march. It was being in the march, as more than a marcher, being a part of the machinery. I loved it. I loved seeing it work. I loved seeing how the pieces fit together and how the plan was carried out. You planned for something to go wrong, and when something went wrong you had a plan for it, whether it was having water and raisins for the marchers so they wouldn't collapse, or how to deal with a disrupter. We had one. We surrounded him with linked arms and it worked.

I think it created a pathway in my brain that said, "These things aren't magic. They're work." Being a part of that work is really exciting. Something big and dramatic and powerful could happen. You could make it happen: not just see it or be a part of it, but make it happen. I think that was really part of becoming an organizer, not just being an activist.

Not too long ago, I was cleaning my basement and moving some stuff around, and I found some stuff from high school. There was a paper there in a folder from a trip my dad took me to in New York. It was my junior or senior year in high school. I was thinking about what to do for college. My dad knew of my interest in social change and civil rights and the anti-war movement and stuff. He had heard about Saul Alinsky. He wrote to the Industrial Areas Foundation and sent in an application for organizing school. They sent back a letter that said, "You don't do it that way."

But we visited a group in the northeast Bronx, which is a poor neighborhood. It's clear to me, from reading the junk that I saved from this visit, that it was clearly an Alinsky organization. They showed us and gave us stuff about how they did their work and meetings. In this file are minutes of a meeting with the councilman over housing. It was a bunch of stuff about the workings of organizing. It was me considering what I was going to do. It was amazing to see that and remember. It was one of the pathways to what I was going to do.

There are a number of other things that go into the mix of me being an organizer. I was very active in youth work in high school. I was at the State Fellowship of Baptist Youth and the Local Baptist Youth, as well as the Ecumenical Coalition of Youth. In a lot of ways, that's where I learned the machinery of a group: how you make a plan, how you carry it out, how you work with a group of people to get something done, how you organize a big event like a conference or a meeting.

I was in the Harvard-Radcliffe Model UN. A couple of kids from each

> • • • I think it created a pathway in my brain that said, "These things aren't magic. They're work." Being a part of that work is really exciting. Something big and dramatic and powerful could happen. You could make it happen: not just see it or be a part of it, but make it happen. I think that was really part of becoming an organizer, not just being an activist. • • •

school get to go. That's the place where I learned to use Robert's Rules of Order. It's one of those things that I learned a long time ago and can still do. This is all a mix of what I came to be.

Another formative moment for me was the summer camp of the Massachusetts Baptists Convention. It was called Leadership Development Camp. It was the traditional story. We'd sing songs. We'd do Bible study. We'd learn skills of how to do a youth group. There was a social justice class for two weeks. The agenda was to find an issue around us, in this little community by the sea. Do research. Figure out what you want. Figure out who the target is. Engage them. Come to the conclusion. If there's a protest in there that's good. In that two weeks, we found a clause in the agreement of every property owner in this Baptist community. It was an exclusionary clause, saying that Africans and Mongolians—Chinese people, for some reason—were not allowed to own property there. It was one of those classic exclusionary clauses. It was constitutionally unenforceable, but there it was, in every deed.

So we took this on as our issue. We identified the target, which was the head of the association. We invited him to come talk to us and he didn't want to. So we did a picket in front of his house. We made him come talk to us. He agreed to have that legally removed from all the deeds. It was a magnificent learning experience, probably entirely set up. The poor guy, we viewed him like some kind of devil, but probably that was all arranged. But it was a wonderful doing and reflecting experience, jammed into one period.

I was born in 1950, so when Vietnam came around I was at that magic age. The concept of not getting my ass shot off and not having to play in the scene was quite real for me.

I ended up going to college at the University of Massachusetts at Amherst. In the two and a half years I spent there, I probably took four or five courses seriously. I think in the second semester that I was there I got my first grant. It was through the school of education. They had Ford Foundation money. I took a load of courses that were put together to be essentially an independent study for a semester. I took the grant and went to Pittsfield, Massachusetts. I lived in a commune of kids and helped to put out an underground newspaper and organized kids in high schools against the war.

I was in the SDS [Students for a Democratic Society] chapter at college. I learned a lot about organizing, the use of procedure, and factions and all that organizational drama.

In my sophomore year, I had a semester where I signed up for a bunch of courses where the people agreed not to take attendance. I went to Cuba. I worked side by side with Cubans who had been actively involved in the revolution, not just the idea of the revolution or the bureaucracy of the revolution.

I got to meet with people from all over the world who were also there as a sign of support. Being in the mix of people who were doing all sorts of important work all over the country was really an important part of my education.

I went back to school for one semester and then discovered that it really wasn't interesting or exciting enough. I told my dad that I was going to take a year off. I went to work in a curtain factory. After a year in the curtain factory, a friend who I had been with in Cuba, who was in seminary, got recruited by a guy named Stan Holt in Rhode Island. He called me up and said, "There's this thing, this organizing thing. You should really check it out."

Somehow I got through an interview with a real serious organizer who thought it was worthwhile to give me a chance to see if I could do this. His challenge to me was: "I don't have any money, so you're going to have to think of a way to make a living. I'll let you work here." He sent me to see someone at an anti-poverty jobs program. I made up this sad story about how I'd fallen on hard times and wasn't working and how I really needed to be rehabilitated and learn skills. I said that I would love to have a placement in this community work because I really wanted to learn how to work with people. I got assigned to this community organizing job. It was fifty-five bucks a week. I think that was 1971.

I worked for Holt for just over a year. It was a very intense year. Stan was in the greater family of Tom Gaudette. He had come to Rhode Island after training with Tom in Chicago. He had stayed in close touch with Tom and was part of Tom's plan to build a bunch of regional training centers.

Stan had an approach which was bring in a lot of people, work them really hard, and see who shapes up. So we worked ridiculous hours. We had staff meetings twice a week, on Tuesday and Thursday nights. They started at 10:00 at night if possible, whenever we could get everyone together. The really, really good staff meetings stopped when the birds started singing and the bread trucks started to roll.

It was a very powerful grounding experience, but very difficult. You went around the room. You talked about what you were doing and why you were doing it that way. Every once in a while it was your turn. It was your turn not to be nurtured but to be attacked. Your work would be questioned. You would report and you would explain.

Occasionally it would transfer into "How do we know what's going on? What information do we need to know in order to find out who to go after to really solve the problem rather than just organizing people?" There were times when it was just magic. It was a political education that provided an analytical approach to the issue and an organizing screen on the political analysis of community dynamics. There were times when that was magic.

It hardwired some different things in my life, too. One of them is that I don't really start to think creatively until ten or eleven at night. That can be a problem. Not everybody has the same schedule.

There were a lot of negatives to that style of organizing. It took me a long time to unlearn the things that were not productive. One of the things was the idea that you interact by attacking. You build these skills by breaking them down. I think that was a mistake. It was clearly a part of the organizing culture when I started. It took me a long time to get past it. It was a very male environment. There were a lot of women in it, but they were held apart. That took a lot of time to get through.

But the idea that this is a living and a skill and a world that you can live in and create change—that was big. I did that for a year. Stan left. One of the staff became the executive director. Stan had worked to plan other organizations around town. One of them got a grant and was looking for a director. I became the director.

It was an organization with half a year's budget already raised. It had nothing but a committee. It was called the Neighborhood Organization of Italian Americans. We soon gobbled up the neighborhood next door, which was Polish. We called it the Congress of the Ethnic Neighborhood Organizations. I worked for that for three years. We soon developed enough money to have a couple of staff. Then we used Stan's approach of two Vista volunteers, three high school volunteers—it was just a crowd of people that developed around this thing.

We had staff meetings twice a week, at night. That's the way you did it. We built a community congress. After three years of doing this, Stan had built a lot of sponsoring committees around town. He had begun to look around New England. This was part of Tom's master plan: he developed a sponsoring committee of priests for the New England Training Center for Community Organizers.

I became the first director of the training center as such. After four years of organizing, I was director of the New England Training Center for Community Organizers. What the hell did I know? I knew nothing in terms of training. The training consisted of me telling people how to be an organizer. It's embarrassing now to think about it.

But we also sent them out to do work with community groups and brought them back and debriefed on how it went. The more I put myself in a position to engage with other people to help them think through what they were doing and why they were doing it that way, it made my work better.

I worked for three years there. I consulted with sponsoring committees that worked to build community organizations. I spent three years in the training center and then I moved to Washington, D.C. I went to work for the Legal Services Corporation, training legal services lawyers and paralegals on how to work with community organizers. I worked with community organizers who worked with lawyers.

Then I went back to work as an organizer in Toledo. After six years of that—three years as director and three years of organizing around economic development issues—I went to work part-time with the local university Urban Affairs center. It was essentially nurturing organizing around the

Toledo area and organizing in community development. The other part-time was with the Center for Community Change. After five years of that I worked full-time for the Center for Community Change. I did that until November of 2002.

Then in 2003, I took a position as executive director of the Needmor Fund, a foundation that funds community organizing around the country. It was a convergence of opportunities. I was looking for a job and they were looking for a director. I thought about it for about one minute and realized that this is the job I have been preparing for all my life: I could direct resources—real money and connections and ideas—to organizers in the field.

I've felt the magic of the work. Not that I did it, but I was in it. Sometimes I get caught in the middle with somebody who's building an organization, has power and is wielding it. That person, who's building that organization, says to me, "I'm scared. Help me." That's when I've been in the magic place. She could have been talking to an answering machine, maybe. But I was able to build a relationship with her. At that moment, when she needed that, I could be that for her. That was good.

I like a fair amount of actually achieving things at the end of day. When I can be part of a group that delivers, that's special. I don't have to say I did it. We do that enough. I had my part even as they did it. It doesn't even have to be that they couldn't have done it without me. They did it, and I got to be in it. That's good.

I think just being around people makes exciting things happen. When

Dave Beckwith (left) visits with Andy Kegley of the low-income housing organization Mountain Shelter.

I was working at Legal Services I helped put together a conference of Vietnam vets who were exposed to Agent Orange. The speaker of the conference was Lois Gibbs, who was at the time building a national support organization for citizens groups working on toxic waste issues.

I got to be there and help a little bit at the moment of convergence of that anti-war and health benefits issues, and this toxic waste movement. To sit up late at night at the meeting and talk about her challenges in building this national organization was pretty exciting. My direct organizing work now is mostly with organizers, so it's a step removed.

What I see people doing is really exciting. I use the example of Montgomery, Alabama, where the bus boycott was many years ago. We work with an organization there that is fighting for a better public transportation system. The White people took over the city and eliminated bus service. The equality was there. You could sit wherever you wanted if there were buses, but there were no buses. So people there organized to get buses back. There's a lady who comes to those meetings who made sandwiches for the leaders of the Montgomery bus boycott. She's now part of the struggle to get the buses back. The feeling of continuity with the great struggles of the past was great.

The Transportation Equity Network [TEN], which they were part of, got something put into the rules of the Transportation Department that says that every three years local transportation decision-makers have to have their authority renewed by the federal government, and that process has to be public. So by that little change in the legislation, that Montgomery transportation group was able to challenge the right of the decision-makers to be decision-makers. Seeing this lady's face when the feds came to town and the people who had given her the cold shoulder all of a sudden started listening—that was pretty good. Again, a lot of magic is to see people change.

I remember Lucy Masmanian, one of my earliest leaders. She was a lady I door-knocked in Rhode Island. She taught me that every true Armenian household had a couch in the kitchen. She worked as a maid in the downtown hotel. She was shy. She didn't want to come to the meetings. She thought I was a nice young man who was just misguided to think that anything could be done, because she knew better. I enticed her into coming around. She became an active part of the organization, starting with trying to get her landlord to take better care of her house. Part of what brought her along in the organization was that she felt like a mom to the organizers. She'd bring food and stuff.

Lucy Masmanian was very shy and concerned that anything she said would lead to her being in trouble. She learned very slowly, by doing a little something and not getting in trouble, that she really could have a voice. Lucy Masmanian's crowning glory as a leader was when we had a meeting with the mayor. He didn't show up. She led us on the buses to the hotel where she worked, up the elevator to a room that she cleaned, where she knew the mayor would be with his girlfriend. His wife didn't know he was there. The newspaper that was with us didn't know he would be there. But Lucy Masmanian took us to the mayor's room. We knocked very politely on the door. He came to the door in a towel and Lucy Masmanian was the most powerful woman on the planet at that moment. We didn't make her speak. She didn't have to show herself to the administration of the hotel. But Lucy Masmanian was not a meek little Armenian woman who provided food for the staff any more. She was the most powerful person on the planet. She never forgot that.

Then there was Sharon Hess, whose original training as a leader came from the Cub Scouts. She was a very good den mother. She knew how to make people do things. My first week as an organizer in Toledo, the city stopped picking up the trash, which they were doing twice a week, because people voted against the tax levy. They decided to pick up the trash once every two weeks. They limited the number of bags to three per household, once every two weeks.

As organizers, we just went crazy. This was the most wonderful thing they could have done to help build an organization. We swept through neighborhoods. We had to work way beyond our reach.

We'd call through the phone record on the street until we got someone who was mad enough to say they would be the organizer for their block. We'd bring them the organizing kit. We'd give them sixty-two flyers and a rap sheet and a Xerox of the phone list. They were the organizers for their block.

We hit the whole neighborhood. We didn't have much of a leadership structure for the whole neighborhood, so those leaders became our call lists for the planning meetings. Whoever came were leaders. Whoever did things were the ones who got to do things. It was going way too fast for the old, ineffective, staff-directed way.

Sharon Hess rose through that system like that [snaps his fingers]. She said, "Yes, I'll do my block. Do you need any blocks around me in case there's someone that doesn't do it?" After she got rid of all the flyers she called back to say, "Can I come in and pick up some more? And by the way, when is that leadership meeting?" She stood up at the leadership meeting. This was my first week on the job. I had been hired by this community organization that said they wanted to really rebuild.

Then this first week this whole thing exploded. We had this action. "On the first trash day that you're not going to get picked up, bring your trash to the bridge that connects our neighborhood to downtown." The mythology is that we blocked the bridge with garbage and rats were sticking out. Really, we had this very carefully selected place on the side of the road where everyone could stand on the sidewalk and the trash could be in a nice little neat pile.

It was pouring down rain. Who knew who was going to come? My leadership were the spokespeople. It came time for the thing to start, in

What makes a good organizer?

A good listener. Someone who can push and pull at the same time. Listen to people in an active way to find ways to bring them along. Move them through their excuses to action and through action to learning. Move them through learning to more action.

I think a good organizer is a teacher and a learner at the same time. Moves people along. I think it takes great security of self to move people along. Move people from where they are to where they want to be or to where they didn't want to be before they met the organizer.

I think excellent organizers are very clear about their own politics and values. They know what they care about and they act on it. I think there are gradations. It's such a continuum.

You have the need to win and the need to take on things that you can't always win. There is the need to listen to people but move them. There is the need to work hard but to have a life. I think those balances are all very difficult.

It's a balance between winning and building, a balance between life and work and a balance between changing people and using people. It's a balance between listening and telling. It's a balance between having politics and listening to the community. An organizer can be very good in three out of five categories. They can live with imbalance for a certain amount of time. But to be in it for a long time and do it well, I think they have to be good at all the balances. I think a truly great, exciting organizer has all those balances figured.

I don't think there's a simple formula for it. I think you have to live with the tension and remember the opposite side of where you are at any given time. You have to have a life. You have to have relationships and whatever kind of family you can get. You have to take care of your dog. Occasionally you have to violate all that and just work flat-out. You have to push people where they don't want to go. That's different from listening to them. Sometimes you have to just push. At the same time, you have to find the line and move on. If all you do is find the line you'll never build anything important.

I'm not saying that there are simple formulas. I'm saying that there are a bunch of complex analyses that you're going to have to learn to live with. I think about my own story and I think about the people that I consider to be truly great leaders and organizers. They are people who live with those balances. They violate them on both sides all the time, but they keep with them.

—Dave Beckwith

the pouring rain. The president of the organization resigned and went home. "This is wrong. I can't stand it. I didn't know this is what you meant by conflict. I can't take it." The vice president of the organization said, "I'll get in trouble with my boss. I can't speak." There we were. The press was there. We were having the big radical action and there was no one to talk. I looked around and said, "Who wants to talk?" Sharon Hess said, "If no one else will do it, I will." She was shaking like a leaf. She'd never spoken to a TV camera before. In the course of the next two years that I worked in that neighborhood organization, Sharon continually did things that she was scared of and that she was not ready for. She did them anyway and asked us to help her get better at it. She listened to us. She really became a sophisticated, politically astute, bold leader in her own community and in her life. I saw that personal transformation. I learned so much from her about courage. I learned a lot about her managing her family in the course of doing that. I learned a lot about her ability to reason through issues.

I believe there are two ways to organize people. One is to use them and the other is to build them. She refused to be used and she taught me to be a better organizer by making me explain why and asking me to help her figure out what to do. It was not just to tell her what to do. It was to help her figure out what to do. She was a great teacher for me, but she was also just fun. She was great.

Of course, there've been disappointments, too. I've always believed that part of organizing is building other organizers and helping people come into the work and stay in the work. So there's been a disappointment when people couldn't figure out a way to stay. There was a period of time, as an executive director working with staff, that the door just kept revolving. It was very frustrating. People seemed to have good potential but wouldn't stay. I can think of a number of individuals who really had a lot to offer. They were smart and passionate, but just couldn't make it work. Sometimes it really broke my heart to see them go. There's no way to make people stay.

I learned a number of lessons the hard way. I have to remember that I'm a White man and that I grew up middle class. My way of listening to people and my way of communicating with people is changed by that. It doesn't make me better or worse than anybody. Learning how to maneuver that relationship with other people has really been important. I've had such good teachers. I've been attacked in really large public meetings. I've been beaten up in my own office. There were bomb threats. It made me a better organizer. I wouldn't say that I would regret those failures. But they were difficult learning experiences.

What Organizers Read and Watch

We asked our interviewees to think of books they would recommend to someone considering becoming an organizer or to someone who has been in organizing for some time. The variety of books they named is staggering. Ancient Chinese philosophy, the Bible, modern corporate management manuals, novels, poetry—even some books about organizing!

Organizing

A frequently mentioned book was *Organizing for Social Change* by Kim Bobo, Jackie Kendall, and Steve Max. As James Mumm said, "This is the best book in the English language on how to do organizing. Everyone should read it cover to cover and copy out sections and work with their leaders on it."

Another favorite was *Cold Anger: A Story of Faith and Power Politics* by Mary Beth Rogers, a book which focuses on the work of Ernesto Cortes, an organizer with the Industrial Areas Foundation (IAF).

More recent books by organizers include Rinku Sen's *Stir It Up*, Michael Gecan's *Going Public*, and Edward T. Chambers' *Roots for Radicals*.

Other books about organizing include *Roots of Justice: Stories of Organizing in Communities of Color* by Larry Soloman; Linda Stout's *Bridging the Class Divide and Other Lessons for Grassroots Organizing*; Si Kahn's *Organizing: A Guide for Grassroots Organizers*; *Roots to Power* by Lee Staples; *Democracy in Action* by Kristina Smock; *Building Powerful Community Organizations: A Personal Guide to Creating Groups That Can Solve Problems and Change the World* by Michael Jacoby Brown; and Paul Wellstone's *How The Rural People Got Power: Narrative of a Grass-Roots Organizer.* Also check out Gary Delgado's two books, *Organizing the Movement: The Roots and Growth of ACORN* and *Beyond the Politics of Place: New Directions in Community Organizing in the 1990s.*

For an historical perspective, there is *Let the People Decide: Neighborhood Organizing in America* by Robert Fisher and *The Roots of Community Organizing, 1917–1939* by Neil Betten and Michael J. Austin.

Three important works on Appalachian organizing are *Fighting Back in Appalachia: Traditions of Resistance and Change*, edited by Stephen L. Fisher; Richard A. Couto's *Making Democracy Work Better*; and *Making History: The First Ten Years of KFTC* (Kentuckians For The Commonwealth), compiled and edited by Melanie A. Zuercher.

Faith-based organizing

Faith-based (also known as congregation-based) organizing has been the model most written about, and organizers recommend the following works: Richard L. Wood's *Faith in Action: Religion, Race, and Democratic Organizing in America*; Mark Warren's *Dry Bones Rattling: Community Building to Revitalize American Democracy*; *Doing Justice: Congregations and Community Organizing* by Dennis A. Jacobsen; and *Activism that Makes Sense: Congregations and Community Organization* by Gregory F.A. Pierce.

Two of Robert Linthicum's books explain community organizing from a scriptural point of view—*Transforming Power: Biblical Strategies for Making a Difference in Your Community* and *City of God, City of Satan: A Biblical Theology of the Urban Church*.

Also important for organizing with people of faith is "finding scriptural texts, whether it be from the Torah, from the Bible, or from the Koran," said Makiva Harper. "I always try to understand the different stances that each of those books hold for doing justice and understanding what God's call is for justice in the city."

Alinsky

Saul Alinsky has influenced community organizing in the United States more than any other writer, and most organizers have at least one of his books: *Rules for Radicals, Reveille for Radicals,* and *John L. Lewis: An Unauthorized Biography*. Books about Alinsky include Sanford D. Horwitt's *Let Them Call Me A Rebel: Saul Alinksy—His Life and Legacy* and David P. Finks' *The Radical Vision of Saul Alinsky*.

Other icons

Organizers can benefit from reading books about, and by, the icons of social change—Jesus, Gandhi, Martin Luther King, Jr., Paulo Freire, Myles Horton, Emma Goldman. . . .

Leah Ottersbach really likes *The Long Haul: An Autobiography* by Myles Horton (with Judith Kohl and Herbert Kohl). "I think that part of why it's so great is that so many of the 'Ah-ha' moments of organizing are in that book. Also, they're presented as if you're sitting down with Myles and you're just talking together and he's telling the story. It's very critical of things that are overly academic and overly intellectualized."

Movements

A sense of history and historical movements is important, many organizers said. Among the books mentioned by the interviewees were Lawrence Goodwyn's *The Populist Moment,* Howard Zinn's *A People's History of the United States; Poor People's Movements: Why They Succeed, How They Fail* by Richard A. Cloward and Frances Fox Piven; *An Interracial Movement of the Poor: Community Organizing and the New Left* by Jennifer Frost; and *Political Prairie Fire: The Nonpartisan League 1915–1922* by Robert L. Moran.

Civil rights

The Civil Rights Movement has rich lessons for any organizer.

"One of the greatest books, I think, is Charles Payne's *I've Got the Light of Freedom,* which really gets at the micro-level of SNCC [Student Nonviolent Coordinating Committee] and the patient, deliberate, participatory leadership development and organizing. I think it's just a great model," Jon Liss said.

Other books about the Civil Rights Movement mentioned by the interviewees included:

Andrew Young, *An Easy Burden: The Civil Rights Movement and the Transformation of America*
Howell Raines, *My Soul is Rested: Movement Days in the Deep South Remembered*
Aldon D. Morris, *Origins of the Civil Rights Movement: Black Communities Organizing for Change*
Diane McWhorter, *Carry Me Home: Birmingham, Alabama—The Climactic Battle of the Civil Rights Movement*
John Lewis, *Walking with the Wind: A Memoir of the Movement*
Nicholas Lemann, *The Promised Land: The Great Black Migration and How It Changed America*
David Garrow, *Bearing the Cross: Martin Luther King, Jr. and the Southern Christian Leadership Conference*
John Ditttmer, *Local People: The Struggle for Civil Rights in Mississippi*
Taylor Branch, *Pillar of Fire: America in the King Years 1963–65*
Taylor Branch, *Parting the Waters*
Anne Braden, *Between the Wall*
Ella Baker, *Freedom Bound*

Democracy

Kevin Williams had this to say about C. Douglas Lummis' *Radical Democracy:* "Lummis argues that a democratic faith is really where we need to focus our attention, which means trusting people and believing in what people can be, based on how they sometimes are. To me, that sort of sums up organizing in a lot of respects."

Other books that have a democratic theme are William Greider's *Who Will Tell The People: The Betrayal of American Democracy*; Paul Rogat Loeb's *Soul of a Citizen: Living with Conviction in a Cynical Time*; *Back of the Yards: The Making of a Local Democracy* by Robert A. Slayton; *Free Spaces: The Sources of Democratic Change in America* by Sara M. Evans and Harry C. Boyte; and *Democracy Is In The Streets* by James Miller.

Power/Politics

All organizers need to know about power and politics. Some key books are Robert Caro's books about Lyndon Johnson: *Path to Power, Means of Ascent* and *Master of the Senate*; John Gaventa's *Power and Powerlessness*; Machiavelli's *The Prince*; Alexis de Tocqueville's *Democracy in America*; and *In Defense of Politics* by Bernard Crick. Also, books by Al Franken, E.J. Dionne, and Thomas Jefferson were recommended.

"I think that reading history and politics is helpful," Allen Cooper said. "I think Robert Caro's stuff is really essential; I don't think there is any substitute for *The Power Broker* in terms of understanding power in institutions, and how decisions really get made in a city."

Biography/Autobiography

"I know that one book I just had the most fun with was William Sloan Coffin's autobiography, *Once to Every Man: An Autobiography*. I mean this is a guy that spoke out against the powers that be and really threw himself into it with a vengeance," Kimble Forrister said. "It was very engaging."

Biographies that organizers have found useful are Mary Beth Rogers' *Barbara Jordan: An American Hero*; *Lush Life: A Biography of Bill Strayhorn* by David Hajdu, Dave Eggers' *Heartbreaking Work of Staggering Genius, Lincoln* by David Herbert Donald, and *Dreams from My Father* by Barack Obama.

Betty Garman Robinson said that "Barbara Ransby's *Ella Baker and the Black Freedom Movement: A Radical Democratic Vision* is a phenomenal book showing her development as a person. It's got a lot of information in it about different organizing styles as well."

Diversity

A lot of books recommended by organizers fall into this broad category, such as Angela Davis' *Women, Race, and Class;* Mike Davis' *Prisoners of the American Dream: Politics and Economy in the History of the U.S. Working Class;* Frantz Fanon's *Wretched of the Earth;* Isabel Fonseca's *Bury Me Standing: The Gypsies and Their Journey; How The Irish Became White* by Noel Ignatiev; and *Uprooting Racism: How White People Can Work for Racial Justice* by Paul Kivel. And anything by bell hooks.

Others include John Anner's *Beyond Identity Politics; White Men Challenging Racism: 35 Personal Stories* by Cooper Thompson, Emmett Schaefer, and Harry Boyd; *Why Are All the Black Kids Sitting Together in the Cafeteria? and Other Conversations About Race* by Beverly Daniel Tatum; *Fool's Crow* by James Welch; *Yo Hija de Los Maya* by Rigoberta Menchu; and Barbara Smith's *The Truth That Never Hurts: Writings on Race, Gender, and Freedom.*

Arlene Stein's *The Stranger Next Door* and Martin Duberman's *Stonewall* focus on sexual orientation issues.

"Considering that my focus has really been on the intersections between race, class, gender, and sexual orientation, I'd have to say Audre Lord's *Sister Outsider* is one of the fundamental texts for someone who's interested in approaching the work from that perspective," Ana Lara said.

Learning from other countries

Much can be learned from the experiences of people organizing in other countries, such as those in Benjamin Medea's *Don't Be Afraid, Gringo: A Honduran Woman Speaks from the Heart: The Story of Elvia Alvarado; Life and Debt* by Stephanie Black; Rogue Dolton's *Miguel Marmol: Los Sucesos de 1932 en El Salvador;* and *Our Weapon is Our Word* by Subcommandante Marcos and Juana Ponce de Leon.

Labor and economics

"Barbara Ehrenreich's *Nickel and Dimed: On (Not) Getting By in America* is a great analysis of what's happening in the struggle of working people in this country who are forced into the kind of worst jobs or below minimum jobs, how it's difficult to make ends meet with those kinds of wages, and the horrible stark contrast in this country between the very rich and the very poor," Pamela Miller said.

Other books include Henry Kraus' *The Many and the Few,* a book about the 1936 Flint sit-down strike ("a great book about strategy" according to Betty Garman Robinson), Barbara Kingsolver's *Holding the Line: Women in the Great Arizona Mine Strike of 1983; We Can't Eat Prestige: The Women Who Orga-*

nized Harvard by John Hoerr; Philip Foner's *History of the Labor Movement in the United States;* and *The Communist Manifesto* by Karl Marx and Friedrich Engels.

Education

Many organizers work on education issues. Two books they have found helpful are Jonathan Kozol's *Savage Inequalities: Children in America's Schools* and James W. Loewen's *Lies My Teacher Told Me: Everything Your History Textbook Got Wrong.*

"Ira Shor's *Critical Teaching for Everyday Life* is about City College in New York, which had open enrollment; anyone could go to college," Ellen Ryan said. "So, everybody was coming in, and there were a whole lot of people without your proper college-prep background suddenly enrolling in college courses. Ira Shor talks a lot about how to make complex concepts real to ordinary people. There is a wonderful little piece in there about using a hamburger. One of the students came into class with a fast-food hamburger . . . the students were all bringing fast food in to eat for their evening classes, and I think Shor was trying to get at the economy as a whole and used the hamburger as an example to illustrate how the corporate economy works. So, those kinds of skills, those kinds of critical teaching skills that Ira Shor talks about in an American context, are similar to those of Paulo Freire, the Brazilian educator."

Environment

Rachel Carson's *Silent Spring,* Mary Clark's *Ariadne's Thread: The Search for New Modes of Thinking,* and Andrew Revkin's *The Burning Season: The Murder of Chico Mendes and the Fight for the Amazon Forest* are among the environmental books organizers suggested.

Agriculture

Organizers working on agriculture issues recommend Wendell Berry's *The Unsettling of America: Culture and Agriculture* and Osha Gray Davidson's *Broken Heartland: The Rise of America's Rural Ghetto.*

Robin Bagley said, "If you ever had an inkling that factory farms aren't that bad, if you read *Cesspools of Shame* by the Natural Resource Defense Council, you'll never go back."

Victor Davis Hansen's *Fields Without Dreams* is "about agriculture and how our country's policy works to impoverish farmers and ruin our whole system of food production and distribution," according to Mark Trechock.

Books without a category

Some organizers stressed the importance of reading things you don't agree with, such as books by Rush Limbaugh or Ralph Reed. Others said that Victor Frankel's *Man's Search for Meaning* was important to them. Huey P. Newton's *Revolutionary Suicide* also made the "suggested" reading list, as did Alisdair MacIntyre's *Dependent Rational Animals: Why Human Beings Need the Virtues.*

"It sounds crazy, but Fritjof Capra's *The Tao of Physics* is an organizing book to me," Ellen Ryan said. "Understanding how we thought the universe was organized, and then finding other ways to think about it is what organizing is about."

Kimble Forrister suggested reading *Brother to a Dragonfly* by Will Campbell. "The notion that the Ku Klux Klan, the low-income Whites in the Ku Klux Klan really had more in common that they realized with low-income Blacks down the road from them, and that the real enemy is the corporate board of directors. That was a very moving book for me. When I read it, I was a displaced Southerner, so my homesickness helped make it a moving book for me."

And then there is Jim Hightower's *There's Nothing in the Middle of the Road but Yellow Stripes and Dead Armadillos.* "It's really not about organizing, but it's irreverent and funny and it just paints this picture of, 'Man, corporations are in charge," Teresa Erickson said. "He arms you with humor and with wit."

Management

Four management books were mentioned as helpful: Jim Collins' *Good to Great,* Peter Drucker's *The Effective Executive,* and two by Peter Senge—*The Dance of Change: The Challenges to Sustaining Momentum in Learning Organizations* and *The Fifth Discipline: The Art & Practice of the Learning Organization.*

Personal development

"I think that *Smart Questions* [by Dorothy Leeds] is very helpful for organizers to read because I think one of the most important things about being an organizer is being able to ask critical questions of members," Aaron Browning said.

Alan Lakein's *How To Control Your Time and Your Life* was also recommended.

Poetry

Maya Angelou, Mary Oliver, and Adrienne Rich were poets that the interviewees suggested.

The poetry of Pablo Neruda "has inspired me about the beauty and the understanding we have of the natural world but also the struggles of working people and their struggles to right the injustices that exist in this world," Pamela Miller said.

Novels

Novels were important to many organizers who included the following on their list of books organizers should read:

Harriet Arnow, *The Doll Maker*
Bebe Moore Campbell, *Your Blues Ain't Like Mine*
Denise Giardina, *Saints and Villains* and *Storming Heaven*
Barbara Kingsolver, *Animal Dreams*
Jeffrey Lent, *In the Fall*
Jack London, *The Iron Heel* ("A great Stalinist story of tough-edged
     Communist organizing," according to Dave Beckwith)
Myra Page, *Daughter of the Hills: A Woman's Part in the Coal Miners'
     Struggle*
Mario Puzo, *The Godfather*
John Steinbeck, *In Dubious Battle*
Julia Alvarez, *In the Time of the Butterflies*
Robert Penn Warren, *All the King's Men*

Diana Bustamante recommends *Hasta No Verte Jesus Mio* by Elena Poniatowska. "She has this character named Jesusa who travels throughout Mexico. What Elena Poniatowska has done is to fictionalize all the women that she's interviewed into one person. Poniatowska gets involved in the community, becoming a voice for that community. In this book, Jesusa is the one traveling, but in fact what Elena is doing is speaking about what's going on in those communities. When I gave the book to new organizers, they couldn't understand why. I said, 'Because you need to capture those nuances. You need to capture the voice and describe the face of the people with whom you work.' It's ethnography, but also being able to look beyond the picture. You have to look at the background of the picture and tell me what's going on in the community. To me that's a really good way of doing it."

Movies

Movies that were suggested include Lee Mun Wah's *The Color of Fear*; the Public Broadcasting System (PBS) series from 1987, *Eyes on the Prize*; *Lakota Woman: Seige at Wounded Knee*; John Sayles' *Matewan*; Marlon Riggs' *Tongues Untied: Black Men Loving Black Men*; *Cold Mountain*, directed by Anthony Minghella;

and Michael Moore's *Roger and Me: A Humorous Look at How General Motors Destroyed Flint, Michigan.*

John Frankenheimer directs *The Burning Season: The Chico Mendes Sustainable Rainforest Campaign.* "It's about an organizing campaign in Latin America. It's pretty interesting and insightful, in a Hollywood way," LeeAnn Hall said.

Many organizers think *Salt of the Earth* is a "must see." "I think it is still one of the best organizing movies," said Vivian Chang.

Other videos that were recommended were *Chicken Run,* directed by Peter Lord and Nick Park; *Slam,* directed by Marc Levin; Barbara Kopple's *Harlan County, USA; Northern Lights,* directed by Jim Hanson; *Fundi—The Story of Ella Baker* by Joanne Grant; and *At the River I Stand* by David Appleby, Allison Graham, and Steven Ross.

Where Organizers Work

ACORN (Association of Community
Organizations for Reform Now)
2–4 Nevins Street, Second Floor
Brooklyn, NY 11217
718.246.7900
www.acorn.org

Action for Grassroots Economic and
Neighborhood Development Alternatives
(AGENDA)
1715 West Florence Avenue
Los Angeles, CA 90047
323.789.7920
www.scopela.org/agenda

AFL-CIO's Voice@Work
AFL-CIO
815 16th Street NW
Washington, DC 20006
www.aflcio.org/joinaunion/voiceatwork

Alabama Arise
Post Office Box 612
Montgomery, AL 36101
334.832.9060
www.alarise.org

Alaska Community Action on Toxics (ACAT)
505 W. Northern Lights Blvd., Suite 205
Anchorage, AK 99503
907.222.7714
www.akaction.org

Alaska Youth for
Environmental Action
750 West Second Avenue, Suite 200
Anchorage, AK 99501
907.258.4825
www.akcenter.org/take_action/
youth_action.html

Alternate ROOTS
1083 Austin Avenue NE
Atlanta, GA 30307
404.577.1079
www.alternateroots.org

American Friends Service Committee
1501 Cherry Street
Philadelphia, PA 19102
215.241.7000
www.afsc.org

Amigos Bravos: Friends of the Wild Rivers
Post Office Box 238
Taos, NM 87571
505.758.3874
www.amigosbravos.org

Appalachia Service Project (ASP)
4523 Bristol Highway
Johnson City, TN 37601
423.854.8800
www.asphome.org

Appalachian Voices
703 West King Street, Suite 105
Boone, NC 28607
828.262.1500
www.appvoices.org

Asian Immigrant Women Advocates
310 Eighth Street #301
Oakland, CA 94607
510.268.0192
www.aiwa.org

Asian Pacific Environmental Network (APEN)
310 Eighth Street #309
Oakland, CA 94607
510.834.8920
www.apen4ej.org

Black Panthers
www.blackpanther.org

Bread for the World
50 F Street, NW, Suite 500
Washington, DC 20001
202.639.9400
800.82-BREAD
www.bread.org

Broward County ACORN
2700 W. Oakland Park Blvd. #23
Ft. Lauderdale, FL 33311
954.484.6990
www.acorn.org/index.php?id=7890

Californians for Justice
1611 Telegraph Avenue #317
Oakland, CA 94612
510.452.2728
www.caljustice.org

Center for Community Change
1536 U Street NW
Washington, DC 20009
202.339.9300
www.communitychange.org

Center for Health, Environment and Justice
Post Office Box 6806
Falls Church, VA 22043
703.237.2249
www.chej.org

Center for Third World Organizing (CTWO)
1218 East 21st Street
Oakland, CA 94606
510.533.7583
www.ctwo.org

Citizens Clearinghouse for Hazardous Wastes
is now called Center for Health, Environment
and Justice

Citizens of Louisville Organized and United
Together (CLOUT)
1113 South Fourth Street
Louisville, KY 40203
502.583.1267
www.thedartcenter.org/CLOUT.html

Colonias Development Council
1050 Monte Vista
Las Cruces, NM 88001
505.647.2744
www.colonias.org

Colorado Public Interest Research Group
(CoPIRG)
1536 Wynkoop Street, Suite 100
Denver, CO 80202
303.573.7474
www.copirg.org

Dakota Resource Council (DRC)
Post Office Box 1095
Dickinson, ND 58602
701.483.2851
www.drcinfo.com

Dakota Rural Action
Post Office Box 549
Brookings, SD 57006
605.697.5204
www.dakotarural.org

Direct Action and Research Training Center
(DART)
314 NE 26th Terrace
Miami, FL 33137
305.576.8020
www.thedartcenter.org

Faith and Action for Strength Together (FAST)
Post Office Box 10421
St. Petersburg, FL 33733
727.823.9197
http://www.thedartcenter.org/FAST.html

Family Matters
7731 N. Marshfield Avenue
Chicago, IL 60626
773.465.6011
www.familymatterschicago.org

Federation of Southern Cooperatives
2769 Church Street
East Point, GA 30344
404.765.0991
www.federationsoutherncoop.com

Freedom to Marry Coalition
116 West 23rd Street, Suite 500
New York, NY 10011
212.851.8418
www.freedomtomarry.org

Gamaliel Foundation
203 North Wabash Avenue, Suite 808
Chicago, IL 60601
312.357.2639
www.gamaliel.org

Greater Birmingham Ministries
2304 12th Avenue North
Birmingham, AL 35234
205.326.6821
www.gbm.org

Highlander Research and Education Center
1959 Highlander Way
New Market, TN 37820
865.933.3443
www.highlandercenter.org

Idealist
Action Without Borders
360 West 31st Street, Suite 1510
New York, NY 10001
www.idealist.org

Industrial Areas Foundation (IAF)
220 West Kinzie Street, 5th Floor
Chicago, IL 60610
312.245.9211
www.industrialareasfoundation.org

Institute for Agriculture and Trade Policy
(IATP)
2105 First Avenue S.
Minneapolis, MN 55404
612.870.0453
www.iatp.org

Interchurch Coalition for Action,
Reconciliation, and Empowerment (ICARE)
118 East Monroe Street
Jacksonville, FL 32202
904.633.9340
http://www.thedartcenter.org/ICARE.html

InterValley Project
95 Fair Oaks Avenue
Newton, MA 02460
617.796.8836
www.intervalleyproject.org

Justice Action Mercy (JAM)
201 N. Limestone Street
Springfield, OH 45503
937.328.3378
http://www.thedartcenter.org/JAM.html

Kentuckians For The Commonwealth (KFTC)
Post Office Box 1450
London, KY 40743
606.878.2161
www.kftc.org

Kentucky Fair Tax Coalition is now called
Kentuckians For The Commonwealth

Laramie Resource Council
see Powder River Resource Council

Los Angeles Metropolitan Alliance
1715 West Florence Avenue
Los Angeles, CA 90047
323.789.7920
www.scopela.org/ma

Massachusetts Immigrant and Refugee
Advocacy Coalition
105 Chauncy Street, Suite 901
Boston, MA 02111
617.350.5480
www.miracoalition.org

Metro Organizations for People
1980 Dahlia Street
Denver, CO 80220
303.399.2425
www.mopdenver.org

Minnesota Alliance for Progressive Action
(MAPA) is now called TakeAction Minnesota

Missouri Coalition for the Environment
6267 Delmar Blvd., Suite 2E
St. Louis, MO 63130
314.727.0600
www.moenviron.org

Montana Environmental Information Center
Post Office Box 1184
107 West Lawrence Street #10
Helena, MT 59624
406.443.2520
www.meic.org

Mothers on the Move
928 Intervale Avenue
Bronx, NY 10459
718.842.2224
www.mothersonthemove.org

National Housing Law Project (NHLP)
614 Grand Avenue, Suite 320
Oakland, CA 94610
510.251.9400
www.nhlp.org

National Organizers Alliance (NOA)
715 G Street SE
Washington, DC 20003
202.543.6603
www.noacentral.org

National People's Action (NPA)
810 N. Milwaukee Avenue
Chicago, IL 60622
312.243.3038
www.npa-us.org

National Training and Information Center
(NTIC)
810 N. Milwaukee Avenue
Chicago, IL 60622
312.243.3035
www.ntic-us.org

NC Justice Center
Post Office Box 28068
Raleigh, NC 27611
919.856.2570
www.ncjustice.org

Needmor Fund
42 S. St. Clair Street
Toledo, OH 43602
419.255.5560
www.needmorfund.org

New Orleans ACORN
1024 Elysian Fields Avenue
New Orleans, LA 70117
504.943.0044
www.acorn.org/index.php?id=8219

Northeast Action/Citizen Action
30 Germania Street, Building L
Boston, MA 02130
617.541.0500
www.neaction.org

Northern Plains Resource Council (NPRC)
227 South 27th Street
Billings, MT 59101
406.248.1154
www.northernplains.org

Northwest Bronx Community and Clergy
Coalition
103 East 196th Street
Bronx. NY 10468
718.584.0515

Northwest Federation of Community
Organizations
1265 South Main Street, Suite 305
Seattle, WA 98144
206.568.5400
www.nwfco.org

Oak Ridge Environmental Peace Alliance
Post Office Box 5743
Oak Ridge, TN 37831
865.483.8202
www.stopthebombs.org

Oregon Rural Action
Post Office Box 1231
La Grande, OR 97850
541.975.2411
www.oraction.org

People Improving Communities
through Organizing
(PICO National Network)
171 Santa Rosa Avenue
Oakland, CA 94610
510.655.2801
www.piconetwork.org

Planned Parenthood Advocates of Virginia
Post Office Box 1046
Charlottesville, VA 22902
434.971.5700
www.ppav.org

Powder River Basin Resource Council
934 North Main
Sheridan, WY 82801
307.672.5809
www.powderriverbasin.org

Project South: Institute for the
Elimination of Poverty and Genocide
9 Gammon Avenue
Atlanta, GA 30315
404.622.0602
www.projectsouth.org

Public Housing Association of Residents
(PHAR)
1000 Preston Avenue, Suite C
Charlottesville, VA 22903
434.984.3255
www.phar.typepad.com

Quality Community Council (QCC)
327 West Main Street, Suite 101
Charlottesville, VA 22903
434.977.3045
http://cvilleqcc.com/default.aspx

Save Our Cumberland Mountains (SOCM)
Post Office Box 479
Lake City, TN 37769
865.426.9455
www.socm.org

Shenandoah Ecosystems Defense Group is now
called Wild Virginia

Sierra Club Environmental Justice Program
85 Second Street, Second Floor
San Francisco, CA 94105
415.977.5500
www.sierraclub.org/environmental_justice/

Solutions
3204 East Magnolia Avenue
Knoxville, TN 37914
865.523.8009
www.discoveret.org/solutions

Southern Christian Leadership Conference
(SCLC)
Post Office Box 89128
Atlanta, GA 30312
404.522.1420
www.sclcnational.org

Southern Echo
Post Office Box 9306
Jackson, MS 39286
601.982.6400
www.southernecho.org

Southern Organizing Committee for Social
and Economic Justice
Post Office Box 10518
Atlanta, GA 30313
404.755.2855

Southwest Organizing Project (SWOP)
211 10th Street SW
Albuquerque, NM 87102
505.247.8832
www.swop.net

Stillwater Protective Association
Post Office Box 267
Absarokee, MT 59001
http://www.northernplains.org/affiliates/spa

Stop Prisoner Rape
3325 Wilshire Blvd., Suite 340
Los Angeles, CA 90010
213.384.1400
www.spr.org

Student Environmental Action Coalition
(SEAC)
Post Office Box 31909
Philadelphia, PA 19104
215.222.4711
www.seac.org

Student Peace Action Network (SPAN)
1100 Wayne Avenue, Suite 1020
Silver Spring, MD 20910
301.565.4050
www.studentpeaceaction.org

Students Transforming and Resisting
Corporations (STARC)
Post Office Box 11125
Berkeley, CA 94712
510.848.1818
www.starcalliance.org

TakeAction Minnesota
(formerly Minnesota Alliance for Progressive
Action (MAPA))
2484 University Avenue
St. Paul, MN 55114
615.641.6199
www.mapa-mn.org

Tenants and Workers United
(formerly Tenants' and Workers' Support
Committee)
3801 Mt. Vernon Avenue
Alexandria, VA 22305
703.684.5697
www.twsc.org

Tennessee Economic Renewal Network
(TERN)
Post Office 6779
Knoxville, TN 37917
865.637.1576
www.tneconomicrenewal.net/

Transportation Equity Network
Center for Community Change
1536 U Street NW
Washington, DC 20009
202.339.9300
www.transportationequity.org
www.communitychange.
org/issues/transportation/ten/

United Farmworkers of America
Post Office Box 62
Keene, CA 93531
661.823.6250
www.ufw.org

United Mine Workers of America (UMWA)
8315 Lee Highway
Fairfax, VA 22031
703.208.7200
www.umwa.org

Virginia Organizing Project (VOP)
703 Concord Avenue
Charlottesville, VA 22903
434.984.4655
www.virginia-organizing.org

Warren/Conner Development Coalition
11148 Harper
Detroit, MI 48213
313.571.2800
www.warrenconner.org

Western Colorado Congress (WCC)
Post Office Box 1931
Grand Junction, CO 81502
970.256.7650
www.wccongress.org

Western Organization of Resource Councils
(WORC)
227 South 27th Street
Billings, MT 59101
406.252.9672
www.worc.org

Western States Center
Post Office Box 40305
Portland, OR 97240
503.228.8866
www.westernstatescenter.org

Wild Virginia
Post Office Box 1065
Charlottesville, VA 22902
434.971.1553
www.wildvirginia.org

What They're Doing Now

Lisa Abbott is the Organizing and Leadership Development Director for Kentuckians For The Commonwealth. From her Berea, Kentucky, office, she coordinates the leadership development training programs and supervises organizers working in offices in Whitesburg, Louisville, Lexington, and Richmond.

Jana Adams is the Training Coordinator for DART, Direct Action and Research Training Center Network, a national network of grassroots, metropolitan, congregation-based, community organizations across the United States. She lives in Dayton, Ohio.

Rhonda Anderson is an Environmental Justice Organizer for the National Sierra Club's Environmental Justice Program. She assists residents, communities, and organizations to organize around environmental justice issues such as air and water pollution, illegal dumping, soil contamination, poverty, unemployment, health care, and crime.

Robin E. H. Bagley is the Lead Organizer for Dakota Rural Action. She oversees all chapter and issue team campaigns and supervises the organizing staff. She works out of the field office in Newell, South Dakota.

Dr. Marie Coles Baker is a retired educator. She was previously associate professor at the State University of New York College at Buffalo and associate dean at the Howard University School of Social Work.

Bob Becker is now a City Councilor of Knoxville, Tennessee. At the time of the interview, he was an organizer with the Tennessee Industrial Renewal Network in Knoxville, working primarily on the Knoxville Living Wage Campaign.

Dave Beckwith is in Toledo, Ohio, where he has been the Executive Director of The Needmor Fund since early 2003. Needmor is a private family foundation that funds community organizing across the United States.

Stephen Bradberry is Head Organizer for New Orleans ACORN in Louisiana. He oversees all ACORN operations in New Orleans, including the training of organizing staff, the establishment and maintenance of neighborhood groups, campaigns and actions on neighborhood and citywide issues, fundraising, and coalition building.

Donna Uma Aisha Brown is the founder and Director of Culture Spirit, Inc. and a co-founder of Sisters Working to Manifest Awesome Change. She has worked as interim director of the Tennessee Economic Renewal Network, coordinator of Carpetbag Theater's Knoxville American Festival Project, and popular education team member at the Highlander Research and Education Center.

Aaron Browning is Director of Organizing and Campaigns for the Northern Plains Resource Council in Montana. He supervises six field organizers who work on issues as varied as coal bed methane development, hard rock mining, and protecting Montana's system of family agriculture from the increasing threats of globalization. He also serves as Lead Organizer for NPRC's Good Neighbor Agreement with Stillwater Mining Company.

Diana Bustamante is Executive Director of the Colonias Development Council in New Mexico, which works in community and economic development, education, youth organizing, farmworker issues, and environmental health and justice.

Vivian Chang is the Executive Director of the Asian Pacific Environmental Network (APEN) in Oakland, California. Her primary role is to build a collective vision of the group's work and provide leadership, motivation, and support to staff and board members to achieve this vision. At the time of the interview, she was Organizing Director of APEN.

Allen Cooper works for the Equal Justice Center in Austin, Texas, on a project organizing poultry workers in East Texas. At the time of the interview, he was Lead and Senior Organizer of Industrial Areas Foundation projects in Austin and San Antonio.

Paul Cromwell is a minister in the United Church of Christ and has served in his ministry as a community organizer for more than twenty-five years. At the time of the interview, he was Head Organizer for the Interchurch Coalition for Action, Reconciliation, and Empowerment (ICARE) in Jacksonville, Florida. He is currently living in Germany with the support of the National Protestant Church (Evangelische Kirche in Deutschland) in cooperation with the Forum on Community Organizing, working to develop community organizing projects in Germany and elsewhere in Europe.

Jane Crowe is Program Development Coordinator for the Tennessee Migrant and Seasonal Head Start Program, developing education and recreation programs for the children of migrant and seasonal farmworkers. At the time of the interview, she was a Community Organizer for Solutions in Knoxville, Tennessee, where she was responsible for recruiting and sustaining the group's membership base while working with members to develop strategies for social and economic justice campaigns.

Scott Douglas is Executive Director of Greater Birmingham Ministries in Birmingham, Alabama. The group's current work includes re-igniting civic imagination and participation in a campaign to change Alabama's outdated and racist state Constitution through a delegated citizens' constitutional convention.

Don Elmer is Northwest Regional Organizer for the Center for Community Change, mentoring and consulting with directors of community organizations around the country. He works with CCC Teams on rural and Native American initiatives as well as a team thinking through how to do a better job of recruiting, developing, and retaining community organizers, especially organizers of color. He lives in Issaquah, Washington.

Teresa Erickson is Staff Director for the Northern Plains Resource Council in Montana. NPRC organizes Montana citizens to protect their water quality, family farms and ranches, and unique quality of life.

Kim Fellner writes about social, racial, and economic justice issues from her home in Washington, D.C. She is the former director of the National Organizers Alliance.

Kimble Forrister is State Coordinator for Alabama Arise and Executive Director for Arise Citizens' Policy Project, the 501(c)(3) sister organization to Alabama Arise. He supervises a staff of four organizers, three policy analysts, and directors of communication, development, and legislative advocacy.

Ken Galdston is the Director/Lead Organizer of the InterValley Project (IVP), a New England organizing network based in West Newton, Massachusetts. He advises the staff and leadership teams of each of IVP's member groups, coordinates common organizing campaigns and joint fundraising, and develops IVP's relationships with allies and new resources. He also oversees IVP's Training, Congregational/Organizational Development, and Clergy Leadership Development staff.

Lamar Glover is Core Member of the Los Angeles Local Organizing Committee (LALOC), a group which brings young progressive artists, organizers, activists, and others together across issue, geography, class, race, and gender, with the goal of building power that will translate into a powerful youth voting bloc. At the time of the interview, he was a fourth-year student at the University of Virginia.

Vickie Goodwin retired from her position as Organizer with the Powder River Basin Resource Council in March 2004. She now works with citizens around Douglas, Wyoming, in the effort to stop or curtail some gravel mining activities around the area, and serves on the board of the Social Justice Fund NW, a member foundation that funds social change through community organizing. She is also writing a novel with a community organizing theme.

Nicholas Graber-Grace is Head Organizer for Broward County ACORN in Florida. He recruits, trains, and manages the staff of organizers; oversees recruitment and development of community leaders and new neighborhood chapters; and works with the group's board of directors to implement policy initiatives and run campaigns at the neighborhood, city, county, and state level.

Janet Groat is taking time off to parent her son after the family's move to Portsmouth, New Hampshire. At the time of the interview, she was Senior Associate and Director of the Money and Politics Project at Northeast Action, a center for Citizen Action organizations and statewide progressive coalitions in the Northeast, with offices in Boston and in Hartford, Connecticut.

Haley Grossman is Lead Organizer with Faith and Action for Strength Together (FAST), an organization of diverse congregations building power to address justice issues in Pinellas County, Florida. She trains and develops new organizers, assists leaders in developing issue campaigns on issues such as affordable housing, access to transportation, and education, and teaches leaders to build power through organized people.

Emily Gruszka is the Development Director for Family Matters in Chicago, a family-centered organization in the North of Howard neighborhood that seeks to be a catalyst for change—building and strengthening the community through programs that support personal leadership. At the time of the interview, she was Director of Community Organizing with Family Matters.

LeeAnn Hall is the Executive Director of the Northwest Federation of Community Organizations (NWFCO), a regional network of four grassroots organizations—Idaho Community Action Network, Montana People's Action, Oregon Action, and Washington Citizen Action. NWFCO's mission is to achieve systemic change by building strong state affiliate organizations and by executing national and regional campaigns that advance economic, racial, and social justice.

Jerry Hardt is Communications Director of Kentuckians For The Commonwealth. He is responsible for the development and implementation of communications strategies and work plans in support of KFTC's goals.

Makiva L. Harper is the Lead Organizer for Justice Action Mercy (JAM), a sixteen-member congregation organization of Christian, Jewish, and Muslim traditions. She supervises one associate organizer and is responsible for organizing several campaigns in Springfield, Ohio.

Presdelane Harris is a Team Leader for Organizers at Alabama Arise. She coordinates the development of short- and long-term organizing strategies related to the group's issues, establishes realistic work priorities based on annual goals and objectives, and coordinates the work of team members.

Tiffany Hartung is Regional Organizer for Tennesseans for Fair Taxation, working with local organizing committees in East Tennessee and statewide issue committees. At the time of the interview, she was an organizer for Save Our Cumberland Mountains in Tennessee.

Holly Hatcher is Director of Programs at the Charlottesville Area Community Foundation. At the time of the interview, she was Director of Statewide Organizing for Planned Parenthood Advocates of Virginia.

Ray Higgins, Jr. is Teacher of Theology at Roanoke (Virginia) Catholic's Upper School, where his work in social justice is at the center of his teaching. At the time of interview, he was Executive Director of Faith Works in the Roanoke Valley.

Brian Johns is Political/Community Organizing Coordinator for the Service Employees International Union, District 1100P in Philadelphia. He is in the long-term care division, organizing senior citizens and civic organizations around health care and statewide nursing home and home health care issues. At the time of the interview, he was an organizer with the Virginia Organizing Project.

Julie Jones is a Program Officer at the Virginia Health Care Foundation. She helps to manage all aspects of the grantmaking operations of VHCF, which funds community-based organizations that are working to increase access to primary health care for uninsured and medically underserved Virginians. At the time of the interview, she was Director of the Virginia Health and Environmental Project.

Brett Kelver is Assistant Planner for the City of Milwaukie, Oregon. He works on land use planning issues, including building permit review, code enforcement, land use applications, and planning and zoning questions. At the time of the interview, he was an organizer with Oregon Rural Action.

Sara Kendall is the Washington, D.C., Office Director of the Western Organization of Resource Councils (WORC). She tracks WORC's federal legislative strategies and coordinates lobby activities in Washington.

Sheila Kingsberry-Burt, at the time of the interview, was Outreach Coordinator for the North Carolina Budget and Tax Center.

Ana-Maurine Lara works as a writer, healer, and organizer with bustingbinaries.com. She uses fiction, creative nonfiction, poetry, and essays to engage in social justice dialogues.

Burt Lauderdale is the Executive Director of Kentuckians For The Commonwealth, a state-wide citizens' social justice organization based in London, Kentucky. He works with the Steering Committee, directs the staff team and oversees strategy development and organizational development.

Jon Liss is Executive Director of Tenants and Workers United/Inquilinos y Trabajadores Unidos. He oversees all of the group's campaigns and is currently running its taxi driver organizing efforts.

Jeff Malachowsky is a consultant on projects for public interest organizations and foundations. A long-time public interest activist who has worked as a community organizer leading and founding a number of citizen-based efforts at statewide, regional, and national levels, he lives in Portland, Oregon.

Dave Mann works as a consultant, helping organizations to create practices of strategic reflection, planning, and action that are then incorporated into the organization's culture. He works primarily with organizations that are organizing for power to systemically address the disparities in economic wealth and opportunity and who see their work as part of building a larger movement. He is an Associate with the Grassroots Policy Project and lives in Minneapolis.

John McCown is Executive Director of the John L. McCown Center for Rural Economics in Sparta, Georgia. The center uses community organizing, resource assessment, and strategic visioning exercises to assist communities in their efforts to spawn viable, sustainable economies using available local resources. At the time of the interview he was Co-Director of the Sierra Club's National Environmental Justice Program.

Pamela Miller is the Director of Alaska Community Action on Toxics in Anchorage. She coordinates the organization's work for environmental health and justice, including water protection, pesticide use right-to-know, military toxics, northern contaminants, and health campaigns. She organizes with other staff members, workers, and community members to find solutions to contamination from the military, mining, and other industries. At the time of the interview, she was Program Director for the organization.

James Mumm is the Executive Director of the Northwest Bronx Community and Clergy Coalition (NWBCCC) in New York City. NWBCCC is a thirty-two year old multi-issue, broad-based community organization in Northwest Bronx. At the time of this interview, he was Co-Director of Mothers on the Move in Bronx, New York.

R. Dennis Olson is the Director of the Institute for Agriculture and Trade Policy's Trade and Agriculture Project in Minnesota, which advocates for farmers and peasants in the U.S. and around the world, within the context of global trade debates. At the time of the interview, he was an organizer for the Northern Plains Resource Council in Montana.

Leah Ottersbach is an Administrative Assistant for the Center for Genetics and Society, which works for responsive policies for new human genetic technologies and supports women's health and productive rights. At the time of the interview, she was an organizer and legislative coordinator for Kentuckians For The Commonwealth.

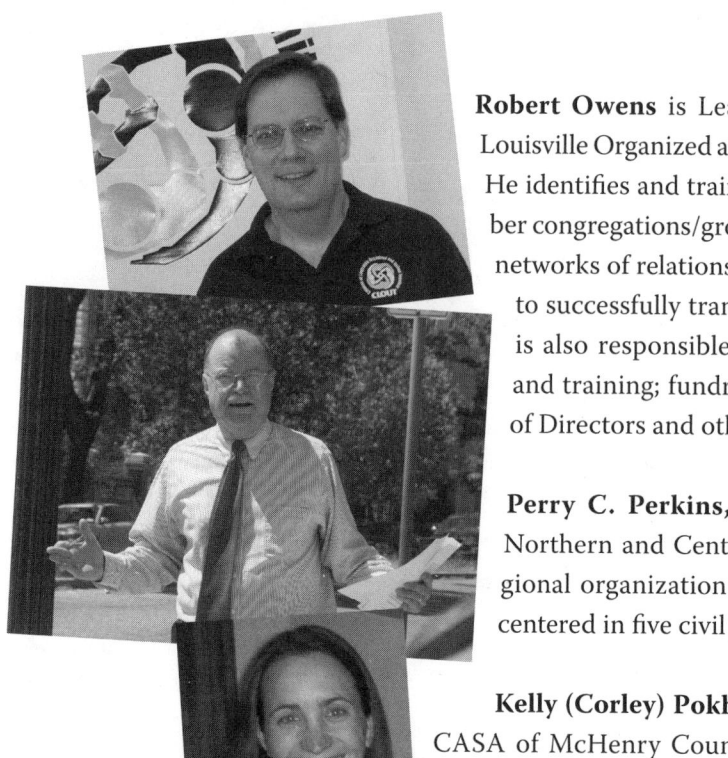

Robert Owens is Lead Organizer for Citizens of Louisville Organized and United Together (CLOUT). He identifies and trains grassroots leaders in member congregations/groups to build and develop their networks of relationship and therefore their power to successfully transform their communities. He is also responsible for staff hiring, supervision, and training; fundraising; and staffing the Board of Directors and other committees.

Perry C. Perkins, Jr. is Lead Organizer with Northern and Central Louisiana Interfaith, a regional organization of more than 80 institutions centered in five civil parishes.

Kelly (Corley) Pokharel is Executive Director of CASA of McHenry County, Illinois, where she trains and works with volunteers to advocate for abused and neglected children involved in the court system. At the time of the interview, she was an organizer for the Northern Plains Resource Council in Montana.

Guillermo Quinteros has been working to support the candidacy of John Bonifaz for Massachusetts Secretary of State, to pass a cross-initiative ballot initiative, and to organize a Working Families Party in the state. At the time of the interview, he was Executive Director of the Commonwealth Coalition in Boston.

Edgar Rivera is an Organizer with Tenants and Workers United in Northern Virginia. He organizes communities of color through community door knocking. He lives in Lorton, Virginia.

Lisbeth Meléndez Rivera is the National Mobilization Coordinator of the Freedom to Marry Coalition in Silver Springs, Maryland. She works with non-gay allies in historically underrepresented communities to highlight, raise, and organize local voices working towards the elimination of heterosexism in marriage. She also works with local non-profits and statewide federations to develop a diverse cadre of leaders.

Betty Garman Robinson is an Organizer with the Baltimore Education Network, building an independent, citywide parent organization that can hold the school system, school board, mayor, and other elected officials accountable for providing a quality education for all Baltimore's children.

Robby Rodriguez is Executive Director of the Southwest Organizing Project (SWOP) based in Albuquerque, New Mexico, a grassroots membership-based organization working to empower the disenfranchised of the southwest to realize racial and gender equality and social and economic justice. At the time of the interview, he was Organizing Coordinator for SWOP.

June Rostan is a Lead Campaign Community Organizer for the AFL-CIO's Voice@Work. She coordinates a team of community organizers who are building community support for the United Mine Workers of America to organize the coal mines of Peabody Energy. For seventeen years she served as the director of the Southern Empowerment Project, the position she held at the time of the interview.

Alicia Ruiz is an Organizer for Tenants and Workers United in Northern Virginia. She is directly organizing day laborers in Culmore (Fairfax County) and leading organizing efforts to create a chapter in Woodbridge (Prince William County).

Ellen Ryan worked for the Virginia Organizing Project from 1999 to 2005. Beginning in the fall of 2005, she is taking a leave from organizing to study Christian ethics, with plans to return to organizing work in 2007.

Wanda Salaman is Executive Director of Mothers on the Move in the Bronx, New York, a membership-based organization working on issues of education, youth, environmental justice, and housing.

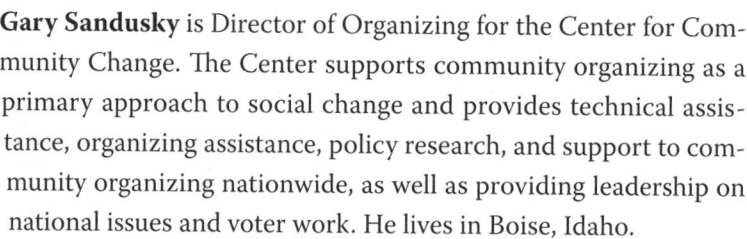

Gary Sandusky is Director of Organizing for the Center for Community Change. The Center supports community organizing as a primary approach to social change and provides technical assistance, organizing assistance, policy research, and support to community organizing nationwide, as well as providing leadership on national issues and voter work. He lives in Boise, Idaho.

Jerome Scott is Executive Director of Project South: Institute for the Elimination of Poverty and Genocide in Atlanta, Georgia. He brings activists and scholars together for popular economic and political education and action research to develop new leadership for a bottom-up movement for fundamental social change. He also writes articles and popular education materials on political economy, race and class, and the anti-globalism and popular movements for justice, equality and popular democracy.

Brian Shields is Executive Director of Amigos Bravos, Friends of the Wild Rivers, a statewide river advocacy organization with offices in Taos and Albuquerque, New Mexico. For the past fifteen years he has been instrumental in creating a community-based "river's movement" along the Río Grande and in the communities of northern New Mexico. He works with Native Americans, environmental justice activists, and environmentalists on a process for collaborative intercultural policy development.

Abigail Singer is an organizer for Katuah Earth First!, working to stop mountaintop removal coal mining. She is based in Wilmette, Illinois. At the time of the interview, she was Coordinator of Organizing for the Oak Ridge Environmental Peace Alliance in Tennessee.

John Smillie is Campaign Director for the Western Organization of Resource Councils (WORC), where he has worked since 1984, after being a community organizer for the Northern Plains Resource Council from 1979 to 1984.

Matt Sura is the Energy Director for Western Colorado Congress. He works with landowners to achieve greater protection for their rights in the face of gas development throughout Western Colorado. He lives in Grand Junction.

Patrick Sweeney is the Regional Director for the Western Organization of Resource Councils. WORC is a regional network of seven grassroots community organizations that include 9,500 members and fifty local chapters.

Ben Thacker-Gwaltney is the Lead Organizer for the Virginia Organizing Project. He supervises the organizing staff and works with the Williamsburg and Peninsula VOP Chapters. He also staffs the statewide tax reform campaign.

Mark Trechock is Staff Director of Dakota Resource Council. He supervises a staff of eight, including six organizers, working with seven different chapters and several statewide issue campaigns. He works with an elected board of twenty-five, is in charge of fundraising and communications for the group, and still gets out in the field every month.

Carlton Turner is the Regional Development Director for Alternate ROOTS, a non-profit member service organization for community artists in the Southeastern United States. He is also a founding member of the performing group M.U.G.A.B.E.E. (Men Under Guidance Acting Before Early Extinction). At the time of the interview, he was the Artistic Director for My Mississippi Eyes.

Pennie Vance now is the owner/manager of The Book Shop in Sheridan, Wyoming, "because I believe that reading and good books are essential ingredients to healthy communities and a democratic society." At the time of her interview, she was an Organizer with the Powder River Basin Resource Council in Wyoming.

Octavia Ware is a vocational specialist with The Daily Planet in Richmond, Virginia, where she teaches a four-week job readiness class for homeless clients. At the time of the interview, she was an apprentice organizer with the Virginia Organizing Project.

Karen Waters is the Executive Director of the Quality Community Council (QCC) in Charlottesville, Virginia, a community coalition addressing quality of life issues in eight targeted city neighborhoods.

Kelley Weigel is Field Director of the Western States Center. She coordinates the training and organizing programs of the Center, whose programs support the culture and practice of community organizing to facilitate connections between grassroots organizations in the region and contribute to the movement for social justice.

Kevin Williams is Director of Organizing for the Western Organization of Resource Councils (WORC). He leads the staff for WORC's leadership and capacity building program, oversees trainings, and coordinates the delivery of assistance and support to member groups. He is based in Montrose, Colorado.

Cathy Woodson is an Organizer with the Virginia Organizing Project, responsible for chapters in the Richmond area, coordinating Dismantling Racism and leadership workshops around the state, and staffing the minimum wage campaign strategy committee.

DeAnna Woolston is Community Relations Director for the American Red Cross Southwest Washington Chapter. At the time of the interview she was an organizer for the Western Colorado Congress.

Christina Wulf is Appalachian Treasures Outreach Coordinator with Appalachian Voices. She is in charge of keeping the Appalachian Treasures outreach tour on the road, encouraging involvement by citizens in target Congressional districts in stopping the environmental and human rights catastrophe caused by mountaintop removal coal mining. At the time of the interview, she was an organizer for Virginia Forest Watch.

Larry Yates is the Shenandoah Valley Organizer with the Virginia Organizing Project, reaching out and building new chapters of VOP in the Shenandoah Valley of Virginia. He also staffs the statewide racial profiling campaign and is editor of the VOP news magazine, *virginia.organizing*.

Rochelle Ziyad is a community organizer with Save Our Cumberland Mountains (SOCM) in Tennessee. She is responsible for the Maury County Chapter and staffs the Social Progress Committee and SOCM's work on a statewide campaign to restore voting rights for former felons who have completed their sentences. She also works part-time in the Columbia State College Office of Minority Affairs.